D1236341

THE GENESIS OF THE
CANADIAN CRIMINAL CODE OF 1892

During the 1892 session of Parliament in Ottawa, Sir John Thompson introduced a bill in the Commons to codify the criminal law of Canada. It came into force the following year. Canada thus became the first self-governing jurisdiction in the British empire to codify its criminal law. Britain had tried to do the same thing three times before and failed; today, it still does not have a criminal code.

In this study of a remarkable legal and political achievement, Desmond Brown explores the far-reaching impact of this legislation and the means by which it was realized. He explains the conditions in the British North American colonies that led legislators to enact codes of statute law. After Confederation the famous (such as John A. Macdonald), the not-so-famous, and the obscure continued this process to its logical conclusion: the integration of criminal statute law and common law. At the centre of the story is John Thompson, the brilliant jurist and parliamentary magician.

The enactment of a criminal code made Canada's criminal law process systematic and rational. It changed the focus of the development of the criminal justice system from the judiciary to Parliament, and the Code has become a model followed by many British jurisdictions since that time. Desmond Brown provides an illuminating account of that process, including an epilogue that traces the history of the Code from 1892 to the present day.

DESMOND H. BROWN is assistant professor of history, University of Alberta.

The Genesis
of the Canadian
Criminal Code
of 1892

DESMOND H. BROWN

The Osgoode Society

ISBN 0-8020-5833-7

Printed on acid-free paper

Canadian Cataloguing in Publication Data

Brown, Desmond Haldane, 1930–
The genesis of the Canadian Criminal Code of 1892

Includes bibliographical references.
ISBN 0–8020–5833–7

1. Criminal code – Canada – Codification – History.
2. Canada. Criminal code.   I. Osgoode Society.
II. Title.

KE8809.B76 1989   345.71'009   C89-093957-8   KF9219.B76 1989

To my wife, Inge

Contents

PUBLICATIONS OF THE OSGOODE SOCIETY

Foreword

THE OSGOODE SOCIETY

The purpose of The Osgoode Society is to encourage research and writing in the history of Canadian law. The Society, which was incorporated in 1979 and is registered as a charity, was founded at the initiative of the Honourable R. Roy McMurtry, at that time attorney general of Ontario, and officials of the Law Society of Upper Canada. Its efforts to stimulate legal history in Canada include the sponsorship of a fellowship, research support programs, and work in the field of oral history and legal archives. The Society publishes volumes that contribute to legal-historical scholarship in Canada and that are of interest to the Society's members. Included are studies of the courts, the judiciary, and the legal profession, biographies, collections of documents, studies in criminology and penology, accounts of great trials, and work in the social and economic history of the law.

The current directors of The Osgoode Society are Brian Bucknall, Mr Justice Archie Campbell, Douglas Ewart, Martin Friedland, Jane Banfield Haynes, John D. Honsberger, Kenneth Jarvis, Mr Justice Allen Linden, James Lisson, Brendan O'Brien, Peter Oliver, James Spence and Richard Tinsley. The attorney general for Ontario and the treasurer of the Law Society of Upper Canada are directors ex officio. The Society's honorary president is the Honourable R. Roy McMurtry. The annual report and information about membership may be obtained by writing The Osgoode Society, Osgoode Hall, 130 Queen Street West, Toronto,

Ontario M5H 2N6. Members receive the annual volumes published by the Society.

In 1892 the minister of justice introduced legislation into the Canadian House of Commons to codify the criminal law of Canada. With this enactment Canada became the first self-governing jurisdiction in the British empire to codify its criminal law. The impact of this rationalization and simplification was far-reaching. It changed the focus of development of the criminal law from the judiciary to Parliament, and the Code became a model followed by many jurisdictions since that time – although not by Great Britain itself, which still does not have a criminal code.

In *The Genesis of the Canadian Criminal Code of 1892*, Desmond Brown explains the origins of the Code in the context of the social and political circumstances of nineteenth-century Canada. This authoritative study of the events leading to the enactment of the Code adds significantly to our understanding of nineteenth-century Canadian legal processes.

Brendan O'Brien
President

Peter N. Oliver
Editor-in-Chief

Preface

The idea for this work originated in a remark made by Lillian Mac-
Pherson, then the acting law librarian of the University of Alberta. I was
investigating the charges of sedition laid against the leaders of the Winnipeg Strike of 1919, and I was curious to know why 'sedition' was not
defined in the Criminal Code of the day. I asked Lillian if there was a
history of the Code. She replied, 'No. Are you going to write one?' I
thought this a most interesting and worthwhile project and one that
was long overdue. My then supervisor, Roderick Macleod, agreed. I
would like to record my debt to him for his aid and encouragement
through some very dark days. I am also grateful to Professors F.D.
Blackley, Wilbur F. Bowker, and William H. Jones, as well as to the late
Professor Lewis H. Thomas. Whatever literary merit the work has was
enhanced by the painstaking analysis and criticism it was subjected to
by my good friends Ann Henderson-Nichol and Stanley Gordon. I am,
of course, responsible for the errors and infelicities that remain. I wish
to extend my sincere thanks to the staff of the Law Library of the University of Alberta, particularly to Peter Freeman, Patricia Remple, Neil
Campbell and Elsie Rothrock, and to the staff of the Cambridge University Library Archives.

I was fortunate enough to have been awarded fellowships by the
Canada Council, the Izaak Walton Killam Trustees, and the University
of Alberta. These awards enabled me to work full-time on my studies;
I am profoundly grateful for this privilege.

The Genesis of the Canadian Criminal Code of 1892

The laws of the most kingdoms and states have been like buildings of many pieces, and patched up from time to time according to occasions, without frame or model.

... this continual heaping up of laws without digesting them maketh but a chaos and confusion, and turneth the laws many times to become but snares for the people.

Then look into the state of your laws and justice of your land: purge out multiplicity of laws: clear the incertainty of them: repeal those that are snaring; and press the execution of those that are wholesome and necessary ...

Francis Bacon

Introduction

A year after the passage of the Great Reform Bill of 1832 in the imperial Parliament, one of its principal and most eloquent advocates began a process intended to effect another great and necessary reform: the amelioration and systematization of the cruel, capricious, and obscure criminal law by a process of substantive amendment and codification. In a commission issued to several eminent jurists and barristers, Henry Brougham, lord chancellor, instructed them, in part, to

> digest into one Statute all the Statutes and enactments touching Crimes, and the trial and punishment thereof, and also to digest into one other Statute all the provisions of the common or unwritten Law touching the same, and to inquire and report how far it may be expedient to combine both those Statutes into one body of the Criminal Law, repealing all other statutory provisions, or how far it may be expedient to pass into a law the first-mentioned only of the said Statutes, and generally to inquire and report how far it may be expedient to consolidate the other branches of the existing Statute Law, or any of them.[1]

Although the movement for reform by codification had begun some fifty years earlier, this was the first time in nearly two hundred years that it had been made policy. Although the efforts of the commission were to no avail, in that none of the legislation proposed by it was enacted, the movement gathered strength over the years, and several later commissions pondered the reform of the criminal law. Learned reports were produced, and some specific areas of the criminal law were rationalized by consolidated acts. But this is all that was achieved, for although several codes were drafted and introduced in Parliament, they were withdrawn or became null and void by prorogation or dissolution prior to third reading. The movement culminated in 1880, when a bill drafted by the eminent jurist Sir James Fitzjames Stephen, and amended by a commission of distinguished judges, was introduced in the House of Commons a few days after the opening of Parliament. In his opening remarks on first reading, the bill's sponsor, Attorney General Sir John Holker, said that 'it attempted what had never, he believed, been attempted before – the codification of a substantial part of the law. It proposed to state in a number of terse, lucid, and comprehensive sentences, the law of England and Ireland upon the subject of ordinary crime, and also the law relating to the procedure by indictment against those who committed such crimes. This codification was exceedingly desirable, and would, if accomplished in this instance, set an example for codification of the law generally.'[2] This bill, too, was left on the order paper when Disraeli dissolved Parliament prematurely two weeks later over the question of Irish home rule and then lost the ensuing election. In this way the movement toward codification of the criminal law was halted after fifty years of progress and the expenditure of much time and money.[3]

In contrast, eleven years later, with no fanfare and with little advance warning, the Canadian minister of justice, Sir John Thompson, introduced in the Canadian Parliament a bill that incorporated many of the reforms and innovations proposed by Stephen and his judicial colleagues. Some fourteen months later, on 9 July 1892, a Canadian Criminal Code received royal assent. Canada thus became the first self-governing jurisdiction in the British empire to codify its criminal law.

Why was this so? Why was it possible to do in Canada in a few months what could not be done at all in England? How was Thompson able to convince legislators in the Canadian Parliament that such a bill was necessary, and why did he not wait to see how affairs progressed in other British jurisdictions that were preparing to pass similar legislation? Why was the measure adopted in 1892? Why not in the 1870s or 1880s, when codification bills were before the imperial Parliament and when assemblymen enacted criminal codes in several of the United States? The Canadian act is much longer than the English draft. Why should a dominion with far fewer inhabitants and with a less complex social structure require more law than the mother country? This in turn raises the question of the origins of the Canadian bill: who drafted it, and what were his or their guidelines? Was it enacted to effect a reform of the substantive law as well as systematization, or was it merely an administrative measure, an attempt to tidy up the tangled mass of statutes and common law precedents that then constituted the criminal law?

The aim of this study is to provide answers to these questions. But in order to lay a firm foundation for the work and to give the reader a historical perspective, it is first necessary to define the terms that will be used in the discussion. What, for example, is a 'code'? When and where did the concept of codification evolve? Why did it develop in different forms in those jurisdictions that have provided the models on which most modern codes are based – that is, in England, France, and Germany?

1

Definitions and Descriptions

In the legal sense the verb 'to codify' was first noted in the English language about 1800, when Jeremy Bentham said, 'I propose to codify this.'[1] What he proposed to codify was the vast and impenetrable forest of eighteenth-century English statute and common law; the remark was made with specific reference to his essay 'A General View of a Complete Code of Laws,'[2] in which he set forth a detailed plan to achieve his aim. Although he did not define the term in so many words, the essence of his argument can be summarized, in general terms, by either of the current definitions of 'codify' in the *Oxford English Dictionary*: 'To reduce (laws) to a code; to digest ... to reduce to a general system; to systematize.'[3] The derivative of the verb, the noun 'codification,' was also invented by Bentham, or, at least, his was the first noted use of the word in print, in the title of another essay, 'Papers relative to Codification and Public Instruction,' published in 1817.[4] Again, he did not offer a definition of the term, but an examination of his writings leaves us in no doubt about the process he advocated to formulate a code. The work, he said, should be 'a complete digest: such is the first rule. Whatever is not in the code of laws should not be law.'[5] The main part of the compendium would be made by undertaking 'a general revision of the existing laws, the rejection of the antiquated and useless portions ... and the reduction of those parts which should be preserved, to a clear order, and to precise and intelligible language.'[6] In this revision all law, enacted and judge-made, would be included,[7] and would be separated into substantive law – authoritative orders creating and regulating rights – and 'adjectival' or 'procedural' law, both of which terms were also invented and defined by Bentham.[8] The substantive law would then be subdivided by subject, and each collection would form a subgroup of the code.[9] When new law was required, either to fill the gap created by the abrogation of previous provisions or to regulate predictable but as yet unforeseen events, it should be written in accordance with rational principles and enacted by the legislature to complete the collection.[10] Inevitably, with use, errors and omissions would be discovered in the code by the bench, the bar, and the public at large. Such flaws should be pointed out to the legislature, preferably accompanied by suggestions for correcting the defects. On the basis of this input, periodic reviews would integrate such improvements as the legislators thought beneficial, and the task of amendment would be much facilitated by having the whole body of the law before the assembly in a rational and coherent format.[11]

Clearly, Bentham contemplated not only the systematization but the reform of existing law. Now the process of codification itself implies reform, but administrative reform only: literally, a codification reformulates disparate elements and so constitutes a cohesive whole. But except in matters of minor detail, codification is not synonymous with reform of the substantive law, progressive or otherwise.[12] The reader must therefore distinguish carefully between Bentham's plan to codify the law current in his day and his proposals for substantive reform, since he himself did not make that distinction explicit.

All things considered, however, Bentham's failure to point out this difference was a minor flaw in a conception of genius, and one that was rectified as draftsmen of codified legislation gained experience. For example, the distinction is made over and over again in a discussion of the Bills of Exchange Act, 1882, the first codifying enactment to pass safely the rocks and shoals of debate in the imperial Parliament and to receive royal assent.[13] Its draftsman was an experienced lawyer in the field, Sir MacKenzie Chalmers, who was told that the act must be 'introduced in a form which did nothing more than codify the existing law, and that all amendments should be left to Parliament.'[14] Accordingly, his aim was to 'reproduce as exactly as possible the existing law, whether it seemed good, bad, or indifferent'; although he did stipulate that 'codification pure and simple is an impossibility' because occasional doubtful points of law must be decided one way or the other.[15]

That he was successful is self-evident. His experience is in direct contrast to that of the draftsman of the abortive Partnership Bill of 1882, which 'codified the law of partnership' but failed when it 'encountered the adverse trade wind of hostile mercantile opposition' because 'it also proposed to effect some considerable changes in the existing law.'[16] In contrast with this variant, but in line with Chalmers's concept of codification, the *OED* defines the term as the 'reduction (of laws) to a code ... systematization,'; *Jowitt's Dictionary of English Law* renders it as 'the collection of all the principles of any system of law into one body after the manner of the Codex Justinianius and other codes.'[17]

In the civil law jurisdictions across the Channel, where codified law had been the norm for centuries,[18] events moved more quickly than in England, but terminology lagged behind. Although the Napoleonic Codes were promulgated in the first decade of the nineteenth century, the term 'codification' was not noted in French literature until 1819, and the verb 'codifier' not until 1836.[19] Although the process whereby these words entered the French language is unknown, there is a possibility that they are also attributable to Jeremy Bentham. His work began to gain recognition in France in the 1780s. After the revolution broke out, many of his essays were addressed directly to the National Assembly, to such effect that he was made a French citizen by that body in 1792.[20] Moreover, in 1802 his Genevan editor and translator, Etienne Dumont, began the systematic publication of a French edition of Bentham's works.[21] There is no doubt that these had an impact on French legislation. One has only to compare the Benthamite plan as set out in 'A General View of a Complete Code of Laws'[22] with the enacted elements of the Napoleonic legislation to see many points of similarity, to say nothing of the public acknowledgment of Bentham's advice and assistance by the French draftsmen.[23] It is not unreasonable to assume that the draftsmen also adopted the English terminology, even though the *OED* would have it the other way round.[24] However, if the plan of the French code is along Benthamite lines and is characterized by the integration of substantive reform with codification, definitions of current terminology are similar in content to those in the English dictionaries and are equally brief and unspecific. For example, 'codifier' is given in the *Grand Larousse* as 'Réunir en un code unique des textes législatifs ou réglementaires des coutumes, etc.' Similarly, 'codification' is defined as 'Action de codifier, de réunir des lois en un code; résultat de cette action.'[25] The fourth edition of the *Lexique de termes juridiques* renders it 'Regroupement dans un texte d'origine Généralement gouvernementale d'un ensemble souvent complexe de dispositions législatives ou réglementaires interessant une même matière.'

Similar terminology was invented and defined even later in Germany. The great *Deutsches Wörterbuch*, which began to be compiled in 1854, lists no terms cognate with 'codify' and 'codification.' However, the verb *kodifizieren* and its derivative *Kodifikation* appear in the 1905 edition of *Muret-Sanders Enzyklopädisches Wörterbuch*, with abbreviated definitions and with no literary quotations to give their first noted use in the language. It is possible, though, to make an educated guess as to why they were coined and defined at the end of the nineteenth century and why no first appearance is cited. From 1874 to 1896 a public debate took place concerning the codification of civil law for the new German empire. The result was the much-imitated *Bürgerliches Gesetzbuch* (BGB).[26] In all probability several of the authors who criticized the first draft of the BGB in a 'flood of papers, pamphlets and books'[27] copied English and French practice and coined both words simultaneously as substitutes for the multi-word descriptions which had had to be used before that time. But this is conjecture. What is not in doubt is that irrespective of their mode of coinage, their current definitions are similar to their English and French cognates and are equally brief and unspecific. Thus, the *Duden* renders *kodifizieren* as *Gesetze, Rechtsnormen in einem Gesetzwerk zusammenfassen* and *Kodifikation* as *Gesetzessammlung, die das gesamte Recht oder einzelne Gebiete des Rechts, systematisch erfaßt.*[28] In the 1971 edition of the *Ullstein Lexikon des Rechts, Kodifikation* is given as *Schaffung eines Gesetzwerkes, insbes.durch Zusammenfassung verschiedener Gesetze bzw. Rechtsnormen des Gewohnheitsrechts.*[29]

Unlike the mutlilingual forms of 'codify' and 'codification,' which are of relatively recent origin, the first products of the action described by these words – codices or books of laws – have been in use at least since the early years of the first Christian millennium, and the concept of a 'code' is almost as old as the first use of writing.[30] Moreover, it has been identified by a specific name in the vernacular tongues of England, France, and Germany from the fourteenth century or earlier. 'Code' is defined in the *OED* as 'a systematic collection or digest of the laws of a country, or of those relating to a particular subject.' Similar meanings are given in the *Grand Larousse*, which specifies that a code is a 'Recueil de lois et de dispositions ayant force de loi dans un pays,' and in the *Duden*, which, with commendable brevity, equates 'code' to *Gesetzbuch.* *Gesetzbuch* in turn, is said to be a *Buch, in dem alle Gesetze über Verordnungen zu einem bestimmten Sachgebiet enthalten sind.*[31] Legal dictionaries use many of the same words to say the same thing. In *Jowitt's Dictionary* a code is defined as 'a collection or system of laws'; in the *Lexique de terms juridiques*, it is given as an Ensemble de lois ordonnées regroupant les matières qui font partie d'une même branche du droit. In the *Ullstein Lexikon*, *Gesetzbuch* is rendered as *ein Gesetz, das eine Rechtsmaterie (z.B. Handelsrecht) weitgehehend regelt (z.B. Handelsgesetzbuch).*[32]

In contrast to the rigorous and minute definition of most legal terms, all the definitions of 'codify' and its derivatives and their various French and German cognates appear to be of a very general nature and patently loosely formulated. But there is good reason for this apparent imprecision. The lexicographers have had to come to terms not only with the theoretical constructs of legal philosophers such as Bentham, but also with the historical fact that enacted codes have been as diverse in form, content, arrangement, and emphasis as the disparate jurisdictions that brought them into being. For example, the body of law promulgated under Justinian I, which 'is distinguished by the appellation of "The Code" by way of eminence,'[33] was drafted to include all the statute law of its day, the written 'Constitutions,' which were arranged by title in a topical order. On promulgation the code abrogated all previous enacted law.[34] Similarly, the United States Code (1970) comprises all the statutes in force collected, consolidated, and arranged in a coherent order, by subject and title. It does not, however, repeal any of the original statutes, nor does it include any part of the common law. In contrast, the French Code civil is based on old Roman models not noted for their rational formats.[35] It is a digest or condensation of the prior statutory and customary law that was not abolished during the revolution, various old royal ordinances, and the revolutionary laws. All of this material was expressly repealed when the Code came into force.[36] For the most part the work is a collection of short, pithy paragraphs which summarize private law in 'rules or principles of relatively narrow scope and of an intensely practical kind.'[37] In its brevity it was not unlike the penal code adopted by the German empire soon after its creation in 1871. That work, which was closely modelled on the French Code pénal of 1810,[38] was a clear and systematic treatment of the indigenous criminal law, and was typical of Continental penal codes in that it was divided into general and special parts.[39] It too abrogated all previous common or statutory law in the individual German states.[40] Therefore, any definition that purports to be inclusive of all past experience must be very general and unspecific, comprising only the element that is common to that experience, namely, the systematization of an existing body of law.

The Canadian Criminal Code of 1892 was yet another variant. Sir John Thompson, who conceived the legislation and who was its most able and informed advocate, did not suggest that the Canadian bill was drafted from first principles. But it was fair to say, as he did when he moved second reading, that it would effect 'a reduction of the law to an orderly written system, freed from needless technicalities, obscurities and other defects which the experience of its administration has disclosed.'[41] He went on to say, however, that although both statute and common law would be codified, only the statute law would be abrogated, and the common law would be left in full effect.[42]

It is apparent that there may be as many variants of the concept of 'code' as there are codes themselves; it is equally apparent that all of those discussed above are codes within the accepted legal definition of the word as laid down in authoritative English, French, and German sources. This point needs not only to be made but to be emphasized, because many Canadian legal writers have held that the Criminal Code of 1892 was not really a code at all, but something much less – a collection or compilation without benefit of unifying principle. For example, in his essay 'Codes and Codification,' J.D. Cameron said, 'Our Criminal Code, though called such in the Act, is not a code but a compilation or consolidation.'[43] This view is also epitomized in the proposals of the Law Reform Commission of Canada, which state that the dominion legislation was not a 'genuine code' but 'merely the first step towards a true codification.'[44]

These views differ sharply from those of the progenitors of the 1892 legislation and of the foremost legal draftsman of the day, James R. Gowan, who said that the Canadian Criminal Code was 'by far and away the most complete codification that has ever been submitted to any legislative body.'[45] In general, eminent contemporary specialists such as Frederick H. Lawson, a professor of comparative law at Oxford, and Glanville Williams, the author of several authoritative works on the criminal law, are in agreement with Gowan's view of Sir John Thompson's very considerable accomplishment.[46] However, to put the Canadian experience in perspective it is first necessary to glance at the untidy and unsystematic evolution of the law in England before the nineteenth century, and then to follow more closely the several unsuccessful attempts that were made to codify English criminal law after that time.

2

Attempts to Codify English Criminal Law

In an assembly that came to be dominated by common lawyers from the late thirteenth century on, English legislation reflected their ethos and method. Statutes were, for the most part, intensely practical and narrowly defined instruments which dealt with a precise and pressing issue.[1] Perhaps William Pitt put it most succinctly when he said, with specific reference to the criminal law, 'The statute laws of this country were not the result of a systematic code. They had grown up to what they were by an accumulation of provisions made to suit offences as they occurred.'[2] They were also unconnected and uncoordinated, and over the years they proliferated. When Henry VIII died in 1547, there were in excess of 2,000 statutes, and by the mid-eighteenth century there were 16,000 or more.[3] To make matters more difficult, parliaments of different eras would deal with the same issues in happy ignorance of legislation already on the books. For example, when Robert Peel was home secretary in 1826, he reported to the House that there were twenty acts dealing with the theft of or wilful damage to trees, each of which prescribed separate and specific penalties ranging from death to a twenty-pound fine.[4] If the statutes were in an untidy tangle, the common law – the unwritten law of precedent – came to constitute a virtually impenetrable labyrinth formed by thousands of judicial decisions delivered over hundreds of years.[5]

From very early days there was dissatisfaction with this state of affairs. Lawyers such as Thomas More, historians such as Raphael Holinshed, and playwrights such as Ben Jonson criticized and lampooned the system unmercifully.[6] The government, in the person of successive lord chancellors, wanted to consolidate and codify the enacted law, and was particularly eager to bring some order to the penal statutes.[7] During the period from about 1540 to 1660 at least fifteen parliamentary committees were struck to draft measures to systematize part or all of the statute law, and four bills to effect this end were introduced – all to no avail.[8]

The most systematic of these attempts was that of Sir Francis Bacon during his tenure as attorney general in 1616. His scheme was based on the plan Justinian had used to codify Roman law in the sixth century.[9] The law officers of the Crown would digest the common law into an authoritative two- or three-volume edition modelled on the *Digest*. At the same time Parliament would be asked to codify the statute law in emulation of the Justinian Code. To accomplish this, Bacon recommended that both Houses nominate members to a joint committee to draft enabling legislation which Parliament could then consider, because '[t]he houses will best like that which themselves guide, and the persons that themselves employ.'[10] He was careful to disavow any intention to make changes in the common law during the process of digesting it, because he knew it would arouse the hostility of the common lawyers, who formed the largest professional group in the House, and thus ensure the defeat of his scheme.[11] The common lawyers' hostility to such proposals was understandable. Any major change in the law, common or statute, would cause much disruption and uncertainty in the profession. Because all the commissions or committees to bring order to the law were largely or entirely composed of lawyers, and because, in matters that affected the profession, they controlled Parliament, they had the means to defeat any such legislation, and they did so consistently.[12]

After the achievement of parliamentary supremacy in the mid-seventeenth century, no more was heard of reform or systematization of the statutes. The climate of opinion that eventually brought on such changes in the criminal law was the result of a reform movement which slowly gathered momentum in the next century. In large measure the impetus for reform came from the writings of Continental legalists, and particularly from Cesare Beccaria's seminal work *On Crimes and Punishments*, published in 1764.[13] In England, *Of Public Wrongs*, the fourth volume of William Blackstone's *Commentaries*, came out five years later,[14] and Jeremy Bentham began his long campaign for reform with his *View of the Hard Labour Bill* of 1778.[15] But in a conservative institution like Parliament the idea of far-reaching change in the law takes time to germinate and grow, and no progressive reforms in systematization received legislative sanction until more than half a century after Blackstone's strictures appeared. In the interim, however, Parliament was responsible for a measure that greatly facilitated the reforms, if indeed it was not an absolute prerequisite for them: the publication of the Statutes of the Realm (SOR).

The process began in 1800 when, in an address to the Crown respecting the public records, the House of Commons reported that in many of the important departments of state such records were 'wholly unarranged, undescribed, and unascertained; that some of them are exposed to Erasure, Alteration, and Embezzlement, and others are lodged in Places where they are daily perishing by Damp, or incurring a continual Risk of Destruction by Fire.'[16]

The House asked the Crown to authorize the printing of the records to preserve the 'ancient and valuable Monuments of our History, Laws and Government.' The request was granted, committees were appointed, and work began. One result was the production of the SOR, which included all the public general acts passed between 1235 and 1714, as well as the charters of the kings before Henry III. Except for the latter, all statutes that had been enacted in Latin or French were translated into English, with the original appearing on one side and the translation on the other side of a double-column page. This monumental work, which was longer than Justinian's Code and rivalled it in the span of time covered, appeared between 1811 and 1824 in nine folio volumes.[17] Like the Code, it contained only statutory enactments, but there were differences: the acts were in chronological order, not topical, and they were reprinted as originally published, with no additions, deletions, or amendments, and with all necessary emendations footnoted.

The significance of this work is that it made possible the eventual reduction of the mass to more manageable proportions, because it was now a simple process to determine which acts were in force. Moreover, because the edition bore the imprimatur of the legislature, argument or litigation over the text as rendered and the text of previous unofficial editions or of the translations was unlikely.[18] Its efficacy in these respects is shown by the fact that in 1825, the year after the final volume was issued, the first major consolidation of statute law was enacted, after the head of the Customs Branch had digested the essence of 452 statutes on customs law in 10 bills. A separate Statute Law Revision Bill repealed the obsolete acts.[19] This process of expurgation continued for the next forty years with or without consolidation, and was virtually complete by 1863.[20] With respect to the penal law, consolidation and statute law revision occurred simultaneously.

On 9 March, in the short session of 1826, Robert Peel, the home secretary in the Tory government of Lord Liverpool, rose in the House of Commons to introduce measures which he said would 'break [the] sleep of a century.'[21] These were bills to consolidate the statute law relating to larceny and to criminal procedure. The former would unite 'into one statute all the enactments that exist, and are fit to be retained, relating to the crime of theft, and to offences immediately connected with theft.'[22] After reintroduction, the larceny bill became law in the following session; the procedure bill received royal assent a few weeks after Peel spoke.

Of course, like most major legislative innovations, these measures did not constitute a sudden and isolated occurrence. Rather, they came as the culmination of many frustrating and abortive attempts to achieve the same ends by distinguished private members such as Sir Samuel Romilly and Sir James Mackintosh.[23] However, by their very efforts they had begun to cause a change of temper in the legislators. This may be seen in the recommendation of a select committee in 1819 that the law of a limited class of penal offences be codified.[24] The change of temper is detectable, too, in the statement of a subsequent committee in 1824 'that it is expedient that the Statutes relating to the Criminal Law, should be consolidated under their several heads,' if it could be done 'without amendment or alteration.'[25] Not only was there a modicum of progressive reform of the substantive law in the bills of 1826 and in subsequent similar measures sponsored by Peel, but they passed through both chambers with no discernible opposition and with evident approbation from both sides of the Commons.[26] It seems that the home secretary had laid the groundwork carefully.

His method of procedure was to separate out all acts of Parliament or parts thereof relating to a specific topic (in this instance, larceny), and to compare their provisions. If the comparison showed an omission, it was supplied,[27] when a principle was only partly applied, it was extended.[28] The substantive portion of each act thus scrutinized was then set down under an appropriate rubric, either in the language of the original or in a paraphrase if the language was archaic. Both indictable and summary offences were included. If different penalties had been specified for the same offence, they were reconciled, and, in a few instances, the death penalty was mitigated in favour of a lesser punishment.[29] Since an addendum to the bill referred the reader to the source of each clause,[30] it was an easy matter to compare the proposal with the original enactments in the SOR, and so to ensure that there had been no change in the substantive law other than that specified by the home secretary.[31] The draft bills were prepared by ministerial staff assisted by an eminent barrister, which kept costs to a minimum, and when they were ready they were submitted to the judges of the senior benches for comment on the detail of the subject matter. Several judges, whom Peel named, responded with 'very useful suggestions.'[32] He invited the members at large to do likewise.[33] All of this information was in his speech of 9 March, which began with his reference to Francis Bacon's proposal of 1616.

In fact, he quoted the lord chancellor's opening argument clause by clause, and thus cut the ground from under any opposition by anticipating and answering all probable objections. Furthermore, he was able to improve on Bacon's answer to the objection that English laws were no more prolix or obscure than those of other jurisdictions by noting that since Bacon's time many 'foreign nations [had] condensed and simplified their laws.'[34] When he said this, Peel was undoubtedly referring not only to the civil law jurisdictions of the Continent and the codified legislation of Louisiana, but also to the considerable number of common law jurisdictions in the United States that had systematized their statute law before the date of his speech.[35] He went on to buttress his argument for consolidation with copious and relevant statistics. For those members who were curious why the home secretary and not a law officer was introducing such measures, he informed them that he was 'placed in an office which devolves upon me the duty of superintending, in many important respects, the administration of justice, which entitles me to advise the Crown as to the remission or execution of almost every sentence of the law, and which gives me daily, I might say, hourly opportunities of witnessing the practical operation of the statutes which I am attempting to simplify and amend. These considerations will probably relieve me from the charge of any unwarranted and presumptuous interference in matters which I do not comprehend.'[36] Moreover, his saying this provided Peel with the opportunity to describe how expert legal aid had been employed in the drafting of his bills, to give profuse thanks to the judges for their assistance, and, by implication, to suggest that the bench had given its unreserved support to the measures. And this brought him to the legal members, who still formed the largest professional group in the Commons – 112 members, or 17 per cent of those sitting.[37] 'It is the fashion to impute to that profession an unwillingness to remove the uncertainty and obscurity of the law, from the sordid desire to benefit from its complexity. This is a calumny which I know to be unfounded; for I have never made, in the progress of this work, a single application to any member of the profession of the law, which has not been received in the spirit which becomes a generous mind, rising above the narrow prejudices of habit, and the paltry view of private gain.'[38] Most significantly, he assured the House on several occasions that there would be little substantive change because, like Bacon's, his work tended 'to pruning and grafting the law, and not to ploughing up and planting it again ...'[39] and he disavowed any intention to meddle with the common law.

Peel's speech was a virtuoso performance. It was cogent, logical, beautifully phrased, and calculated to appeal to the deep-rooted conservatism of the members. But above and beyond this it was also a plea from a non-lawyer member to the majority of the House, who were of like standing, to help him put through vital legislation. At the same time, he propitiated bench and bar, the traditional sources of opposition to such legislation, and so made it virtually impossible for the profession to attack either the detail or the principle of his bills. No wonder he concluded his presentation 'amidst loud cheers.'[40]

Peel's later performances were no less carefully planned and no less successful.[41] By the time his tenure as home secretary ended in 1830, well over half the criminal law had been consolidated in a manner which, allowing for the differences between the French and the British systems, was not unlike Napoleon's methodical procedure prior to the enactment of the Code civil.[42] Among the most important of Peel's acts were those concerning procedure, larceny, malicious damage to property, offences against the person, and forgery.[43] These relatively short pieces of legislation covered forty-five folio pages in total. But the almost mechanical technique used to draft them, and the fact that each section, regardless of length, was one interminable sentence, complete with enacting words, produced the most stultifying prose.[44] Furthermore, much procedural matter remained embedded in substantive provisions. A fair sample is section 8 of 7 & 8 Geo. 4, 1827, c. 30, the statute concerning malicious damage to property, which, in 11 lines, replaced four redundant statutes containing a total of 171 lines, or about three folio pages:

And be it enacted, That if any Persons, riotously and tumultuously assembled together to the Disturbance of the Public Peace, shall unlawfully and with Force demolish, pull down, or destroy, or begin to demolish, pull down, or destroy, any Church or Chapel, or any Chapel for the Religious Worship of Persons dissenting from the United Church of England and Ireland, duly registered or recorded, or any House, Stable, Coach-house, Outhouse, Warehouse, Office, Shop, Mill, Malthouse, Hop Oast, Barn, or Granary, or any Building or Erection used in carrying on any Trade or Manufacture, or any Branch thereof, or any Machinery, whether fixed or moveable, prepared for or employed in any Manufacture, or in any Branch thereof, or any Steam Engine or other Engine for sinking, draining, or working any Mine, or any Staith, Building, or Erection used in conducting the Business of any Mine, or any Bridge, Waggonway, or Trunk for conveying Minerals from any Mine, every such Offender shall be guilty of Felony, and, being convicted thereof, shall suffer Death as a Felon.[45]

Although it is mind-numbing to attempt to read and comprehend these redundant phrases and long lists of nouns, it is important to realize what a change had been wrought in the statute-book and how the achievement was viewed by Peel. He took great pride in pointing out that a dozen or so short acts, in which a modest number of changes in the substantive law had been made, had now replaced hundreds of penal statutes enacted over the past six hundred years.[46] Given the clarity and force of his own use of English, he may not have been gratified by the phraseology of his acts, but he was a pragmatist. He was willing to settle for a bird in the hand rather than several in the bush. He gave Parliament what it wanted in terms of continuity with the past, and proposed no radical reform of words or content 'for the chance of speculative and uncertain improvement.'[47] In return, his bills were enacted.

Henry Brougham was less accommodating. While he was probably the most eloquent advocate of reform in or out of the Commons, this brilliant but unpredictable and caustic polymath also had a remarkable ability to alienate everyone who did not wholly agree with his proposals. With respect to the legal system these were radical enough, for he had long been an intimate of Jeremy Bentham, and from his first days in Parliament had advocated sweeping changes in accordance with Benthamite principles.[48] In need of Brougham's continuing support, but unwilling to allow him to harangue the House from the treasury bench, Lord Grey elevated him to lord chancellor on the Whig accession to power in 1830. Promotion to the peerage may have deprived Brougham of his accustomed forum, but it did not prevent him from launching many reform measures from the upper chamber.

Among these was the Commission of 1833, in which he directed a group of eminent practitioners to digest the criminal statute law into

one bill and the common law on the subject into another, and to recommend whether it would be expedient to combine both in a single
enactment.[49] After answering this question in the affirmative in their
first report, the commissioners proceeded to implement their recommendations.[50] The process took more than ten years, during which time
they made a comparative study of codified legislation from the Continent, the United States, and India, and subjected English legislation to
the most 'thorough examination [it] has received at an official level before
or since.'[51] Seven more reports were submitted; the seventh (1843) and
the eighth (1845) were, respectively, a draft code of indictable offences
and a procedural code following the French model.[52] While the former
would have made only a modest number of changes in the substantive
law, and thus would have called for little rewording of a specific section,
it would have made a decided change in the overall form of the law.[53]
On 170 folio pages a systematic exposition of indictable offences and
punishments was set out, in which related crimes were grouped under
general chapter titles, such as 'Offences against the Administration of
Justice' and 'Offences against Public Health'; a 'Chapter of Penalties'
defined forty-five specific punishments. But perhaps the most striking
innovation was the form of the code. Drawing from Continental models
and from codes from the common law jurisdictions of the United States,
the draftsmen divided the work into consecutively numbered chapters,
each of which contained numbered sections beginning at '1' in each
chapter. Each section contained one or more articles numbered inde-
pendently of the first two systems, so that subsequent amendments
would not disarrange the numbering of succeeding sections and chapters.[54] Furthermore, the words of enactment were omitted from all but
the preamble. However, unlike the French code, which was exhaustive
of the penal law, the commissioners' draft did not include offences
punishable on summary conviction. From their first report it seems that
they had intended to deal with such offences,[55] but nothing more is
heard of the matter until the seventh report, which mentions the omission in passing but gives no reason for it, other than to say that 'it would
not be desirable that such provisions should be incorporated with the
crimes of a higher and more general nature.'[56]

Although Brougham had long ceased to be chancellor and was, in
fact, in opposition when the draft code came out in 1843, he nevertheless
introduced it in the House of Lords as a private bill the following year.[57]
Later, in long and eloquent (if not always politic) speeches, he urged
the House to support the measure and so reduce the penal law to a

coherent, orderly system. To no avail: neither the Tory chancellor, Lord Lyndhurst, nor learned colleagues from Brougham's side of the chamber were impressed. In the main they objected to the inclusion of relevant portions of the common law in the bill, and it was given second reading only after Lyndhurst had made it clear that it would go no further in that session, but would be sent to a new commission which he would convene.[58] This was done; five reports were issued during the next five years, with the fourth (1848) and the fifth (1849) containing revisions of the code of indictable offences and the procedure code, reworked and shortened, but not otherwise altered, except for a provision that abrogated the common law on the subject.[59]

When the Whigs returned to power in 1846, Lord John Russell formed a ministry in which Brougham had no place. Nevertheless, he again took the initiative and introduced the Indictable Offences Bill in the session of 1848. Since Parliament's prevailing attitude toward reform had expressed itself in the recent enforcement of an otherwise forgotten seventeenth-century statute to prevent the Chartists from presenting their monster petition to Parliament en masse,[60] and since revolution was raging in the country that had provided the model for the legislation, it was not a particularly auspicious occasion. Perhaps this is the reason he did not press for its passage in that session, but urged the members to give it their attention during prorogation. Lord Cottenham, the Whig chancellor, sounded relieved at this turn of events, since the bill 'related to a subject upon which many different opinions existed and one which required serious consideration.' Lord Campbell, a future chief justice and chancellor, also sounded relieved, but he took the opportunity to remark that if Brougham 'had communicated privately with the Judges, and with other persons conversant with this subject, he might have brought his Bill to something like perfection before he had submitted it to the House.'[61] Brougham might have been able to take such criticism from a party colleague without visible ire, but he was not prepared to see the bill criticized by a much younger man, the Earl of Powis, from the other side of the chamber. After Powis's speech, in which he commented unfavourably on a provision in the chapter on treason, Brougham said he 'rejoiced to see the earnestness and zeal with which the noble Earl had taken up this subject; but he might be allowed to observe that zeal was more valuable when it was accompanied by knowledge, than when it was dissociated from it.'[62] Debate petered out soon after this exchange, and no one cheered when Brougham sat down. The bill was sent to a select committee, where it remained in limbo until 1852.

In that year Lord St Leonards, the chancellor in the short-lived Conservative administration of Lord Derby, was prevailed upon to proceed with the codification of the criminal law. To effect that end, he instructed the legal draftsman Charles Greaves and a colleague to prepare a series of separate bills based on the chapters of the criminal law commissioners' drafts. Like those drafts, the new bills were to incorporate both common and statute law; they were to be confined to indictable offences and would abrogate all common law on the subject not incorporated in the text. Lord Cranworth, who succeeded St Leonards as chancellor in Lord Aberdeen's coalition government in 1852, carried on the work by introducing one of the new bills in the Lords, where it was referred to a committee.[63] Perhaps mindful of Campbell's rebuke to Brougham for not consulting the judiciary, Cranworth also sent the draft legislation to the personnel of the senior benches. Unlike Peel, who had requested only comment from the judges on the detail of his bills, Cranworth asked whether 'they consider[ed] that the bringing of the whole criminal law, as far as relates to offences and their punishment, into one or more statute or statutes ... would be a measure likely to produce benefit in the administration of criminal justice, or the reverse.'[64] Their replies, which were published in *Parliamentary Papers*, were unanimous: they were opposed to the change. Although several respondents made searching and detailed criticisms of the substance of the proposed legislation, the primary objection was, as it had been in 1844, that Parliament should not tamper with the common law. This view was epitomized by Mr Justice Alderson, who said, 'Let the Bill ... be confined to consolidating and amending, if necessary, the statute law as to these crimes, and adding new provisions where doubts have arisen ... but let us retain the rules and principles of the common law as they have been handed down to us from our predecessors,' and by Mr Justice Talfourd, who argued that 'to reduce unwritten law to statute is to disregard one of the greatest blessings we have for ages enjoyed in rules capable of flexible interpretation.'[65] After this devastating rebuff, nothing more was heard of codification for more than twenty years.

However, criminal law was still perceived to be unsystematic; thus, Parliament, moving in the direction pointed by the judiciary, instructed Greaves to draw up legislation to consolidate the major divisions of the statute penal law. In turn, he made a strong and convincing argument to the lord chancellor that each bill should be exhaustive of a particular branch of the law, and should thus include both summary and indictable offences.[66] This was done, and in 1861, in a remarkably effective speech,

Solicitor-General Sir William Atherton introduced the seven measures that have since become known as Greaves's Criminal Consolidation Acts. In particular, he stressed that the bills had been drafted by experts working under the direction of a parliamentary committee; that no attempt had been made to codify the law or to integrate any part of the common law in the bill; that there had been no interference with the common law; and that members were invited to settle in committee those provisions concerning punishments that might prove controversial.[67]

Thus, Atherton took a line that is reminiscent of Peel's approach in the 1820s, and it will be observed that the wheel had also turned full circle with respect to the legislation itself. This was by design, for Greaves was of the opinion that Peel had pursued a systematic course which had 'worked extremely well' in producing beneficial legislation; he therefore 'determined to frame as many of the new Bills as could be in accordance with [Peel's] Acts.'[68] Moreover, Greaves, like Sir Robert, was a pragmatist, for although he held 'that a code of the Criminal Law embodying the unwritten as well as the written law, can be framed,' he was emphatic that 'it is a very different question, whether such a code could ever be passed through Parliament, and my strong impression is that it never could be so passed. Neither House of Parliament would adopt bills prepared on such a principle without examination.'[69] In the event, Greaves's bills were all enacted with little alteration. Since they had been drafted on the earlier model, however, they had the same defects and merits. On the one hand, they employed the same tedious and redundant phraseology and concentrated on particulars rather than principles. Furthermore, apart from the omission of words of enactment from all but the first section of an act, they resembled Peel's acts in appearance, since Greaves did not employ the technical innovations introduced by Brougham's draftsmen.[70] On the other hand, much consolidation was effected, and 106 redundant statutes were abrogated. In particular, seventeen lines of Greaves's Malicious Damage to Property Act replaced a total of fifty-five lines from Peel's act and two other repealed statutes.[71]

But if limited consolidation was still the order of the day in the imperial Parliament of 1861, other common law jurisdictions were forging ahead with comprehensive codification projects. Massachusetts, for example, had advanced to the forefront of the codification movement in 1836 with an elegant code of all its statute law.[72] In New York, David Dudley Field and his fellow commissioners were progressing well with the draft state penal and procedural codes.[73] Moreover, even before these were enacted, they served as the models for similar codes in several of the other states, including Georgia, where they were adopted in 1863, and California, where they came into force in 1866.[74] On the other side of the world, the Indian Penal Code was promulgated in 1861 after a long gestation.[75] It was the product of two law commissions, and the initial draft, written by Thomas Babington Macaulay in 1837, was the 'first specimen of an entirely new and original method of legislative expression.' But though it may have been a model code and much admired abroad, it was one of a kind and would not have seen the light of day in a self-governing dominion.[76] No Indian was employed in drafting the bill, and no indigenous criminal law was included; it was English law written by English legalists. Not unnaturally, this was resented by the Indian intelligentsia.[77] To add insult to injury, the bill was promulgated as law by the Legislative Council, a body of twenty men, all of whom were British and had been appointed by the secretary of state for India or by the governor general in accordance with the India Act of 1861.[78] One such appointee was the legal member, whose duty it was to draft legislation as directed by the autocratic council. The first incumbent was the eminent legal scholar, Sir Henry Maine, who taught law at Cambridge in the 1850s.

Maine's successor in 1869 was one of his former students, James Fitzjames Stephen. Born in 1829, the son of the evangelical 'Mr Over Secretary Stephen' of the Colonial Office, he grew up with all the advantages enjoyed by the son of an upper-class literary family.[79] Nevertheless, he did not distinguish himself academically at Eton, Cambridge, or the Inns of Court. At the time of his appointment Stephen was a practising barrister of no great forensic talent with a large family to provide for.[80] He had a way with the written word, however, and wrote a prodigious number of editorials, reviews, articles, and books.[81] Although his interests were catholic, he tended to legal subjects, and, as a Benthamite, to the systematization of the law.[82] On his own testimony, Stephen was the epitome of the Victorian legalist: fair, and a staunch supporter of the rule of law, but uncompromising and élitist.[83] Since he was also an articulate critic of democracy and its possible ramifications, and of parliamentary government as then practised, he was admirably fitted by experience and inclination for his new appointment. He worked well in the Indian system, and 'left the Legislative Council breathless and staggering' with his 'unprecedented labours.'[84] To be precise: in just over two years Stephen was either the sole or the principal author of twenty-two major measures, including codes of evidence and criminal procedure, which were duly promulgated.[85] Considering the leisurely pace at which legislation usually proceeded through Westminster, the contrast between the two systems is at once apparent.

After returning to England in 1872, Stephen again became immersed in work at the bar and in journalism. But he concerned himself increasingly with the drafting of penal legislation and especially with codification, in the hope that such employment would secure him a place on the bench, and with it financial security and the opportunity to pursue his own interests.[86] Articles on codification flowed from his pen, and within months of his return he was commissioned to draft an evidence bill modelled on his Indian code; it was introduced in the Commons, but did not get beyond first reading.[87] Concurrently, he drafted the unsuccessful Homicide Bill, and in 1874 he was retained by the Colonial Office to revise the recently completed draft Jamaican Criminal Code, a measure that was intended to serve as a model for all British dependencies.[88] But his major work of the period, which he also began in 1874, was his *Digest of the Criminal Law*, an octavo volume of 411 pages divided into 6 parts, 46 chapters, and 398 articles.[89]

This work, which was three years in the writing and is now in its ninth edition, is a systematic treatment of indictable offences, both from statute and common law, and accomplished a significant compression of both sources.[90] However, its subject-matter was predetermined, and Stephen had a multitude of models from which to draw. For example, in its general layout and in the use of technical innovations in its structure it is not unlike the draft codes of 1843 and 1848; the fact that, unlike previous writers such as Blackstone, he did not make even a reference to summary offences also points to the influence of Brougham's commissioners. Similarly, the inclusion of detailed examples after most substantive articles is reminiscent of Macaulay's draft Indian Penal Code of 1837. It is emphasized that, while the *Digest* was not unlike the French or German penal codes in appearance and text, it was not a code in the sense that they were. It did not constitute authority: that is to say, a barrister could not quote the text of the *Digest* to support his case; he was required instead to quote from the judgment or statute cited by the author. But this is not to disparage Stephen's accomplishment, for the *Digest* pointed a new direction in English legal writing. Instead of attempting to enumerate particulars, he 'boiled down' all the redundant material, to use his favourite expression, and reduced it to a principle. This not only cut down the bulk of the law, but also reduced much tedious repetition. Stephen himself explained his method in his 'Penal Code': 'I will take a section from an Act of Parliament in the exact words in which it stands and then I will give its meaning in other words, which

I say are identically the same, only that they are arranged in a different manner.'[91] He then quoted section 11 of the Malicious Damage to Properties Act of 1861:

If any persons riotously and tumultuously assembled together to the disturbance of the public peace, shall unlawfully and with force demolish or pull down or destroy, or begin to demolish, pull down or destroy, any church, chapel, meeting-house, or other place of divine worship, or any house, stable, coach-house, out-house, warehouse, office, shop, mill, malt-house, hop-oast, barn, granary, shed, hovel, or fold, or any building or erection used in farming land, or in carrying on any trade or manufacture, or any branch thereof, or any building other than such as are in this section before mentioned, belonging to the Queen or to any county, riding, division, city, borough, poor-law union, parish, or place, or belonging to any university or college, or hall of any university, or to any inn of court, or devoted or dedicated to public use or ornament, or erected or maintained by public subscription or contribution, or any machinery, whether fixed or movable, prepared for or employed in any manufacture, or in any branch thereof, or any steam engine or other engine for sinking, working, ventilating, or draining any mine or any staith, building, or erection used in conducting the business of any mine, or any bridge, waggon-way, or trunk for conveying minerals from any mine, every such offender shall be guilty of felony, and being convicted thereof shall be liable at the discretion of the Court to be kept in penal servitude for life, or for any term not less than three years, or to be imprisoned for any term not exceeding two years with or without hard labour, and with or without solitary confinement.

The section is set out in 17 folio lines of print, and contains 276 words. Stephen set out the same section 'expressed in a different manner':

All persons are guilty of felony, and on conviction are liable to penal servitude for life as a maximum punishment, who being riotously and tumultuously assembled together to the disturbance of the public peace, unlawfully and with force demolish, or pull down, or destroy any of the buildings, public buildings, machinery, or mining plant mentioned in the notes hereto, or begin to do so [notes omitted].

This runs to 64 words; the notes define the various types of building and machinery specified in the 1861 act. However:

The meaning of these two statements is identically the same ... but the one is perfectly clear and can be understood in a moment; the other leaves on the mind only a confused impression of a multitude of words. The difference between the two is as follows: – In the one the verb follows the nominative case. 'Every one commits felony who,' & c. In the other the mind is kept in suspense till the end of an interminable sentence before it learns what is to be the consequence if persons riotously assembled do any one of a vast number of things specified ... The shorter form has the advantage of suggesting to the mind the possibility of dispensing with the notes altogether, reading 'building' for 'buildings,' and striking out the words 'of the,' 'public buildings,' and 'mentioned in the notes hereto.'

The section is thus reduced to 55 words, or less than 20 per cent of the original. The successive efforts of Peel, Greaves, and Stephen had reduced seven statutes, with a total of 226 lines occupying between four and five folio pages, to 4 lines of print; and the principle had been laid down that it was an offence to destroy any building, machinery, or mining plant. Stephen was equally succinct when he coined his definitions from the common law. For example, he reduced many pages of description and explanation in judgments and books of practice to one line of print when he defined homicide as 'the killing of a human being by a human being.'[92]

'A Penal Code' came out in March 1877, and was an edited version of a speech given by Stephen to the Trade Union Congress (TUC) in February.[93] Lord Coleridge, chief justice of the Court of Common Pleas, was in the chair, and many distinguished legalists and politicians were present in the audience, which cheered loudly at the close of Stephen's remarks. The event was reported in *The Times* the next day in a long and favourable article, and was further broadcast two days later in *The Law Times*.[94] The latter account also included the text of a resolution urging the government to codify the law, which was proposed and given unanimous approval after Stephen's address. In addition to the articulate and influential members of the upper classes which these publications had reached, he now had a large and approving audience among the lower classes. To complete his coverage, as it were, he sent presentation copies of the *Digest* to many of the more influential members of the government and nobility after it was published early in April.[95] Considering all his other activities and that he had to earn a living, this was an unusual flurry of activity even for Stephen, but some light may be shed on it by his correspondence with senior legal officials.

'Sleepy Jack' Holker, the attorney general in Disraeli's second administration, was a contemporary of Stephen, but he had come to prominence by a very different route. Born in 1828, the son of a manufacturer in an obscure Midlands cotton town, he attended the local grammar school, went on to article for a county solicitor, and eventually was entered at Gray's Inn. Holker was characterized by his biographer as 'a tall lumbering Lancashire man ... somewhat dull but altogether honest.' Unlike Stephen, he was an accomplished advocate; his 'persuasiveness, shrewdness, and tact [made] him extraordinarily successful in winning verdicts,' and enabled him to earn, in his best years, upwards of £20,000 per annum.[96] Before his appointment as attorney general in 1875, Holker had become interested in the abortive Homicide Bill, and had redrawn the measure. Correspondence with Stephen followed,[97] and a friendship evidently developed, because Stephen rejoiced that in the attorney general he had secured 'at least one real convert' to his codification project.[98] On 20 January 1877 Stephen sent a letter to Holker which was in effect a proposal for, and an outline of, a penal code.[99] Although it was to be based on his *Digest*, he proposed to do what the *Digest* could not – namely, make many major alterations to the law. In the first paragraphs he recapitulated a previous conversation with the attorney general, and it is evident that he expected a sympathetic reception for a proposition that was obviously drafted for a larger audience. On 5 March, after the TUC speech but just before 'A Penal Code' was issued, Holker sent Stephen's proposal to Lord Chancellor Cairns with a covering letter that deserves extensive quotation:

PRIVATE

My Dear Lord Chancellor,

I have good reason to believe that the question of the consolidation or codification of some portion of the law, will before long be brought before the House of Commons.

There is a feeling in the country which is rapidly gaining strength that something ought to be done in this direction.

Being a good deal interested in the matter myself I have lately been in communication with Sir James Stephen, who as you are aware has paid much attention to the subject, and in consequence of what has happened between us, he has addressed to me a letter containing suggestions for a measure for the amendment of the criminal law, which would be a fitting preparation for its ultimate codification ...

If after consideration of the letter you should come to the conclusion that it will be advisable to introduce some such measure as the one suggested, I am fully convinced that Sir James Stephen would merely in consequence of the deep interest he takes in the question and not with any expectation of remuneration for his labour, afford every assistance in his power to secure the production of a satisfactory Bill, and need hardly say I would devote all my energies to the same object ...[100]

Cairns, a strong-minded, enigmatic man and 'the first lawyer of his time,' was, as Disraeli's chief political adviser, one of the most powerful Victorian chancellors.[101] He was also an early advocate and practitioner of the systematization of the enacted law.[102] In 1868, after the consolidation of the statutes begun in 1825 was complete and soon after his appointment as chancellor, he issued a commission to publish a revised edition of the statutes containing only the acts in force, and appointed a statute law committee consisting of Sir Francis Reilly, the parliamentary draftsman, and senior law officers of the Crown to supervise the work and sundry other matters connected with the enacted law.[103] In 1877, during Cairns's second appointment as lord chancellor, the last volumes of this work were in the press. Thus, when Stephen mounted his campaign for codification, much of the tangled legislative underbrush of the previous six centuries had already been cleared away, and it is likely that, far from needing to be pressured or prodded to proceed with codification – and Cairns was not the man to be coerced – he welcomed Stephen's initiative to codify the penal law, especially since much of it had been consolidated by Peel and Greaves. The lord chancellor was evidently convinced of the need for action, since he scribbled a note to himself on the back of an envelope to instruct his secretary to inform Stephen that he (Cairns) was in agreement with the attorney general regarding codification, and to commission Stephen to draft a penal code and a code of criminal procedure.[104]

But the lord chancellor did not act on his *aide-mémoire* immediately. Instead, he sent Stephen's outline to Sir Francis Reilly and copies to the other members of the statute law committee, who would thus be able to compare the measure with a recent report on consolidation of the penal law prepared for them by Robert S. Wright, the London barrister who had written the draft Jamaican Criminal Code.[105] Meanwhile Stephen, who may have learned indirectly of Cairns's interest in a procedural code, sent a proposal directly to the lord chancellor in which he offered to amend and codify both the substantive and administrative criminal law. Unlike Holker, he raised the question of payment, but said he would accept any remuneration Cairns considered fair, so long as his drafts would receive serious consideration, such as referral to a royal commission.[106] Two weeks later he followed up his proposal with an eight-page printed outline of a code of procedure.[107]

Then Holker again took up his pen on Stephen's behalf. In another effective memorandum to the lord chancellor, he stressed the advantages that would accrue to the government if the law were codified; he pointed out that Assheton Cross, the home secretary, thought the 'codification of the criminal law ... very desirable,' and urged Cairns to allow Stephen to begin work, so as to 'have the drafts settled by the commencement of the [next] session.'[108] Shortly after this, Reilly reported to Cairns. He had canvassed his colleagues of the statute law committee and had found that they were not enthusiastic about allowing Stephen to proceed with codification. But Reilly did recommend that Stephen be employed to make emendations to the criminal law, since he had 'certainly prepared public opinion to expect and support improvements ...'[109] The upshot of all this activity, and notwithstanding Reilly's recommendations, was that on 2 August Cairns commissioned Stephen 'to draw a Penal Code and a Code of Criminal Procedure at once.'[110] However, the letter from Treasury which authorized a payment to Stephen of twelve hundred pounds (later increased to fifteen hundred guineas) stipulated that it would be made on the completion 'of the three bills for consolidating and codifying the Criminal Law of this Country.'[111] In accordance with past practice, and with the actual organization of the draft code of 1878, the third bill was undoubtedly to be a statute law revision act to repeal the enactments made redundant by the code.[112]

Stephen set to work immediately. The result was a draft code of indictable offences, employing the economical style of the *Digest*. The mammoth sentences of Greaves's acts were reduced on average to less than a quarter of their original length. More important, the terse definitions of crimes which Stephen had coined in the *Digest* were maintained, and the common law was specifically abrogated.[113] If the draft code became law, homicide, rape, and robbery, for example, would be defined by statute for the first time. By this revolutionary means Stephen hoped to make the law 'distinct and certain' and thus reduce or eliminate the 'quasi-legislative authority'[114] of the bench which allowed judges to bestow 'liberal mercy ... in the one case [and] exemplary severity in the next.'[115] He completed the work early in October. Such speed was possible because, as Stephen himself observed, 'with a little alteration [the *Digest of the Criminal Law*] would make a Draft Penal Code.'[116] A comparison of the *Digest* and the draft code of 1878 bears him out.[117]

But in effecting this transformation Stephen either did not have the time or saw no need to make the modification that was essential if the draft code was to be read with comprehension by any person other than a legalist. A reading of any substantive article in his *Digest* (the draft section on riotous destruction quoted above is a good example; it is a copy of article 74 of the *Digest*) reveals that it is essentially a statute in miniature. It begins by defining a particular crime, classifies it as a felony or misdemeanour, and specifies the punishment. This form of construction seems to obviate the necessity, if not the desirability, for the code to contain a 'general part' in the Continental style. Such a feature defines terms, lays down principles on which the code is based, specifies the classification of offences and details the range of punishments for each class of offence.[118] However, one of the many alterations Stephen proposed to make in the law was the abolition of the now meaningless procedural distinction between 'felony' and 'misdemeanour,' a laudable aim. To accomplish this, the two words were to be expunged from the legal vocabulary and replaced by the term 'indictable offence.'[119] There was no intention to alter the substantive provisions of the law. All felonies and misdemeanours would be redesignated simply as indictable offences, to be subject to one and the same process – that which had been reserved for felony – and, increasingly, to similar punishments. The problem was that the words 'felony' and 'misdemeanour' were ancient terms, widely known to and used by the general public as classes of crime differentiated by punishment and procedure, in which the accused had a right to trial by jury.[120] An indictment was merely a piece of paper on which the particulars of a specific offence were described, a detail in the administrative procedure developed to deal with crime. In view of the legal lore implicit in the proposed change, it was not difficult for the politician who considered the legislation and for the legal professionals who would administer it to deduce that a person charged with an indictable offence would be entitled to trial by jury. But this was not clear to the lay reader; to him it appeared that what had been part of an administrative process was now something to do with the crime itself. He got no help from Stephen. Despite the fact that the term 'indictable offence' was used over and over again in the bill in connection with specific crimes, it was nowhere defined. In this one instance, if in no other, the change from *Digest* to draft code created the necessity for a 'general part,' if the work was to be read with any degree of comprehension by a non-professional. Stephen did not supply that need in his submission to the lord chancellor.[121]

Again, Cairns sent the draft to the statute law committee for its comments. Furthermore, he also asked that any material on criminal law prepared for the committee by R.S. Wright be made available to him. In a turnabout, the work of the other prominent codifier of the day was now to be used by Cairns and his law officers 'as a test of the completeness and correctness' of Stephen's work.[122]

The committee members complied with the chancellor's request for Wright's material, but 'doubt[ed] whether it [was] within their province to offer a collective opinion on the Draft Code.' However, they did recommend to Cairns the observations of Sir Francis Reilly, which were appended to their memorandum.[123] Coming from one whose business it was to draft legislation that would become law, Reilly's remarks were cogent and to the point. In the main, he thought it inexpedient to combine large alterations in the law with codification, and he was not happy with the reduction of common law to statute. His chief recommendation was that any changes in the law should be the subject of a separate bill, which should be enacted prior to the code. As before, Reilly's criticism had no discernible effect on Cairns. Nor did Wright's work change his thinking, for Stephen continued with codification unhindered.

In the meantime Stephen kept his name and the subject in the public eye. In September 1877 *The Nineteenth Century* published his 'Improvement of the Law by Private Enterprise,' which outlined a scheme to codify all law and gave, as a starting-point, a statistical outline of its bulk, both statutes and reported cases.[124] 'Suggestions as to the Reform of the Criminal Law,' an argument for the codification of criminal procedure, appeared in the same journal in December.[125] But Stephen did not neglect his legislative drafting, and indeed claimed to have persuaded Cairns and other senior legal officers to accept an innovative change in the format of the legislation: when his draft was ready for the printer early in January 1878, both the penal and the procedural matter had been integrated in one criminal code.[126] At that time Stephen had high hopes that the bill would be introduced early in February. Much to his disgust, the weeks went by and no action was taken. Never one to wait on events, he went to work behind the scenes and lobbied the influential. In a letter to Lord Lytton, the viceroy of India, for example, he recorded that he had 'used all manner of arts trying on the one hand to land Stafford Northcote (who as leader of the House of Commons is the unfortunate person) by appealing to the Lord Chancellor and the Attorney General in accents something like despair, and on the other to stir up action in the shape of the United Trade Unions of all England, who take a deep interest in the subject and are quite willing (to my great satisfaction) to agitate about it.'[127]

All of this demonstrates that Stephen was a persuasive writer and a skilful lobbyist. But, unlike Peel, he was not attuned to political reality as manifested in the legislature, a fact he made abundantly clear in print. His 'Parliamentary Government,' for example, was a lucid, rational, and wide-ranging critique, which compared the British system adversely with the Indian and asserted that 'Parliament is ill fitted for the task of elaborating the details of legislation, especially when it is complicated and relates to special subjects.'[128] He had been even more specific in 'A Penal Code,' when, in addressing the problem of how to prepare such legislation, he stipulated: '[I]t is a work which Parliament can no more do for itself than it could have built the house in which it sits.'[129] There may have been some truth in these assertions, but it is unlikely that they would have encouraged many parliamentarians to support legislation drafted by their author. Thus, while Stephen was creating a constituency for his ideas among influential friends and the public at large, he was alienating men who held the power to implement or reject his bill.

When, eventually, late at night on 14 May, the attorney general introduced the bill for first reading in the Commons, his speech did nothing to improve the situation, for his style and the content and arrangement of the subject-matter were strongly reminiscent of an argument by Stephen.[130] Holker's presentation was a lucid and systematic exposition of the history and content of the measure, but its main theme was the need for change in the law and an examination of the large alterations proposed by Stephen, including the measures to eliminate the 'irrational rules' of the common law pertaining to larceny.[131] All very true, no doubt, but not on the whole the best way to appeal either to a chamber composed largely of barristers and those charged with the administration of criminal law or to a Liberal opposition, which venerated the common law as the foundation of parliamentary supremacy.[132] Unlike Peel and Atherton, who had followed a Baconian approach, Holker did not invite members to participate in the process, nor did he suggest that Stephen's draft should be analysed and amended by a special committee or other such body. The few opposition back-benchers who followed Holker gave the bill a restrained welcome, although one did anticipate subsequent developments when he remarked that 'the changes proposed were of so extensive a character that they would require the gravest possible consideration.'[133] Second reading, which also came on late at night, was dominated by this theme. There was general support for the measure, but since the opposition claimed that it proposed so many large alterations in the law that the principle and detail of the bill must be discussed in committee, the government was pressed to give assurances that such debate would be allowed for.[134]

Obviously, the draft code was going to face hostile and detailed scrutiny, and it is reasonable to suppose that the lord chancellor asked Sir Henry James, a prominent Liberal legal critic and Holker's successor as attorney general in Gladstone's second administration, to canvass opposition members for their views on the measure. In any event, James reported to Cairns that they were in favour of it, but 'would like to see it sent first to some body in the nature of a Royal Commission.'[135] For his part, Stephen kept the subject before the public by responding to a leader in *The Times*, which called for the new matter to 'be pointed out for public information,' with a letter to which he appended a list of the proposed changes (which filled four columns on the editorial page).[136]

Probably as a result both of his investigations and of Stephen's activity, Cairns decided to withdraw the bill and to form a royal commission consisting of Stephen and two judges to criticize and amend it for reintroduction in the next session. He so informed the Lords, and also told them that he had considered sending it to a select committee of both Houses, but had decided not to do so on the grounds that members would not have the time to give the measure their undivided attention.[137] This information was then reported to the Commons by Holker, and caused a shift in the focus of the opposition. Now their primary concern was that representation on the commission should be enlarged to include laymen who represented all orders of society. As Sir William Harcourt, a future home secretary, pointed out, in such a diverse work as the criminal code, which had the potential to touch the life of every individual, 'they must have the help of different minds; it must be looked at from various points of view, and not exclusively in a legal aspect ... in the present instance he would warn the Government that if they persisted in constituting a purely legal Commission they would entirely fail in the object they had in view – namely, of inducing Parliament to accept that Bill without discussion, and they would next Session be as far as they were now from any chance of passing it.'[138] But this was not news to Cairns, for the TUC had previously made the same point in a letter which also informed him that the congress would be pleased to nominate suitable men to the commission.[139] Cairns's response was to appoint a third judge.[140]

The commission sat continuously from November to April 1879, during which time Stephen was appointed to the bench. His bill was examined minutely and a large number of alterations were made; but they were mainly matters of detail and did not address the principle of the bill.[141] Nor did the commissioners alter its appearance or layout, other than to change 'chapters' to 'parts' in order to avoid the confusion that would arise if the bill became a chapter in the statute-book. The result of the commissioners' deliberations – the draft code of 1879 – was appended to a comprehensive report which set out the objectives of the bill and an overview of the proposed alterations. The most interesting reading is the commissioners' examination of the arguments for and against codification and, particularly in the context of their recommendation to abrogate the common law, of their discussion of its alleged 'rules of flexible interpretation,' or, to use the commissioners' term, its 'flexibility.'[142]

Unlike the first reading of the previous year, the introduction of the draft code of 1879 turned out to be a full-dress debate in which many of the legal luminaries of both sides of the House were deployed.[143] In general, Holker reiterated what he had said previously, and again laid stress on the large number of alterations the measure would effect, especially the abrogation of the common law. He concluded by telling the members that consolidation and codification could not be 'properly accomplished unless the House will be content to confide the preparation of the Bill to persons who are known to be thoroughly competent, and to accept the result of their labours.'[144] In view of what had been said previously, the reaction to this speech was predictable: opposition members assailed Holker from all sides, but chief among their objections was that their powers had been delegated to the royal commission, which was not responsible to the House.[145] There was a general consensus among them that the draft code could not be taken on trust – that, in short, they would be compelled to 'go clause by clause through the Bill, and examine its minutest details.'[146] In confirmation of Reilly's apprehension, several also asserted that the measure should have been confined to codification and should not have proposed changes in the law; they were dubious about the reduction of the common law to statute.[147] Not all the comments were negative, however. Sir Henry James, for example, suggested that the draft be separated into ten or twelve bills and dealt with as and when possible, a proposal Holker rejected.[148] On that note debate ended. And there the matter rested until second reading, apart from the publication in *The Times* of a memorandum of the commissioners' proposed alterations.[149]

Since debate on second reading came on without notice, Sir Henry James took the opportunity to lead off.[150] He began by summarizing the objections of the opposition, while making it clear that the Liberal argument had been broadened and made more precise. Specifically, James stated that he was opposed to the abrogation of the common law and that the bill was incomplete, since it did not codify all of the criminal law.[151] His colleagues then began to repeat their earlier arguments. It is clear that their chief concern was still that the bill had been drafted by a body outside parliamentary control, and would therefore require a detailed and critical examination. In an obvious attempt to pour oil on the troubled waters, the solicitor general hastened to assure opposition members that they would have every opportunity to examine the measure and to institute changes. He then drifted into a discussion of matters of detail.[152] However, he was unsuccessful in muting the Liberal message, which was epitomized in the words of Farrer Herschell, a future lord chancellor: 'It was no use thinking that the Bill would pass through the House without considerable discussion ... and unless they had taken that into account he warned them that they had better abandon the Bill for the present year rather than waste time discussing it.'[153] Then Holker took the floor to wind up the debate. If any gains had been made by the solicitor general, they were lost by the attorney general. His speech was a shortened and more conciliatory address than he had made previously, but his position was unchanged. In particular, his faith in the commissioners was unshaken, and it was still his opinion that 'the House will do well to take the plain draft which has been very carefully prepared by persons most competent to deal with it.'[154] In short, it seems that the government had pressed ahead with its own plan, uninfluenced by the advice of the opposition. As Harcourt had predicted, it was no nearer to getting the code through Parliament than it had been the previous year. Moreover, any lingering hope Holker might have entertained was extinguished by a long and detailed letter he received from the lord chief justice of England.

Sir Alexander Cockburn had been Lord Chancellor Cranworth's attorney general in 1854, when the judges' replies to the chancellor's circular had put an end to the codification project of that era. He was thus in a position to know how effective the judicial objections had been.

Like that of his earlier brethren, his criticism was lengthy and detailed. But his chief objection to the bill was an elaboration of James's complaint that it was incomplete and, especially, that summary conviction offences had been omitted.[155] There was a major difference between the two events, however: whereas the earlier bench had responded to an official query, Cockburn's letter was gratuitous. Nevertheless, it appears to have been just as devastating to the government's hopes as the earlier missives, for it immediately received wide publicity,[156] after which Holker informed Stephen that the bill would be withdrawn and reintroduced during the following session. In the meantime, he proposed a meeting with Stephen to discuss Cockburn's opposition and any further actions the chief justice might have taken.[157]

What was said at that meeting has not been discovered. But it is apparent that the attorney general suffered a sea-change during this period. Perhaps he did some historical reading; possibly he analysed past events, or he may have received and acted on advice from someone other than Stephen. Whatever happened, it caused him to change his tactics and style – to act, in short, like the persuasive, shrewd, and tactful man described by his biographer. On 6 February 1880, the day after the session began, Holker moved first reading, which was agreed to without debate. When second reading came on two weeks later, he was the personification of tact and diplomacy. He assured the House that the government was anxious to receive from all interested members criticism and suggestions concerning the bill. He specifically thanked Lord Chief Justice Cockburn and John Gorst (a future solicitor general) for their 'most welcome' observations.[158] In a complete reversal of former policy, he informed the House that after second reading the draft code would be sent to a select committee with a large and varied membership, which, if the members agreed, would have the power to divide the measure into several smaller bills if such action would ensure safe and uncontroversial passage.[159]

Sir Henry James led off for the opposition. After first getting it on the record that the government had accepted the sensible suggestions from his side of the House, James congratulated Holker on his change of attitude, and it seemed that there was plain sailing ahead.[160] This was an illusion, for the code disappeared for good when Disraeli dissolved Parliament over the Irish Question and then lost the ensuing election.[161]

Given that the public was well prepared for the introduction of the draft codes of 1878 and 1879 and was generally well disposed to them, why did they fail?[162] So far as the opposition and Sir Alexander Cockburn were concerned, the immediate reasons were that the draft codes were incomplete, that they would abrogate the common law, and that their authors had proposed large alterations in the law, about which Parliament had not been consulted. But perhaps a more fundamental reason was the attitude of the government as exemplified by the attorney general. Instead of seeking the accommodation of the Liberals on the questions at issue, Holker abandoned the courtesy and tact for which he had been famous in the courtroom, and, adopting Stephen's arbitrary attitude, attempted to browbeat the opposition for two years or more. He insisted on elaborating the principle that change was necessary and was to be effected by measures conceived and drafted outside Parliament; he stressed that the measures would abrogate the common law, and he refused to submit them to a special committee for analysis and amendment. When he finally adopted the Baconian approach, it was too late.

3

The Origin and Development
of Legal Systems in
British North America

The law of a modern state is the product of its legislative process and its legal system. With respect to the criminal law of Canada, such institutions began to evolve soon after the newly appointed governor and captain general of the province, Colonel Edward Cornwallis, led three thousand settlers ashore at Chebucto harbour in Nova Scotia in 1749 to found the town of Halifax. For five years thereafter he and his successors were not only the military and political heads of the colony, but also its chief legal officers. Then, on the first day of Michaelmas term in 1754, a newly commissioned chief justice in full-bottomed wig and scarlet gown led a legal procession from St Paul's Church to the courthouse.[1] Seating himself under the judicial canopy, he 'gave some directions for practitioners; the grand jurymen were sworn in and the Chief Justice delivered his charge to them. After this the Court adjourned.'[2] Such was the opening of the first term of the Supreme Court of Nova Scotia: Westminster Hall in miniature, it would seem. But appearances are deceptive. In fact, the Nova Scotia system was twice removed from Westminster, and more closely resembled the systems in its sister colonies to the south than that of the parent body.

In the first North American colonies, legal institutions and the law developed before English courts had given authoritative direction on the reception of English law in a colony acquired by settlement.[3] As Lawrence Friedman points out, 'That a hundred settlers huddled on an island near what is now the city of Newport, or freezing in the Plymouth winter, should have reproduced this [English court] system exactly, would have been both miraculous and insane.'[4] They could not and did not. Neither did they accept the English model for legal education and admission to the bar, or the statute law, except on their own terms. Of necessity they developed their legal institutions largely in isolation, much as the English had done before them.[5] And, just as the English had built on the customs of their Germanic forebears, so the colonists rooted their systems firmly in the common law. Therefore, as in the early English experience, their courts were omnicompetent and only slowly separated into legislative and differentiated judicial bodies. In general, early settlers were averse to lawyers. But as society became more complex, bars evolved; they were staffed by practitioners who were undifferentiated by rank and who received their training as apprentices in their principals' offices or, infrequently, at the Inns of Court. Because there was no similar institution in the colonies, however, admission to the bar was controlled by the bench. Written law was largely codified, and drew from several sources, including English common and statute law, the Bible, and the settlers' own experience. The criminal law in particular was much like that of early seventeenth-century England. Moreover, since economic and social conditions were so different in North America, there was little growth in the substantive criminal law during the period in which there was such a vast proliferation of penal offences in England.[6] Thus, in comparison with English statute criminal law, that of the colonies was short, concise, and relatively benign in the middle years of the eighteenth century. All of this and more, rather than the custom of Westminster, was the heritage of Nova Scotia.

In large part it was the old colonists who ensured that this heritage was passed on. Although the first wave of immigrants was largely British-born, many soon abandoned the colony. New England traders, drawn to the region by the opportunity to profit from the massive expenditures involved in making Halifax a rival to Louisbourg, became the dominant element. These men were not in favour of the county court erected by Cornwallis on his arrival, and they lobbied effectively for change. It was abolished in 1752 and replaced by inferior courts of common pleas on the Massachusetts model. New Englanders soon came to dominate the benches of these tribunals, which were vested with the original civil jurisdiction of the common law courts in Westminster, and therefore regulated private issues at the local level.[7] The remainder of the system instituted by Cornwallis continued as before. Original criminal jurisdiction was exercised by the Court of General Sessions, a body similar to

Quarter Sessions in England.[8] The General Court of Virginia was the model for the Supreme Court, which was vested with original jurisdiction in all criminal and civil causes where the amount in question was over ten pounds, and it was the appellate bench for General Sessions and Common Pleas.[9] Appeal from the Supreme Court lay to the Court of Error, presided over by the governor, who, like many of his gubernatorial colleagues, also retained his equitable jurisdiction in the Court of Chancery.[10] Finally, as in all other colonies, appeal from the senior tribunals lay not to Westminster but to the King in Privy Council.[11]

Bench and bar also corresponded to the colonial norm. When Chief Justice Jonathan Belcher lectured his auditors on that first day of the Michaelmas term in 1754, a person born and educated in Massachusetts, trained for the law in the Middle Temple and whose practice had been in Dublin as a member of the Irish bar,[12] was addressing a heterogeneous magistracy of soldiers and other professionals and a minuscule and indifferently trained bar of perhaps four or five.[13] The precise origin of the first Nova Scotia bar is unknown. By the terms of his commission, Governor Cornwallis had ample authority to grant licences to individuals to practise law, and he may well have done so. But it is more probable that, as in neighbouring colonial jurisdictions, the bench of the senior tribunal assumed the authority to examine and admit candidates to the bar, since the justices of the Supreme Court were eventually vested with these powers by statute in 1811.[14] This statute also clarified other matters concerning qualification to practise. For instance, it provided that if a student-at-law was a university graduate, he had to serve a four-year clerkship under articles before he was eligible to apply to be called to the bar as a barrister and attorney. If a student held no degree, his clerkship was to be for a five-year term, after which he could be admitted to practise as an attorney. He was then required to serve a full year as an attorney before he received his call. On attaining the rank of barrister, he was entitled to plead in all courts in the province, both common law and equity. Provision was also made to admit licensed practitioners from other British dominions. These regulations remained virtually unchanged for over fifty years. Ideally, the scheme was a sound and rational one, but circumstances could (and often did) corrupt the ideal. Speaking of his own experience in the system a century after its inception, Mr Justice Russell commented that 'it was rather a poor way of getting a student to acquire a profession, and it was a poor and wretched way of testing a student's ability to practice his profession.' He described the system in operation:

The young candidate and aspirant for professional honours and professional distinction articled himself to a practicing barrister. If his barrister happened to be a very busy one the chances were that he would have very little time indeed to give to his student, and if per contra it was a man who was blessed with ample leisure, well then, the chances were that his leisure was due to the fact that he was not fit for anything better than to sit and twiddle his thumbs, so that in either case, whichever way you choose to take it, the dilemma seemed to work out that the student had rather a poor chance. I quite well remember that the examination at the end of the term used to be such as perhaps the student of one year in Dalhousie College Law School at the present day [1918] would think a very trivial ordeal indeed for him to be called upon to pass.

... [W]hen I was approaching the ordeal myself, I was confidentially taken into his residence by a friend of mine, who [showed me] a washtub full of manuscripts. I asked him what these were, and I was told they were accumulated examination questions which had come down from generation to generation of law students, and by the diligent perusal of that washtub full of examination questions, or even half of them ... the candidate would invariably pass, and be very likely indeed to pass with high remarks and to obtain first class distinction with honours.[15]

After his call to the bar the new lawyer began to practise his profession, and, according to Beamish Murdoch, one of the most prominent Nova Scotia advocates of the early nineteenth century,

as in other parts of North America, business embraces the whole management of his Client's affairs. He is in the first place called on for his opinion as to the propriety of commencing or defending a suit. If an action be resolved on, he is then, as the Attorney of the party, to prepare all the written proceedings by which it is conducted, and as an Advocate to debate the legal questions that may spring out of it before the Judges, and to speak on the merits and facts of the cause to the Jury. In the variety of Courts, from the highest to the lowest, he is called on as business arises to advise his clients, draw up their papers, or declaim in their behalf. We find the Colonial Lawyer at one moment pleading before the Governor and Council, and perhaps the next, defending a trivial assault at the Sessions, or seeking to recover for his client a small debt of 6 or £8 in the Summary Court. One day he is pleading at the Chancery Bar, the next probably at that of the Vice Admiralty, or before the Commissioner of Escheats.

This is not all, for his practice also embraces Conveyancing, and he even acts in the capacity of a Notary Public. All these avocations he must pursue as occasion presents, or he would not be able to retain business.[16]

Although Murdoch did not say so explicitly, it is clear from his account that this state of affairs was primarily the result of the marginal economic conditions that prevailed in the colonies in the early days (and which were graphically depicted by the jurist and author, Thomas Chandler Haliburton, in his *Sam Slick* stories).

Another consequence of these conditions was that there was little money available for the lawyer to procure legal texts and reports. If he did purchase books, they had to be shipped long distances over land and water, and the odds of their loss or destruction were high, as were the shipping charges. Thus, the legal profession collectively did not have many books, nor did its members have access to large institutional law libraries. In 1835, for example, eighty years or more after the foundation of the Nova Scotia bar, the Law Library at Halifax held only 1,182 volumes.[17] The scarcity of books was especially hard on the impecunious student, who would have great difficulty in learning the law without the appropriate texts. Furthermore, he would find it difficult to secure or retain business after his call if he was unable to purchase or otherwise gain access to the latest texts and reports so as to be able to study and interpret the law for his clients.

In Nova Scotia a large part of that corpus was the common law which, said Haliburton, had 'been considered by the highest jurisdictions in the parent country, and by the legislatures of every colony, to be the prevailing law in all cases not expressly altered by statute, or by an old local usage of the colonists.'[18] The prime manifestation of the common law is the case law, in which courts apply the principles derived from past decisions to the case at bar. This jurisprudence was unusually ample in Nova Scotia because the profession, as exemplified by Beamish Murdoch, took a liberal and comprehensive view of precedent. It was accepted, of course, that the decisions of the courts at Westminster were 'received generally as an obligatory interpretation of law in all the dominions of the British Crown ... yet we find much valuable information bearing directly on our legal learning in the large number of American treatises and reports of the Courts of Law in the United States. In like manner the decisions of the Supreme Court in the sister province of New Brunswick are well worthy of our attention.'[19] A more concrete example of the adoption of the institutions of the common law is the appearance of the grand jury to receive Mr Justice Belcher's instructions in November 1754. No special authority was needed to bring this institution to life in the colony; the summoning of such a body had been customary for centuries, and it was resorted to as a matter of course.

Its functions, which had evolved over the same period of time, were multifarious: on the criminal side it indicted persons of its own volition, and approved or negated accusations brought by Crown officials or by any member of the public; on the civil side, and in conjunction with the bench, it performed many of the functions that are carried out by local government today.[20]

The reception of acts of Parliament was otherwise. Nova Scotia did not accept all English statutes or any enacted after 1497, the year of Cabot's discovery and claim of Acadia, unless they had been introduced by charter or commission from the Crown or expressly adopted by the assembly, or were declared to be law by the courts.[21] This policy was in conformity with colonial practice and is not surprising, considering that the early legislatures were controlled by the New Englanders who had earlier forced the change in the court system and who, by the convention of the first assembly in 1758, had become the 'merchants of Halifax.'[22] For the most part, Nova Scotia statutes were 'home-made' by these men, although they often looked to the old colonies for models. They patterned their criminal law on that of Massachusetts; consequently, in contrast to the hundreds of penal acts enforceable in England, virtually all indictable offences in Nova Scotia were laid down in two short, concise, almost code-like compilations.[23] Moreover, whereas just one English statute, the Waltham Black Act, defined fifty or more felonies and enumerated over two hundred capital offences focusing on the protection of game,[24] the entire substantive criminal law of Nova Scotia specified only sixteen felonies and defined fewer than seventy capital offences.[25]

However, as in England and elsewhere, the winds of change began to blow in Nova Scotia. During the century that followed the enactment of the penal statutes, there was considerable amendment and amelioration of the criminal law. By 1841 paraphrases of Peel's Acts had begun the process of consolidating and rationalizing criminal procedure; multiple offence felonies, with the exception of treason, were eliminated; and capital felonies were reduced to seven.[26] Ten years later, only two capital felonies remained in force: treason and murder.[27] However, the provincial legislators fell into the same trap as those at Westminster had:[28] 'felony' became meaningless as a class of crime punishable by death, and a felon convicted of a non-capital offence could receive a lesser punishment than a convicted misdemeanant.[29] Nevertheless, Nova Scotia became the leader of the jurisdictions in British North America that were attempting to rationalize and humanize the criminal law.

Shortly after the features of the legal landscape in Nova Scotia had assumed a settled and familiar form, New France, with its sixty thousand or more canadien inhabitants – the king's 'new subjects' – was ceded to Great Britain. The colony had been conquered, and consequently the rule first enunciated in *Calvin's Case* in 1608 that 'if a king come to a Christian kingdom by conquest ... he may at his pleasure alter and change the laws of that kingdom'[30] governed the reception of English law and institutions in the new colony of Quebec. The implementation of that rule in 1764 produced what Hilda Neatby has termed 'a sort of noisy chaos' for the ensuing decade.[31] In particular, the civilian law and custom of Canada developed prior to the conquest were replaced by English common law and statute, and the settled French colonial courts were abolished and replaced by a system that bore a superficial resemblance to that of Nova Scotia.[32] Jury trial, mandatory in criminal and optional in private causes, was, of course, a feature of the system, as were the grand jury, Quarter Sessions, and a Court of Chancery. Because of the dearth of legal talent available among the few British Protestants in the province, the senior benches were a heterogeneous group largely untutored in the law, who heard arguments from a predominantly canadien bar.[33]

Fortunately for the king's new subjects, the system did not operate as intended by those who framed the Royal Proclamation of 1763.[34] Chaos lasted for a decade or more; then the Quebec Act, which began to function in 1777, brought on a more equitable system for the majority.[35] Chancery was abolished: below a Court of Appeal consisting of the Governor in Council, there were thereafter two separate, equal, and mutually exclusive tribunals. Common Pleas sat weekly, following the French rather than the English practice, and it adjudicated only in civil suits by inquisitorial process – that is, without the intervention of a jury. But jury trial was mandatory in King's Bench, which kept terms and heard only pleas of the Crown and criminal appeals from Quarter Sessions.[36] To implement these changes, the governor was instructed to enlarge and reorganize the bench. There were to be six justices of Common Pleas, two of whom were to be canadien.[37] Only one of the six, Pierre Panet, had been trained in the discipline of the civil law under the French regime; two of his British brethren, Adam Mabane and John Fraser, had been educated in civil law jurisdictions.[38] More important than these changes, however, was the requirement that the 'Laws [,] Customs & usages of Canada' were to be enforced in Common Pleas.[39] The old familiar order was to be restored to the canadiens, to the chagrin of the British element of the community.[40] But the criminal courts were to continue to adjudicate using the English penal law, then at its most cruel and pernicious.[41]

The bar, too, had different aspects in Quebec. The system made no provision for attorneys or solicitors as such, since the functions of those officers were performed by civilian notaires. Canadien avocats educated in the civil law in the academic, Continental tradition were the first to be licensed to practise, but were soon joined by old subjects trained in the common law.[42] Ideally, each group should have learned to function in the law of the other and in two languages; accordingly, early initiatives were taken to provide the legal lore of both systems in an academic setting, but to no avail.[43] The only requirement for admission to the bar was the grant of a licence from the governor, issued by virtue of an arbitrary power carried over from the French regime; this licence was a source of increasing discontent in the profession as time went on.[44] The issue finally came to a head in 1784 when Alexandre Dumas, a man whom the profession considered unqualified in every respect, was licensed to practise law as a barrister by the lieutenant-governor. With the attorney general as its spokesman, the bar of Quebec protested the admission of Dumas and petitioned the bench of Common Pleas to make rules for a call to the bar. It was probably this event which led to the Ordinance of 1785, which set out regulations similar to those in effect in Nova Scotia.[45] Students-at-law were required to serve a five-year clerkship with a licensed practitioner, and then to pass an examination administered by bar seniors in the presence of the chief justice or two puisne judges. Licensed practitioners from England and other British jurisdictions were also required to take the examination, but were not required to serve the clerkship.[46] In 1849 the profession was given full authority to regulate its own affairs. Thereafter, the Bar Society of Lower Canada admitted students to practise law in all courts of the province after successful completion of an examination set by the society. As in the previous period, however, five-year articles of clerkship were required prior to admission to the examination: the period was shortened to three years if the candidate had previously completed a program in classical studies, which included a course in law.[47]

The inclusion of the latter qualification in the 1849 legislation became possible only because of the persistence of individuals who wanted to see the academic study of the civil law become a feature of legal education in Lower Canada. There were at least three attempts before 1800 to incorporate an institution of higher learning which would include in its curriculum courses in the civil law and provide students with access to the few hundred legal texts available in institutional holdings.[48] These attempts came to nothing. Thereafter, the bar made a greater effort to provide civil law instruction in professional institutions. Interest in academic instruction picked up again in the 1840s, and within a decade of the appointment of William Badgley, a judge of the Court of Queen's Bench, as lecturer in law at McGill in 1847, there were faculties of law in operation there and at Laval which educated for the degree of bachelor of civil law.[49]

Meanwhile, there had been a fundamental change in the courts. Common Pleas, in which jury trials had been made optional in 1785 for a limited class of commercial cases, was abolished in 1793. Its jurisdiction was assumed by a newly constituted King's Bench, which had permanent divisions in Quebec City and Montreal and which rode circuits to bring justice to other locations in the jurisdiction.[50] Inferior terms of these courts decided in a summary manner the 'small change' of civil pleas, but this practice ceased with the establishment in 1821 of inferior tribunals, which eventually evolved into district courts.[51] There was, however, no change in the laws these several courts administered. The laws, usages, and customs of Canada continued to prevail in all private causes; criminal pleas were tried by English law.

Yet another feature that set Quebec apart from most other North American jurisdictions was its system of government. Nova Scotia, for example, followed the usual colonial practice, and had a representative government with an elected assembly. Quebec, in contrast, was constituted as a 'Crown colony,' governed by an 'appointed council with executive and limited legislative powers.'[52] With respect to the penal law, however, this was no handicap, since offences were defined and charges laid in accordance with the more than ample English law of 1763. Only when the colony wished to change the law was it necessary to have recourse to legislation. It is evident that those in power during this period were not receptive to the amelioration of the substantive criminal law, for no such amendments were enacted during their tenure. In fact, the first such amendment was not made in the new jurisdiction of Lower Canada until 1801, ten years after the granting of representative government, when it was enacted that women found guilty of treason were to be hanged rather than burned to death.[53] Thereafter, there were only weak, sporadic, and random efforts to reduce the vast and tangled thicket of felonies and misdemeanours which then constituted the criminal law of Lower Canada.

During the period of chaos in Quebec, the colony of St John was separated from Nova Scotia and granted independent status; it was renamed Prince Edward Island in 1799. The new regime, authorized in 1769, was impressive on paper but lacking in substance, since there were fewer than eighty old subjects on the island at the time. Nevertheless, a governor was commissioned and instructed to set up courts, commission a council, and convene an assembly.[54] Under the Halifax administration a Court of Common Pleas had been established in Charlottetown, in which the law of Nova Scotia was enforced. It was abolished and replaced in 1770 by a Supreme Court and a Court of Chancery, which were subordinate to a Court of Appeal consisting of the governor and his council.[55] However, Nova Scotia's influence remained strong, for John Duport, the first chief justice of the Supreme Court and its single member, was promoted from the bench of Common Pleas in Halifax, where he had sat for eighteen years.[56] Duport died in 1774, and was succeeded by Peter Stewart, a Scots law clerk whose books and other personal effects were lost when his transport foundered off the coast of the island.[57] Thus, it is probable that for Stewart's first years, at least, the Supreme Court was administered in much the same fashion as it had been under Duport, but with some bias to the civilian law procedure in which the chief justice had been trained. Since no other salaried judge joined him on the bench during his twenty-five-year tenure, and no inferior courts were created for over a century, it is evident that Stewart and, to a lesser extent, Duport exercised a major influence on the character and administration of the courts of Prince Edward Island.

If the island bench was small, the bar was equally so. As late as 1809 there were only five persons trained in the law in the legal establishment, not including Chief Justice Colclough.[58] The reason was well put by Governor Joseph DesBarres a year later: '[T]he profits of the profession of the law will not maintain a gentleman.'[59] Conditions must have improved after the war, for in 1817 a statute was enacted to regulate the admission of students-at-law to practise as barristers and solicitors in the courts of the colony. Candidates were required to serve a four-year clerkship in the office of a licensed practitioner, and to pass an examination conducted by the attorney general or the solicitor general and the senior barrister in the presence of the bench of the Supreme Court. Licensed practitioners from other common law jurisdictions were to be admitted without examination upon proof of their previous call.[60] Unlike Quebec and Nova Scotia, Prince Edward Island would wait seventy years before making a concession for candidates with a degree or other evidence of higher learning. This concession was instituted in principle in 1842,[61] but because the term of clerkship remained at four years for students-at-law with a degree, and was increased to five years for non-graduates, no material benefits accrued to the degree-holders. Moreover, every candidate, graduate or not, was enrolled as an attorney only, and had to practise as such for one year before he received his call as a barrister.[62] Further regulations made in 1852 provided that barristers from other British colonies were required to be examined by a committee of bench and bar prior to their being admitted to the island bar.[63]

There is some doubt about what law was administered by the bench and bar of Prince Edward Island in the early years. Chief Justice Duport's commission of 1770 enjoined him to administer justice in all causes 'according to the Laws, Statutes and Customs of our Kingdom of England.'[64] Since he had been a judge in Nova Scotia for almost two decades, it is probable that he had access to all the relevant statutes and reports that he needed to perform his functions efficiently in that jurisdiction. Conversely, it is unlikely that he would have had all the documents essential to adjudicate in Westminster Hall. Therefore, he probably interpreted his instructions to mean that he was to use the laws and customs of Nova Scotia, as amended or otherwise altered by later island ordinances and statutes. When the first assembly was eventually convened some three years later, it did indeed enact that trials in all causes were to be 'inquired of, heard and determined, and execution awarded thereon according to the laws ... of England.'[65] But the statute-book made no mention of criminal substantive law then or for another twenty years.

Given the primitive conditions obtaining on the island and the loss of Chief Justice Stewart's books, it is likely that he too looked to Nova Scotia for his law. This hypothesis is rendered stronger by the fact that in 1792 a statute was enacted which, for its first twenty-two sections, was an almost verbatim copy of the 1758 Nova Scotia Statute of Treasons and Felonies.[66] Since the remaining sections of the Prince Edward Island Act deal with misdemeanours and their punishment, it is reasonable to assume that whatever law had been in force prior to 1792 was either confirmed or abrogated by this enactment, and that it subsumed all the former law pertaining to indictable offences. Thus, in 1792, the penal statutes of Prince Edward Island became virtually identical to the relatively benign rules in force in Nova Scotia.

But the island legislators moved more quickly – though they did not go so far as those in their sister province – to rationalize the law and to mitigate capital punishment. In emulation of Peel's Acts a decade earlier, two statutes of 1836 paraphrased his legislation and separated the criminal law into procedural and substantive measures. The former provided for the examination, commitment, and bailment of accused persons, the taking of depositions, trial procedure, the process to follow to enter a plea of 'not guilty' for an accused person who stood mute, the abolition of benefit of clergy, and the class of felony that should be capital.[67] It should be noted that in this as in other jurisdictions, the last provision compounded the erosion of the essential distinction between felonies and misdemeanours. On the credit side, however, in the act concerning substantive law,[68] the number of felonies including treason, was reduced from sixteen to twelve, and capital offences from over sixty to about thirty.[69] Apart from the abolition of attempted murder as a felony in 1869, this was the condition of the criminal law when Prince Edward Island entered Confederation in 1873.[70]

As a consequence of the British defeat in the American Revolution, the population of Nova Scotia more than doubled between 1781 and 1783. In the main the immigrants were troops of the loyalist regiments raised in the old colonies. For military reasons they were settled in virgin territory along the banks of the St John river on the mainland, remote from government and population centres. Many of their leaders resented the losses they had incurred through their loyalty, and found the prospect of having to play second fiddle to place-holders in Halifax repugnant and unacceptable. Since they were fortunately situated to do so, they agitated for the creation of a new province that would provide offices and dignities and thus assure them their rightful place in society. Supported by the commander-in-chief, Sir Guy Carleton, their petitions were successful. The colony of New Brunswick, whose institutions and society mirrored those of the old colonies, was the result.[71]

In accordance with his instructions, the first governor, Thomas Carleton, erected a court system similar to that of Nova Scotia, with a supreme court, inferior courts of common pleas, and courts of general sessions.[72] The hierarchy of appeal was also similar, as was the constitution of the Court of Chancery and the institution of the grand jury.[73] Staffing the judicial institutions with highly qualified personnel was, for once, no problem; there was a wealth of talent available among the loyalists. Excepting the governor, who sat in Chancery, the judges and officers of the superior tribunals had all been practising lawyers in the old colonies, and the chief justice, George Ludlow, had been a puisne judge of the Supreme Court of New York.[74]

Similarly, the first bar was made up of practitioners who had learned their law in attorneys' offices from Massachusetts to Virginia. Nine such individuals were admitted to practise in the Supreme Court as barristers and attorneys during its first sitting on 1 February 1785.[75] For eighty years thereafter, the bench retained absolute control over the selection, education, and licensing of students-at-law. While no authoritative regulations for the organization of the bar have been discovered for the early years, other documents shed some light on the system, which, in general, seems to have been similar to that in Nova Scotia. A four-year clerkship served in the chambers of a practising lawyer was evidently the prerequisite to one's being sworn as an attorney. At any rate, that was the period that Gabriel V. Ludlow, the nephew of the chief justice, spent in the office of Ward Chipman, according to a certificate issued to Ludlow, prior to his application to practise in the Supreme Court.[76] After this he was required to serve a further period of apprenticeship as an attorney to become eligible for his call as a barrister. The interval was probably two years, since that was the time specified by the bench in its first recorded order on the subject in 1823.[77] It was also laid down that only college graduates were eligible to serve the four-year clerkship; non-graduates were required to serve a five-year term.

As in other jurisdictions, legal texts were in short supply in New Brunswick, and in 1834 the library of the Law Society held only 348 volumes.[78] In 1843, in an era of growing concern over the state of legal education, the judges followed the lead of their brethren in Westminster and ordered aspiring attorneys to pass an examination set and evaluated by a committee of bench and bar prior to their being sworn; they followed this with a rule that required prospective students-at-law to pass an entrance examination similarly administered.[79] Thus, in addition to his obtaining at least seven years of post-secondary education and training before he was licensed to practise as a barrister, the student was now required to vault two additional hurdles. In a period of rapidly expanding population and economic growth, and with an increasing demand for legal talent, this situation must have become a matter of public concern outside the profession, since in 1863 the assembly made its first legislative intervention in this area, and reduced the periods of clerkship to three years for a degree-holder and four for a non-graduate.

There has been a good deal of academic controversy concerning the reception date of English statute law in New Brunswick.[80] On the whole, D.G. Bell makes the best case for its being the date of the Restoration in 1660.[81] However, with respect to the criminal law at least, it is unlikely that the last word has been said. In contrast to their colleagues in Nova Scotia, the New Brunswick legislators did not consolidate and publish the penal legislation during the first sessions of the assembly. In fact, over the course of four decades they infrequently turned their attention to the substantive criminal law, leaving its development largely to the courts.[82] Since no authoritative reports were made until 1825, there can be no certainty about which criminal statutes were enforced in those tribunals during the early years; but whichever substantive and procedural statutes were in force, they were repealed in 1829 and 1831, together with all the imperial enactments on the subject, in legislation that was a close copy of Peel's Acts.[83] New Brunswick thus became the first jurisdiction in British North America to follow the English lead by consolidating the criminal law and mitigating its severity; the New Brunswick acts retained only ten capital felonies and eliminated multiple offence felonies, except treason and arson.[84] Further legislation in 1845 made some changes in the substantive law, but did not reduce the number of felonies. The amended legislation remained in force until Confederation.[85]

The stream of loyalists that peopled New Brunswick also flowed into Quebec. There the problem of resettlement was more complicated than it had been in the maritime provinces, because French was the common language of the colony, and because the private law and constitutional institutions were different from those of the old colonies. For reasons similar to those that had led to the establishment of New Brunswick in 1784, the solution in Quebec was the same. Loyalist regiments were settled on virgin territory on the lower Great Lakes and the upper St Lawrence, far from the populated areas. To confirm this separation constitutionally and to allow the newcomers to enact law and to develop institutions more in keeping with their needs and traditions, the province was divided into two jurisdictions, Lower Canada and Upper Canada; the latter was a haven for the loyalists.[86]

The Constitutional Act of 1791, which provided for this division, did not repeal the Quebec Act, abrogate the law, or terminate the legal institutions.[87] Each province was given the authority to elect a legislature, and this was the medium through which change was effected in Upper Canada. In 1794 Chief Justice Osgoode, an English barrister, drafted bills to establish courts at the direction of Governor John Graves Simcoe, who 'was an intense Englishman and was determined to make the institutions of the infant Province as much like those of England as possible.'[88] By the terms of subsequent acts the old local courts of common pleas, which heard actions by inquisitorial proceeding, were abolished, and a centralized system was instituted in their stead. A new Court of King's Bench with the civil and criminal jurisdiction of the common law courts at Westminister was to 'be holden in a place certain,' to 'hear and determine all issues of law' with the intervention of a jury empowered to decide all issues of fact.[89] Out of term, its members were to ride circuit to hear the important civil and criminal actions which had been adjudicated formerly by Common Pleas and the commissioners of gaol delivery and oyer and terminer, respectively.[90] To assume the jurisdiction of the Courts of Common Pleas in the smaller-scale private actions, district courts, which also proceeded by jury trial, were erected, while courts of requests staffed by justices of the peace heard minor pleas summarily.[91] Since Quarter Sessions instituted under the Quebec Act remained undisturbed, and since provision was made for probate, the symmetry of this very English model was marred only by the absence of a court of equity.[92] Several reasons have been adduced for this omission; whatever the cause, it was not corrected until the Court of Chancery was erected in 1837.[93]

Apart from this omission, the legal system developed in accordance with English theory and practice. For over twenty years English barristers filled all the seats in King's Bench, and the first three attorneys general also received their call at an Inn of Court.[94] Thus, in contrast to Nova Scotia in the early nineteenth century, 'English precedent dominated legal reasoning in Upper Canada,'[95] notwithstanding that the majority of the early bar had been educated in the law in Quebec or the old colonies.[96] Even with the appointment in 1837 of the first Canadian-born chief justice, John Beverley Robinson, the 'legal community [remained] English in its customs and procedures,' since he 'used his position to root out creeping Americanisms.'[97]

An early manifestation of this trend was the authority exercised over the profession by the Law Society of Upper Canada. In the first years of the province, when trained legal talent was scarce, the custom of the old province of Quebec was revived whereby individuals were authorized to practise by commission from the lieutenant-governor. Then, in 1797, the Law Society was created by an act 'in every line of' which 'the hand of an English Barrister is manifest and particularly the provision looking to the separation of the professions of Barrister and Attorney.'[98] In short, a prospective student-at-law was required to be enrolled on the books of the Law Society before beginning his legal studies, and only its governing body – the treasurer and benchers, as at the Inns of Court – was authorized to issue a call to the bar or to license the aspiring attorney.[99] To qualify as a barrister, the student-at-law had merely to conform to the rules of the Law Society (there were none at that time) and to be on its books for five years; the intending attorney was required to serve a five-year clerkship and to be on the books for three years.[100] Additional sections protected the rights of current practitioners and provided for the admission of qualified practitioners from other jurisdictions. More important, however, the Law Society was 'authorized to form a body of rules and regulations for its own government, under the inspection of the judges of the Province ... as visitors of the said Society.'[101] Thus, in contrast to other jurisdictions in British North America, the legal profession in Upper Canada became self-regulating at a very early date.

As was common in early colonial times, both cash and legal texts were in short supply. The Law Society first attempted to rectify the situation in 1800, but no book purchases were made until 1827, when the solicitor general, Henry Boulton, went to London 'and there bought books amounting to £29/7/9$\frac{1}{2}$,' many of which he retained for some considerable time for his own use.[102] This incident was well described by William Riddell, who also illuminated the hazards of shipping books overseas in those days, and the peripatetic course the texts followed until they were finally lodged in Osgoode Hall sometime in 1831. By 1834 the first catalogue of the Law Society library listed only 380 volumes. Donations and further purchases brought the total to 850 by 1842.

Within a few weeks of its founding, the Law Society convened its first meeting; on this and subsequent occasions the rules of the organization were formulated. On the question of membership, the split in the Law Society between the old world and the new became apparent. It was proposed that all intending barristers would serve a five-year clerkship, and would be enrolled on the Law Society's books for the same term. The motion was put forward by Robert Gray, the solicitor general, in November 1799, and was supported and carried by a large majority of the members who, like Gray, had been trained in North America. The only opposition was from the attorney general, John White, an English barrister. The motion was submitted for approval to the judges – all English barristers – but was referred by them back to the Law Society because of the objection of the attorney general, who was also a bencher. After White's death in a duel the following month, the motion was again proposed, carried, and approved by the bench. In sum, the situation in

Upper Canada with respect to membership in the legal profession was now closer to the North American norm than to English practice. Both barrister and attorney were required to serve a five-year clerkship; the attorney could be licensed after three years on the Law Society's books, but the barrister had to be on the roll for five years before his call. With such rules it is little wonder that almost all students-at-law went on to become both barristers and attorneys in this early period.

In 1820 the Law Society turned its attention to entrance standards. No one was to be admitted to its books unless he had demonstrated his ability in English and Latin composition; the scope of this examination was enlarged in 1825 to include history and mathematics. In a further attempt to approximate the English experience, students enrolled from 1828 onwards were required to keep four terms at King's Bench at York during their clerkship in order to learn the practical side of court work. Presumably to ensure that these measures were effective, in 1831 it was stipulated that intending barristers must pass an examination in open convocation before their call. With the aim of further improving the general education of lawyers, the term of service for a student-at-law with a university degree was reduced from five to three years. Although these regulations were different in detail and wider in scope than those in other jurisdictions, the reminiscences of graduates of the system indicate that legal education in Upper Canada was, in fact, no more rigorous or daunting than in Nova Scotia as described by Mr. Justice Russell.[103]

Later attempts to separate the profession were no more successful than the first had been. Until 1822 the licensing of attorneys was the prerogative of the benchers, and aspiring candidates were required to conform to the Law Society's educational and other requirements. But in that year they were cut loose: in an act to incorporate the Law Society sponsored by the benchers, a section was inserted which terminated their association with the society.[104] As a result, they 'paid no fee, passed no examination and [were] not subject to [the] discipline of the Law Society,'[105] and they could apply to the bench for a licence to practise at the termination of their five-year clerkship. Standards declined, the number of attorneys who did not also become barristers rose, and a separation of the professions looked imminent. Eager to take advantage of the situation that had been created by the act, advocates of separation made several more determined efforts to prohibit an individual from becoming a member of both professions. For the reasons advanced by Beamish Murdoch, the majority of the membership was opposed to these initiatives, and the last bill to divide the professions was defeated in the legislature in 1840. But the standards of the attorneys continued to decline, a development that attracted much public and professional criticism. Finally, in 1857, the legislature forced the Law Society to 'examine and enquire by such ways and means as they shall think proper, touching the fitness and capacity of [an aspiring student-at-law] to act as an attorney or solicitor,' and thus to reassume jurisdiction over the profession.[106] Admission standards and examinations were reintroduced, the level of proficiency rose, and it again became the norm for an attorney to proceed to the degree of barrister.[107]

A prime reason for the division of Quebec was that many loyalists were dissatisfied with canadien law and custom. So important was this matter that in 1792 the first two acts of the first Parliament of Upper Canada rectified the situation by specifying that 'in all matters of controversy relative to property and civil rights, resort shall be had to the Laws of *England*,' and that in all such causes issues of fact were to be decided by a jury.[108] The criminal law was, of course, that of 1763 England, which continued in force by virtue of the Quebec Act. This appears to have been satisfactory, at least for the time being, since the legislature was silent concerning the substantive penal law until 1800. In that year it was enacted that the criminal law of England as it stood in 1792 was to be the law of the province. Among other things, this act abolished absolutely the punishment of branding (and thus improved on the imprecise wording of an English statute of 1779)[109] and substituted banishment for transportation. But apart from these provisions there is no evidence of any attempt to reduce the number of punishments or to mitigate their severity.[110] The act was an administrative measure that incorporated the 'divers amendments and improvements [which] have since been made in the same by the mother country.'[111] It is also possible to discern unannounced but more specific motivations. For instance, English case law up to 1792 could be used directly, without distinguishing statutes and decisions that were not part of the corpus of Upper Canada law. The newer and more accurate collections of English statutes would make the current law readily available; and, perhaps more important from the point of view of judges and practitioners, the latest English commentaries and books of practice could be used to provide authoritative and up-to-date guidance.

That the reform of the substantive criminal law was not contemplated during the Napoleonic Wars in a British jurisdiction that shared a long, open border with the United States is not remarkable. In the years that followed the conflict, however, the harshness of the penal statutes became a matter of increasing concern, and, concurrent with the first stirrings of reform in the 1820s, a movement was begun to ameliorate their severity. After some initial failures it culminated in the third decade of the century,[112] when several statutes were enacted which, though much pruned and attenuated, were modelled on Peel's Acts and followed the imperial wording verbatim in many substantive sections.[113] Much confusing procedural detail was thus left embedded in these provisions, but such relics as 'corruption of the blood' on conviction of felony and benefit of clergy were abolished. The centre-piece of the legislation was an act of 1833 which enumerated the crimes for which 'offenders shall be liable to be punished with death.'[114] There were eleven such felonies, and only two, treason and burglary, defined more than one offence. During the succeeding seven years of the separate existence of the province there were few changes in the criminal law, and the situation respecting capital felonies remained unchanged.

Thus, when Upper and Lower Canada were united as the Province of Canada in 1841, the former had a small body of relatively benign local law which specified few capital felonies. By contrast, Lower Canada still retained, almost unchanged, the vast number of cruel English statutes of 1763. The Act of Union did not alter this. On the contrary, it provided that all the laws of the two jurisdictions were to remain in effect 'in those parts of the Province of *Canada* which now constitute the said Provinces respectively.'[115] Nor did it make any alteration in the two criminal court systems, and thus in the administration of the law. The implications of these provisions were clear and not very pleasant for an inhabitant of the province to contemplate: two standards of justice and two systems of punishment would coexist in one jurisdiction, and he would be subjected arbitrarily to one or the other, depending on his geographical location.

Clearly, this was an intolerable situation, and the administration of Lord Sydenham moved quickly to rectify it. In the first session of the Legislature of Canada in 1841, Henry Black, the MLA for Quebec City and a judge of the Vice-Admiralty Court, introduced bills in the House of Assembly to consolidate the criminal law of both provinces and to repeal all previous legislation on the subject.[116] One bill concerned procedure, and effectively consolidated both legislation paraphrased from imperial acts and local procedural law (of which there was by now a substantial amount).[117] The other three measures concerned the substantive law. Mr Justice Black was a distinguished lawyer and jurist, and it might have been thought that his bills would effect some amelioration of the law. For Lower Canada they did; for Upper Canada they did not. In fact, they were virtually identical to the analogous titles of Peel's Acts.[118] It was true that some of the offences in those statutes that were punishable by death were mitigated to lesser punishments in the Canadian legislation, but in framing his measures Black had simply followed the text of subsequent English amending statutes.[119] The fact remained that the number of capital felonies – eleven – was the same number that had been enforced in Upper Canada since 1833.[120] But the primary object had been achieved: most of the substantive and procedural law relating to penal offences was now uniform across the province. Further amendments to the latter were enacted in 1851 and 1859, but there was no material change in the substantive law and no reduction in the number of capital offences before Confederation.[121]

In passing it will be noticed that the enactment of the criminal statutes assisted in consolidating the quasi-federal system of government that was implicit in the constitutional provisions of the Act of Union. It was most unlikely that Lower Canada would ever agree to the abrogation of the civilian canadien law or that Upper Canada would consider giving up English common law; nevertheless, there would have to be bodies of law common to both sections of the province, such as the criminal acts, so that the emergence of three distinct jurisdictions was a foregone conclusion. And so it proved. By the time of the statute consolidations for Canada and Upper Canada in 1859, and Lower Canada in 1860, clear lines of demarcation had emerged between the 'federal' and the 'provincial' jurisdictions, and the bulk of each of the three statute-books was about equal.

To sum up: the legal system of British North America on the eve of Confederation was quite unlike that of England. To begin with, the parliaments of the colonies had been called into being by royal proclamation or constitutional documents enacted in Westminster over which they had no direct legislative control, and, unlike the imperial Parliament, they were not supreme within their own jurisdictions. Because it was an area of vast distances and separate and distinct jurisdictions, British North America could have no prestigious and authoritative central tribunals such as those at Westminster. Moreover, of the courts in existence, only those in Upper Canada had been erected on the English model, and even there the resemblance was far from exact. A different philosophy guided legal education. There were no centralized institutions of learning such as the Inns of Court, no large institutional libraries;

instead, there was a general dearth of legal texts. Even the profession itself was organized on different principles. The judges of Upper Canada, who had been obliged to learn to be both attorney and barrister and usually to practise as such, came to the bench and saw the law from a perspective different from that of their English brethren. Finally, the body of law they administered, though firmly rooted in English statutes and customs (excepting the civil law of Lower Canada), developed and branched away from its progenitor because of the social, economic, and moral differences between the two societies.

If the sum of British North American experience was unlike that of the English, so, too, was that of each colony different from the others'. If the incipient tribunals of British Columbia and the District of Assiniboia are included, there were seven separate and distinct systems of courts operating on the eve of Confederation. They ranged from Nova Scotia's, which had been functioning for well over a century, to the separate institutions of Vancouver Island and the mainland, which were not united in the Supreme Court of British Columbia until 1870.[122] The antecedents of the courts were as different as the systems themselves: old French patterns dominated in Lower Canada, Nova Scotia drew heavily on the experience of the colonies to the south, and Upper Canada followed the English model. The benchers of the Law Society in Toronto also looked to Westminster and the Inns of Court for inspiration in drafting their rules for legal education. It was otherwise on the lower St Lawrence, where the profession inclined to Continental practice, which saw academic instruction as the best means of imparting knowledge of the civil law. The maritime provinces followed variations of the American system of legal apprenticeship, whereby students-at-law learned both theory and practice in a principal's office. To the west, Assiniboia had no organized bar; in British Columbia no provision had yet been made for legal education, and the bar was composed of individuals who had received their training in other common law jurisdictions.[123] Similar diversity was also evident in the bodies vested with authority to make regulations for the qualification of lawyers in each jurisdiction, and within the regulations themselves. The bench of the Supreme Court of New Brunswick made all such rules for that province, while in Upper Canada the benchers of the Law Society promulgated the regulations. In Lower Canada it could take as few as three years to qualify as a barrister; in Prince Edward Island the minimum period was five years, one of which had to be served in the rank of attorney.[124]

So far as the criminal law was concerned, there were six different statute-books in British North America; although all were rooted in the English experience, each began with the law of a different time.[125] Nova Scotia took its law as of 1497 and modified and adapted later enactments to suit its particular conditions. British Columbia adopted the humane but still massive body of English law of 1858. The starting-points of the penal law in Prince Edward Island, New Brunswick, and the Canadas were at varying dates in between. Much effort had been expended in the first half of the nineteenth century to mitigate the severity of the statutes, and much had been accomplished, but there were still many variations among the colonies. With respect to capital felonies the gap was wide: Nova Scotia had an exemplary low of two, and Prince Edward Island and Canada a punitive high of eleven.[126]

In applying these statutes and in generating precedents, the senior criminal court of each colony was a law unto itself. It was true, of course, that all colonial courts were subordinate to the Judicial Committee of the Privy Council from 1833, and before that to the King in Council, and were thus bound by council decisions. But virtually no body of case law had been generated by these tribunals. As Sir John Coleridge said in his judgment on an Australian appeal in 1867: '[I]nterference by Her Majesty in Council in criminal cases is likely in so many instances to lead to mischief and inconvenience, that in them the Crown will be very slow to entertain an appeal by its Officers on behalf of itself or by individuals. The instances of such appeals being entertained are therefore very rare.'[127] In British North America they were not rare. They were non-existent. No appeal in a criminal cause was ever carried to London before Confederation. It should not be thought that the colonies were particularly law-abiding, or that there were no such cases. Although no reports were published until well into the nineteenth century, and not all cases were reported even then, over one hundred thirty criminal appeals were recorded before 1867 in a representative selection of colonial reports.[128] This not inconsiderable body of case law did not constitute a cohesive source of precedents, however, since a decision enunciated in any given case was binding only on courts within the colony in which it was pronounced, and had merely persuasive authority in the courts of sister colonies. It is thus evident that the high courts of criminal jurisdiction in British North America were, de facto, unsupervised tribunals of equal and concurrent jurisdiction, each of which developed and administered a unique body of law.[129] The system as a whole resembled the decentralized civilian jurisdictions of France and Germany rather than the common law parent in England.

The system was also similar to that which had prevailed in the Canadas before 1841. In part, the legal problems caused by the union were solved by making the criminal law common to both sections of the province and subject to the quasi-federal authority. The equity and utility of this solution, particularly in comparison with the separate criminal jurisdictions operative in the states of the American republic, was obvious. It provided John A. Macdonald with a powerful precedent for arguing that in any new, larger union 'the determination of what is crime and what is not and how crime should be punished' would best be left to the federal government.[130] Those words were spoken in the open debate on Confederation in the Canadian House of Assembly and can thus be quoted; what he said in the closed conferences in Charlottetown, Quebec, and London is not known. But the force and tenor of his argument must have been similar, since the section dealing with this subject in the British North America Act is one that remained unchanged in each successive draft constitution.[131] No record has been found of a voice raised in opposition to the provision, either in the *Debates* or in other published material.[132]

In the event, Macdonald was a successful advocate, and the dominion Parliament was given specific jurisdiction over 'the Criminal Law, except the Constitution of the Courts of Criminal Jurisdiction, but including the Procedure in Criminal Matters.'[133] As in 1841, however, all legal and judicial officers retained their positions and all laws and courts were continued in being until repealed, altered, or abolished by competent dominion or provincial authority.

It is not surprising that over the next twenty-five years there was not much change in the relationship of the provincial legal systems one to another, although there was internal change in each. Certainly the courts of the provinces increased in number and personnel, and adopted more sophisticated forms.[134] But they did so in accordance with priorities set by provincial legislators, and therefore moved separately and at different speeds toward increasing diversity. The dominion government was unable to give the several systems an effective and integrating focus at the appellate level. It attempted to do so in 1875 by erecting the Supreme Court of Canada, which was to 'have, hold, and exercise an appellate civil and criminal jurisdiction within and throughout Canada.'[135] But it did not – could not – abrogate the jurisdiction of the Judicial Committee of the Privy Council. The Supreme Court was subordinate to that tribunal, and a petitioner who lost his cause in Ottawa still retained the right to move for leave to appeal to the Privy Council Chamber or to go to London directly from the provincial superior court.[136] Consequently, problems unique to the Canadian experience were settled by jurists unfamiliar with that experience, often with unexpected and surprising results, and the Supreme Court was not able to generate a definitive body of precedent binding on all lower courts.[137]

Another unsuccessful dominion initiative was the attempt to abolish the grand jury. Following the English model, that institution was, from the outset, 'a sort of county council and local executive,' and was also responsible for the accusation and indictment of malefactors.[138] Together with the magistracy at quarter sessions or the assizes, it was responsible for public works and associated inspection procedures, and for the disbursement of government grants to finance those measures.[139] Well before the mid-century, colonial legislatures began indirectly to chip away at the civil side of the foundations of the grand jury by creating municipal institutions that would levy taxes and oversee their expenditure on the well-being and security of the local population. Of course, such institutions were not popular with the public at large, who had to pay the taxes, or with the grand jurors and magistrates, who stood to lose their prime source of patronage. Governments faced with the necessity of enacting enabling legislation did so at their peril, unless it could be done without opposition, as was the case when the first such measure to be enacted in British North America, the Municipal Districts Ordinance of 1840, was pushed through the Special Council in Lower Canada.[140] It was otherwise in Nova Scotia in 1882. There, in the election of that year, voter resentment at the passage of the County Incorporation Act of 1879, which diminished considerably the civil responsibilities of the grand jury, was a major factor in defeating the Conservative party and thus in bringing down the government of John Thompson, premier pro tem, who as attorney general had given strong support to the bill.[141]

Thompson was a man dedicated to progressive reform; he enjoyed 'clearing away tangles of legal underbrush.'[142] Nevertheless, it must have taken all his political courage to be one of the most prominent advocates of a measure that abolished the main source of patronage for Nova Scotia grand juries – particularly since he ignored the warning given to him five days after its introduction by Senator William Miller, a prominent Nova Scotia power-broker, who advised him that 'very great injustice might be done to the most important interests' if the bill were pushed through without prior consultation with those interests.[143] Moreover, as a practising barrister and legal administrator, he had more knowledge of the privileges and prerogatives, faults and prejudices, of the grand jury than most men, particularly on the criminal side. If, for example, he was counsel for the defence in a criminal action, he was prohibited from appearing before a grand jury on behalf of his client and could thus take no direct action to influence their decision whether to bring in a true bill. Conversely, if he was retained by the Crown to prosecute, he had the inestimable benefit of presenting to the grand jurors evidence that could not be refuted.[144] During his tenure as attorney general of Nova Scotia he was in charge of the criminal justice system, and thus had to deal with the problems raised by these and other medieval remnants from the point of view of a legal administrator.

In Upper Canada such anomalies were the subject of debate in professional literature long before Confederation.[145] They were brought to prominence by the passage of the Indictable Offences Act of 1851, which had been modelled on the English legislation of 1848, and the system of Crown attorneys introduced in 1857.[146] The Indictable Offences Act rationalized the procedure of arrest and the preliminary investigation of an offence; the Crown attorney system – Canadian innovation – set up machinery whereby a salaried legal officer framed a bill of indictment from the findings of an examining magistrate and prosecuted for the Crown in any resulting trial. But the symmetry of this arrangement was marred by the grand jury, which could refuse to return a true bill.[147] Moreover, the jurors could make a presentation of their own volition against a person without any preliminaries by magistrate or prosecutor, or in defiance of a magistrate who had refused to commit an individual for trial in the first instance. After 1867 the grand jury system began to be criticized publicly.[148] One of the first critics was James R. Gowan.[149] His opinion carried considerable weight, for he was a legal scholar and had been the judge of the Simcoe County Court since 1843. Gowan was critical of the grand jury both on its civil and criminal sides. As a legal draftsman of some repute, he had been able to exercise this talent to cut down the civil side of the grand jury and special juries in Upper Canada when he had drafted the Municipal Corporations Act for Robert Baldwin in 1849.[150] Subsequently, it became known that he had been Sir John A. Macdonald's private legal draftsman from the early 1850s, and had in fact lobbied for and drafted the Crown Attorney Act of 1857.[151] He thus had an intimate knowledge of the legislation that was undermining the foundations of the grand jury. In his charge to the local grand jury in 1877, he drew attention to the defects of the system and particularly to the fact that, at their own request, four-fifths of those

committed for trial on criminal charges in Ontario came before the court
directly from the committing magistrate without the intervention of the
grand jury.[152] His message was clear. If this could be done without
injustice in 80 per cent of cases, why not in all cases? In subsequent
terms he returned to this theme, not with any desire 'of [eliciting] an
expression of opinion from these bodies, but as the means of directing
public attention to the subject, and promoting, if possible, an enlightened discussion.'[153]

However, this debate and the eventual outcome were complicated by
a constitutional question: who had jurisdiction over the grand jury?
Oliver Mowat, acting in his capacity as attorney general of Ontario,
contended that 'the abolition of Grand Juries is not within the authority
of the Dominion Government; that the Grand Jury is a part of the constitution of the court and is not a matter of mere procedure.'[154] Ottawa
dissented, and both parties agreed to refer the question to the Supreme
Court in 1879. But Mowat delayed in setting a date for the hearing, and
finally withdrew his consent to the reference the following year. After
that, apart from some provocative legislative manoeuvring by Mowat,[155]
the constitutional issue was left in limbo.[156]

Gowan retired from the bench in 1883, and two years later was called
to the Senate by his old friend, Sir John A. Macdonald. The prime
minister was eager to make use of Gowan's knowledge and experience,
and urged him to accept the appointment on the grounds that the Senate
'is greatly in need of legal ability, and [the minister of justice, Senator
Sir Alexander] Campbell knows from me of what value you were to me
in years gone by.'[157] Within a few months of his appointment Gowan
had become an intimate of the newly recruited minister of justice, John
Thompson, who in the intervening years had seen the grand jury from
yet another perspective when he delivered his charge to it as a justice
of the Supreme Court of Nova Scotia. As a senator Gowan defied the
conventional image of a superannuated party hack dozing away his days
in the upper chamber. He was tireless in his efforts to advance government bills, and Thompson asked for his advice on a variety of measures,
from a franchise bill to a proposed summary jurisdiction act.[158]

There is no mention of the grand jury in the early correspondence
between Thompson and Gowan. Nevertheless, and apparently without
consulting Thompson, Gowan again turned his attention to the institution in a full-dress speech to the Senate in 1889. In the course of his
remarks he pointed out that the grand jury was a medieval institution
that had outlived its usefulness. He catalogued what he perceived to be

the faults of the system, and quoted several senior judges who advocated its abolition. Essentially, his argument was that the deliberations of the grand jury were secret, that on the criminal side the accused had no chance to rebut the charge, that the process was inefficient and uneconomical, and that the functions of the institution could be performed more cheaply and efficiently by appointed officials.[159] It was a well-researched and persuasive speech.[160] But Senator Richard Scott, a distinguished Ottawa lawyer and the leader of the opposition in the upper House, was not moved. He denied that a majority of the bench was for abolition. More important, he made it clear that the grand jury was a popular institution, one which the public supported and wished to see continued. Scott admitted that the system was not perfect, but contended that on balance its faults were outweighed by its advantages. He predicted that the government would not move on the question immediately, and possibly not ever. He concluded by suggesting that the records be searched for a true expression of opinion on the matter from both the bench and the grand jury.[161]

Thompson responded to Gowan's initiative a few days later with a letter in which he congratulated the senator on his speech 'on the question of Grand Juries and County Crown Attorneys which I have read with great pleasure and in the whole of which I concur.'[162] But he made no effort to pursue Scott's suggestions or to take up the question as a matter of governmental policy; he did not refer to it in his replies to subsequent letters from Gowan which elaborated the issue.[163] In fact, not until after Gowan had returned from a European vacation the next year and raised the issue directly with the prime minister was there any further mention of the matter.[164] That mention produced action, however, for a month later Thompson sent out a circular letter to all judges and provincial attorneys general in which he asked for their opinion on the 'expediency of abolishing the functions of grand juries in criminal cases.'[165] Whatever the judges' opinions, it seems that Thompson was by no means convinced that abolition was either feasible or desirable at that time.[166]

During the uproar of dissolution and the general election of 1891 a steady stream of replies to Thompson's circular letter flowed in, from judges and grand juries and, presumably, from the attorneys general. In June, after the new Parliament had settled down, Gowan moved to have the correspondence tabled in the Senate, and gave the members a summary of the replies that had been prepared for him by the Justice Department. According to the senator, 'no less than fifty' of the judges

'are in favour of abolition, thirty-nine against, ten doubtful, and two ...
have declined to answer.'[167] It was by no means an overwhelming vote
to scrap the system. In fact, Gowan and the department seem to have
been somewhat over-optimistic, for when the return was tabled, the
results were even closer: forty-eight were in favour of abolition, forty-
one against; twelve were doubtful. Moreover, Gowan had not mentioned
the opinion of the jurors. Twelve letters from grand juries are printed
in the return: ten opposed abolition and only two were for it. The two
pro-abolition letters were short, three and six lines respectively, and
mentioned only the inefficiency of the system. The anti-abolition letters
were, on the average, much longer, and presented reasoned (albeit traditional) arguments against abolition. In general, the grand jury was
seen as 'the bulwark of our liberties' and the protector of the individual
against appointed officials. The jurors of Northumberland and Durham
were the most blunt in this respect, and suggested that abolition was
predicated on 'the hope that such a change would furnish more fat berths
for office seekers, a class which is very numerous in this county.' The
judges, though more eloquent and lengthy, either supported Senator
Gowan's arguments or elaborated the concerns of the grand jurors opposed to abolition.[168]

Although it may be argued that the grand jury was an outdated institution and that the jurors were partial and biased, there is no doubt
that Senator Scott had been correct in his analysis: the public, as represented by the jurors, was opposed to any substantial change in the
system. That opposition, coupled with the constitutional wrangle with
the provinces that was sure to erupt if the government moved on the
question, suggested that any prudent politician would be wise to take
Scott's advice and postpone to the distant future any measure to change
or abolish the grand jury. No more was heard of the matter in 1891.

Legal education also continued to reflect provincial priorities. There was,
however, a general recognition of the need to require from the intending
student-at-law a higher standard of education than hitherto, and, in the
common law provinces, of the desirability of including academic instruction in the law as a part of legal education.[169] In Nova Scotia, the latter
process began in a university setting as an extension of a liberal arts
education when Dalhousie Law School began its first course of lectures
in 1883.[170] After a series of abortive experiments at the University of
Toronto and with courses of lectures sponsored by the Law Society,
Ontario took a different approach:[171] Osgoode Hall Law School, where

the technical study of law dominated, began operation in 1889 as the educational institution of the Law Society of Upper Canada. These were the forerunners; by the turn of the century most provinces had made some effort to provide systematic education in the law. But the diversity of legal education and bar admission standards in Canada is strikingly illustrated in the text of an address to the American Bar Association in 1899 by Newman W. Hoyles, the principal of Osgoode Hall Law School. In the course of his remarks he touched on British Columbia, Manitoba, the Northwest Territories, and Prince Edward Island, in all of which the student depended on lectures given by bench or bar and on private study to learn his law. Hoyles then detailed the differing courses and curricula offered by the university law schools in Nova Scotia and New Brunswick, as well as the several institutions of Quebec, where the basis of instruction was the civil law, and concluded this portion of his remarks by outlining the curriculum of Osgoode Hall.

It is noteworthy, too, that when explaining the bar admission require-ments for each province, Hoyles was obliged to have recourse to a 'table of variation,' since the regulations were still so diverse that a general statement concerning, for example, the length of service under articles could not have covered all cases.[172] It is instructive to recall that although much spadework had been done to establish a dominion bar society as early as 1876,[173] it was not until 1914, nearly fifty years after Confed-eration, that a national organization of Canadian lawyers, the Canadian Bar Association, was formed. Even then the only mention of standard-ization in the constitution of the association – its aim 'to promote ... the uniformity of legislation throughout Canada' – was carefully qualified by the phrase 'so far as [is] consistent with the preservation of the basic system of law in the respective provinces.'[174] Despite this limiting prov-iso, the task proved to be so complex and time-consuming that in 1918 the bar association spawned a separate organization to do the job. This was the annual Conference of Commissioners on the Uniformity of Leg-islation in Canada, which has done much to bring about a measure of uniformity in provincial legislation, and which still functions.[175]

Although there was little uniformity among the provincial legal profes-sions in the late nineteenth century, some consistency was becoming evident. It was at this time that 'barrister and solicitor' became the profes-sional designation of lawyers in the common law jurisdictions. The de-scription first became current in Ontario after the passage of the Judicature Act of 1881. That statute, which was closely modelled on a previous English enactment, united the existing courts of law and equity in the

High Court of Ontario. As in England, the difference between the attorney, who was an officer of the common law courts, and the solicitor,
whose practice was in Chancery, had become minimal.[176] Since there
would be henceforth a single court, one designation or the other would
be redundant. Therefore, true to the principle that, in any contest between law and equity, equity must prevail,'[177] the title 'attorney' was
abolished and persons entitled to practise as such were thereafter to be
referred to as 'solicitors.'[178] Since almost all such persons were also
barristers, the term 'barrister and solicitor' became the lawyers' technical
appellation in Ontario, and its use eventually became general throughout
common law jurisdictions.[179] The term was also an explicit reminder that
the individual so designated was licensed to practise in both law and
equity.

Although vestiges of colonial criminal law remained on the provincial
statute-books for decades after 1867,[180] Ottawa was able to move quickly
to introduce a large measure of uniformity across Canada. One hundred
ten penal enactments of the former colonies were repealed by the first
Parliament.[181] In their place nineteen disparate statutes laid the foundation of the criminal law of the new jurisdiction. Seven of these concerned procedure, and were largely or wholly of Canadian origin. Most
of them had been based originally on English statutes, but they had
been freely adapted over the years to reflect the reality of colonial conditions and thus to diverge from their English models.
   It was otherwise with the six that contained the bulk of the substantive
law. These were based 'on the Imperial Criminal Law Consolidation
Acts of 1861 [Greaves's Acts] and taken almost textually from them.'[182]
As we have seen, and as Greaves himself was careful to point out, his
bills were 'chiefly re-enactments of the former law, with amendments
and additions. Each bill contains diverse enactments taken from different
statutes, and generally in the terms used in those statutes.'[183] Since most
of the substantive law Greaves had to work with had been consolidated
by Peel, it follows that his acts were essentially a restatement of Peel's
legislation. That was also the source of the colonial legislation, and there
was little difference between the two in fundamental principles. But
there were differences in detail, and since England was a unitary state
some provisions were inappropriate for implementation in a federal state
or were ultra vires the British North America Act. It follows, too, of
course, that because the dominion statutes were such close copies of
Greaves's work, they contained all the merits and defects of the originals.

With respect to capital felonies, the new legislation struck a balance between the humane practice of Nova Scotia, where only murders and traitors were punished by death, and the relatively punitive law of Prince Edward Island and Canada, where eleven felonies were capital offences: the dominion restricted the death penalty to five offences. But the current of opinion was running strongly against the imposition of capital punishment for any crime less than the taking of human life or the threatening of government and society. Accordingly, imprisonment was made an optional punishment for rape in 1873, and the penalty for attempted murder and carnal knowledge of a female under ten years of age was reduced to imprisonment in 1877.[184] Thus, within a decade of Confederation, sentiment and legislation had both moved in the more humane direction taken by Nova Scotia a quarter of a century earlier: treason and murder had become the only crimes punishable by a mandatory death sentence under Canadian statute law.[185] That point having been reached, it is evident that the great majority of Canadians, as epitomized by their members of Parliament, now saw the criminal law as being a 'most liberal and humane' safeguard for society.[186] Their highly moral, and indeed biblical, view is accurately summarized in James Fitzjames Stephen's contemporaneous definition: 'The criminal law may ... be regarded as a detailed exposition of the different ways in which men may so violate their duty to their neighbours as to incur the indignation of society to an extent measured not inaccurately by the various punishments awarded to their misdeeds.'[187]

If there was a large measure of uniformity in the penal law across the dominion twenty-five years after Confederation, there was still little or none in the institutions that applied it. During that time the Judicial Committee of the Privy Council had heard only one Canadian criminal case – R. v. Coote in 1873.[188] Their lordships had given the attorney general of Quebec leave to appeal because the case appeared to turn on a constitutional issue;[189] therefore, it cannot be said that they had departed from their policy respecting criminal appeals as enunciated in R. v. Bertrand and affirmed in their refusal to hear Louis Riel's appeal.[190] In any event, since the Judicial Committee applied its policy evenly to all dominions and colonies, they did not build up a substantial criminal jurisprudence. Nor did the Supreme Court of Canada. Overshadowed from the first by the Judicial Committee, criticized by the legal profession, and threatened with abolition by Parliament, its first years were hesitant and uncertain, and its very survival was in doubt.[191] Even though they did their best 'to catch an appeal case,' the 'six melancholy men' in Ottawa seldom turned their attention to criminal matters.[192] In fact, the Supreme Court heard only thirteen criminal appeals from 1876 to 1892, an average of less than one case per year.[193] In contrast, four hundred or more such cases were noted in a representative group of provincial law reports during the same period.[194] Taken together with the appeals heard up to 1867, at least five hundred decisions, a very respectable body of case law, had been delivered by 1892.

But the situation with regard to the application of the case law had not changed during the intervening twenty-five years. As Senator Gowan reminded the minister of justice in 1892, just as the courts of Bordeaux and Lyons could take different views on a question of law, so 'the decisions in our Province would not be binding on another, and in this respect it would resemble, I incline to think, the condition in France, whereas a decision in Westminster Hall is law throughout England.'[195] He could have said with equal truth that the fragmented legal education system, the provincial legal professions, and the insular courts were also unlike their English progenitors, and, to a greater or lesser extent, unlike each other. Moreover, in constitutional terms, Canadians were creatures of rational, written constitutions. Since public and private law had been codified at the provincial level, they did not have to struggle with a random and incomprehensible collection of statutes scattered through the legislative record of a century or more. For all these reasons the Canadian lawyer and parliamentarian saw the legal system from a perspective quite different from that of their English colleagues.

4

Consolidation and Codification
before Confederation

In view of the fundamental differences between the British North American and English legal and constitutional systems, it was to be expected that the colonials would view attempts to systematize the law differently from their English contemporaries. And so it proved. So far as may be ascertained, there never was the deep-seated and continuing opposition to consolidation and codification that had been characteristic of the English experience, in spite of the fact that in the early dominion Parliaments, at least, there were proportionately more lawyers than in any imperial Parliament.[1] Before we begin to analyse the Canadian experience, it must be made clear exactly what the legislators were dealing with in respect of statute law.

At the beginning of the nineteenth century, when all the contracting jurisdictions to Confederation had been in existence for several years, their statute-books were indistinguishable from the English model.[2] These were large folio volumes, and at the top of each page was printed the year, the regnal year (in Latin), and the chapter number in upper-case roman numerals. Each statute formed one chapter, made up of one or more sections, each consecutively numbered with upper-case roman numerals. Each section was one sentence. All but the first section began with the words 'And be it enacted' or a similar phrase. These words were repeated to ensure that the provisions in the sentence were covered by the enacting formula in the first section.[3] Sections could be, and usually were, seemingly interminable: they were full of enumerations, exceptions, provisos, saving clauses, and redundant words and expressions. There was no attempt to break up the flow of words with internal divisions such as subparagraphs or other independent clauses. A fair example of this style of writing is found in section 8 of Peel's Malicious Damage Act, quoted above in chapter 3, even though it was enacted twenty-five years after the turn of the century, at a time when concerted efforts were being made to reduce surplusage.

A random sampling of colonial acts reveals the same format and the same verbosity. Section 1 of the Nova Scotia Protestant Grantees Act is a sentence of over seven hundred words;[4] in Upper Canada, the first section of the Frivolous and Vexatious Suits Act runs to nearly five hundred words (see figure 1).[5] To make matters worse, there were no indexes in the sessional volumes, merely a randomly ordered list of titles that made up the table of contents. It is not difficult to see that to search the statutes for authority or to determine how the law stood on a particular subject would become an increasingly difficult task as the years went by and the volumes accumulated.

If the statutes were hard to work with, the common law was even more problematic. Decisions from which precedents had been drawn were scattered through the year-books and reports of five centuries, and no one source contained them all. Moreover, case law was not as authoritative as statute law, because precedents could be distinguished by counsel and judge and the meaning of a judgment altered. Books of practice, which attempted to integrate the two sources, were monstrous tomes or multi-volume works, and finding information contained therein baffled even the experts.[6]

Nova Scotia, whose legislature had been functioning since 1758, was the first jurisdiction to recognize and address the problem of the statutes. It had a backlog of 731 acts when, following the lead of Westminster, it began effective reform in 1804. The next year Richard Uniacke, the attorney general, promulgated the Statutes at Large of Nova Scotia by order of the assembly.[7] This was the first authorized collection of the statutes in any jurisdiction in the British empire; it antedated the first volume of the Statutes of the Realm by six years. Like that collection, it is an elegant and accurate production, having been compiled by reference to the original acts. The statutes are ordered chronologically, from the first session of the assembly. But it differs from the SOR in that only the titles and abbreviated headnotes of acts repealed or expired are printed, with marginal notes to indicate subsequent amendments or additions to particular enactments. An alphabetical abridgment of the

CHAP. IV.

AN ACT for the more effectual preventing of Frivolous and Vexatious Suits, and to authorise the Levying of Poundage upon Executions in certain Cases, and to regulate the Sales by Sheriffs and other Officers.

[Passed 9th March, 1809.]

Preamble.

BE it enacted by the King's most Excellent Majesty, by and with the advice and consent of the Legislative Council and Assembly of the Province of Upper Canada, constituted and assembled by virtue of and under the authority of an Act passed in the Parliament of Great Britain, intituled, "An Act to repeal certain parts of an Act passed in the fourteenth year of His Majesty's reign, intituled, 'An Act for making more effectual provision for the Government of the Province of Quebec, in North America,' and to make further provision for the Government of the said Province," and by the authority of the same, That in all actions to

Circumstances under which defendant, when held to special bail, shall be entitled to costs of suit.

be brought in the Province of Upper Canada, from and after the passing of this Act, wherein the defendant or defendants shall be arrested and held to bail, and wherein the plaintiff or plaintiffs, shall not recover the amount of the sum for which the defendant or defendants in such action shall have been so arrested and held to special bail, such defendant or defendants shall be entitled to costs of suit, to be taxed according to the custom of the Court, in which such action shall have been brought; provided it shall be made appear, to the satisfaction of the Court in which such action is brought, upon motion to be made in Court for that purpose, and upon hearing the parties by affidavit, that the plaintiff or plaintiffs in such action, had not any reasonable or probable cause for causing the defendant or defendants to be arrested and held to special bail, in such amount as aforesaid; and provided, that such Court shall thereupon, by rule or order of the same Court, direct that such costs shall be allowed to the defendant or defendants, and the plaintiff or plaintiffs shall, upon such rule or order being made as aforesaid, be disabled from taking out any execution for the sum recovered in any such action, unless the same shall exceed, and then in such sum only, as the same shall exceed the amount of the taxed costs of the defendant or defendants in such action, and in case the sum recovered in any such actions shall be less than the amount of the costs of the defendant or defendants to be taxed as aforesaid, that then the defendant or defendants, shall be entitled, after deducting the sum of money recovered by the plaintiff or plaintiffs in such action, from the amount of his, her or their costs, to be taxed as aforesaid, to take out execution for such costs in like manner as a defendant or defendants may now by law have execution for costs in other cases.

In actions on judgments, plaintiff not entitled to costs, unless by rule of Court.

II. *And be it further enacted by the authority aforesaid,* That in all actions which shall be brought in the Province of Upper Canada after the passing of this Act, upon any judgment recovered, or which shall be

Figure 1 A page from an early nineteenth-century Upper Canada statute consisting of one-sentence sections, each with its enacting formula

statutes in force is appended, and an alphabetical index to the abridgment refers the reader to the statute desired. The index appears to be the earliest example of this feature in any volume of British North American statutes. Three further volumes published in 1818, 1825, and 1835, and compiled along the same lines as the first, update the collection to 1835. However elegant these large volumes are, and notwithstanding that they are a great improvement on what had gone before, they are strictly conventional collections, and use not only an old English title but also Owen Ruffhead's arrangement and layout; they are quite difficult to work with unless one knows exactly what to look for.[8]

Ten years after the first volume of Statutes at Large was issued in 1805, the Acts of the General Assembly of Prince Edward Island, 1773–1814, were published in Charlottetown in two volumes. The edition consisted of a reprinting of the statutes, year by year in chronological order, including the title and heading of repealed acts, but omitting the text. There is an index of acts, but it is not an inspiring collection. Neither were the two volumes that followed it in 1836, nor those issued in 1852, which updated the collection to that year. There was one innovation in this set, however: it was apparently the first to break with the folio or near-folio-size volume, and was issued in a handy octavo format.

In 1838 the Acts of the General Assembly of New Brunswick appeared in one folio volume. This covered the period 1786 to 1836, and it too is an elegant collection. It was ordered by the assembly in 1835, and compiled and edited by George Berton, a barrister, working under the direction of the chief justice of New Brunswick.[9] A table of titles in chronological order precedes the statutes, which are in the same order. Like the Nova Scotia collection, expired or repealed statutes are indicated only by a title and a short headnote; the disposition is given in a marginal note. Statutes in force are copiously annotated with respect to their content and subsequent disposition. The New Brunswick volume has the best index of any collection to that date, with main headings, subheadings, frequent cross-references, and a wide margin for notes on each page.

The Provincial Statutes of Upper Canada were published in strange circumstances. In 1817 a joint committee of the legislative council and the assembly recommended to their respective bodies that the governor general should 'direct proper persons' to revise and print one thousand copies of the provincial statutes.[10] There was no further mention of the project in that year. Early in the next session, a whole series of parliamentary procedures culminated in a joint address to the administrator requesting the revision and reprinting of the statutes. He replied on 6 March that he would 'order immediate measures to be taken' to comply with the request.[11] The next item in the *Journal* on the subject is an order of 21 March for Robert Horne, the printer of the *Upper Canada Gazette*, to attend at the bar of the House to answer questions regarding an advertisement in the *Gazette* of 19 March which was 'an infringement on the rights and privileges of this House.'[12] In essence, the item specified that the legislature had authorized Horne to print additional copies of a collection entitled 'Revised Statutes' for sale to the public. Obviously, he had not been so authorized, and, unless government moved much faster in those days than it does now, it is unlikely that he had received direction even to revise and edit the statutes, let alone to print them. In any event, he was questioned, he apologized, and the assembly ordered him to publish in the *Gazette* the proceedings of the House on the subject. So far as can be established, no such publication was ever made in the *Gazette* or any other journal, and the *Journal* of the assembly did not refer to the subject again that year. Nor is there any further mention of statute law revision until 1825, when an abortive committee was struck to consolidate the acts.[13]

Nevertheless, Horne did print the collection in 1818. The title page announces that they were 'Revised, Corrected and Republished by Authority,' and the administrator's name appears at the bottom of the page. In appearance and size the volume is similar to the Statutes at Large of Nova Scotia, as are the arrangement and chronological layout of the acts and index. There is one innovation, however: where a statute had been amended, the addition or deletion is printed in italic type and a marginal note refers the reader to the amending enactment.

Much the same sequence of events led up to the publication of the Statutes of the Province of Upper Canada, which came out in 1831. Following the fruitless request for a revision in 1825, a similar request was made in 1830, with a similar result.[14] There is no mention of any action in the *Journal* of 1831, until the notation of receipt of a petition from two Kingston publishers for the assembly's patronage of a revised edition of the statutes just off their press.[15] This precipitated a squabble with the King's Printer, the striking of a committee, and the production of a report which recommended the purchase of two hundred copies of the privately printed collection, despite the objections of the King's Printer.[16] This collection, which brought the statutes up to 1830, and was set in a clearer type, was otherwise similar in arrangement and layout to its predecessor of 1818.

Ten more years were to pass before the legislature enacted statutes similar to the British consolidation acts. That innovation was made to implement the policy that had brought about the Act of Union. For example, one of the first bills enacted in Sydenham's Parliament of 1841 was a measure to consolidate and integrate all former Lower and Upper Canadian statutes relating to customs and excise, and then to repeal such acts.[17] It was closely followed by the criminal law bills introduced and managed by the learned jurist Henry Black, which consolidated the penal statutes of the two jurisdictions.[18]

Just before the legislative activity of 1841, a new move to publish an official revised edition of the statutes of Upper Canada had been initiated. That the aim of the revision was to show the statute law of the province as it was at the time of union was probably the reason the attempt was much more businesslike than those of the past, and entirely successful.[19] The initial request from the assembly was made on 9 January 1840; by 25 July commissioners had been appointed and were at work. In part, their instructions were to 'examine and revise the several Statutes from time to time passed, and enacted by the Parliament of Upper Canada, and then in force and effect; and to make such report upon the premises, as in our opinion should be most for the interest, welfare and good government, of the Province.'

Less than three years later the revision was issued. It was published in two large volumes, the first of which contained public acts and the second private acts; it was entirely conventional in layout and arrangement, for reasons the commissioners' report makes clear: 'Before proceeding to execute this Commission, we ascertained that what was contemplated by the Government was, that we should present the Statute Law of Upper Canada as it stood at the time of the Union of the Provinces, having expunged all such parts as had been repealed, either expressly or by clear implication; carefully revising the whole; giving the necessary references in the margin of each Statute; and adding a well compiled index.' They had previously given some thought to classifying and consolidating the acts and then arranging the consolidations in a topical order, but they decided against such a procedure because they were not sure they had a mandate to do so; furthermore, their revision would then have required legislative approval during a prolonged or extra session of the legislature. The report continues: 'Such a re-casting of the Statute Book, by classifying the whole, according to the various subjects, without regard to the order of time, has been frequently proposed in the Mother Country, but never yet attempted, nor has it, so far as we know, been effected in any of the British Colonies, though it has been in some other Countries.'[20] In view of this statement, it may be that the commissioners were surprised when the first report of the commissioners appointed to revise the statutes of Lower Canada was published a few days later.

So far as may be determined, no statute law revision of the British North American variant had ever been proposed or carried through in Lower Canada prior to 1841. In that year, for the same reason that had made the Upper Canada revision necessary, the newly elected Assembly of the Union requested the appointment of a commission to revise the statute law of Lower Canada. But the instructions to the Lower Canadians read somewhat differently from those that had been issued to the Upper Canadian commission. In part, it was specified that they were to 'examine and revise the several Statutes and Ordinances from time to time passed, and enacted and ordained in that part of the Province formerly called Lower Canada, and now in force and effect, and to consolidate such of the said Statutes and Ordinances as relate to the same subjects or can be advantageously consolidated.'[21]

Here was a clear mandate to change the form of the statute-book; but, while the commissioners did so, they moved in a cautious and most conservative manner. In their first report, dated 21 March 1843, they stated that they had determined which of the 3,300 enactments in the statute-book had been repealed and which were in force, and that they had arranged the latter under suitable subject headings with the intention of consolidating like material.[22] However, for reasons that seem tenuous, they backed away from consolidation and stopped instead at a 'halfway house.' The ghosts of Justinian's commissioners might have been peering over their shoulders as they deliberated, because what they produced approximated the layout of his Code. There was a proper table of contents – the first in any British North American collection – with ten topical headings, beginning with 'The Constitution ...' and including penal laws, real property provisions, and so on (see figure 2).[23] In the body of the volume, acts or parts of acts bearing on the same subject were set out under an appropriate rubric, following a rational sequence. But there was no change in the content; each law was set out verbatim as it had been enacted. The pages were not as cluttered as in the past, however, because the regnal year of the act and the chapter number had been shifted from the centre of the page to the margin and printed in small type, and all mention of repealed acts had been omitted. The index was comprehensive and easy to use. As their model for layout,

CONTENTS.

Figure 2 The first topical table of contents in a collection of
British North American revised statutes: page xiv of the Revised Acts and
Ordinances of Lower Canada

format, and size the commissioners chose the Revised Statutes of Massachusetts, and so introduced the octavo volume to Canada.[24] Although the commissioners from Lower Canada had not gone the whole way, they had made a break with the past and pointed the way to the future. Other jurisdictions soon followed their lead.

New Brunswick was the first to do so. In 1849 Lemuel Wilmot, the attorney general and the first premier of the colony, introduced four bills in the assembly to consolidate all the penal statutes and to codify the provisions relating to felonies and misdemeanours. The codification was accomplished by the Indictable Offences Act.[25] Its opening pages were entirely conventional in size and format, and much of the content of the following pages had been developed in New Brunswick. But the format of the following pages was closely modelled on Lord Brougham's draft bill of 1848. The two styles in such close juxtaposition provide a startling contrast. Specifically, the first section of the act covers well over two pages, runs on in a sentence of 1,500 words or more, and employs the conventional words of enactment. The fourth page is an abbreviated copy of Brougham's topical table of contents, often verbatim, and sets out the material covered by chapter, section, and article. There are no words of enactment in any of these divisions.[26] The chapters are numbered consecutively in roman numerals, and the arabic numbers of the sections and articles each start at 1 within their respective subdivisions. Thus, sections and articles could be added or deleted or otherwise amended without disarranging the general numbering.

The New Brunswick draftsmen eliminated many of the explanations and definitions of the imperial model, abbreviated the detail, and did not include a chapter of specific punishments. Therefore, though they followed the wording of the English bill in many substantive clauses, their articles, which still consisted of one sentence, were more conventional than those of the model (see figure 3). For example, the article on riotous destruction of property, one of the longer passages in Brougham's draft, reads as follows:

If any persons, riotously and tumultuously assembled together to the disturbance of the public peace, shall unlawfully and with force demolish, pull down, or destroy, or begin to demolish, pull down or destroy any church or chapel, or any chapel for the religious worship of persons dissenting from the United Church of England and Ireland, or any house, stable, coach-house, out-house, warehouse, office, shop, mill, malt-house, hop-oast, barn or granary, or any building or erection used in carrying on any trade or manufacture, or any branch

CHAPTER VII.

Homicide and other Offences against the Person.

SUMMARY OF CONTENTS.

SECTION 1.

Homicide.

ART. 1.

Murder.

Every person who shall be convicted of Murder, or being an accessory before the fact to Murder, shall suffer death as a Felon; and being an accessory after the fact to Murder, shall be liable to be imprisoned for any term not exceeding four years, and fined if the Court shall so direct.

ART. 2.

Petit Treason made Murder.

Every offence which, before the ninth and tenth years of the Reign of King George the Fourth, would have amounted to Petit Treason, shall be deemed to be Murder only, and no greater offence; and all persons guilty in respect thereof, whether as principals or accessories, shall be punished as principals and accessories in Murder.

ART. 3.

Manslaughter.

Any person convicted of Manslaughter shall be liable to be imprisoned for any term not exceeding fourteen years.

ART. 4.

No punishment or forfeiture when by misfortune, &c.

Provided that no punishment or forfeiture shall be incurred by any person who shall kill another by misfortune, or in his own defence, or in any other manner without Felony.

SECTION 2.

Other Offences against the Person.

ART. 1.

Administering poison, or by means manifesting a design to kill, causing bodily harm, with intent to kill.

Whosoever shall administer to or cause to be taken by any other person any poison, or other destructive thing, or shall by any means manifesting a design to kill, cause bodily harm to any other person, with intent, in any of such cases, to kill, shall be guilty of Felony; and being convicted thereof, shall be liable to be imprisoned for any term not exceeding seven years.

ART. 2.

Figure 3 The first codified enactment of legislation in British North America: a page from the New Brunswick Indictable Offences Act, 1849

thereof, or any machinery, whether fixed or moveable, prepared for or employed in any manufacture or in any branch thereof, or any steam-engine or other engine, for sinking, draining or working any mine, or any staith, building or erection used in conducting the business of any mine, or any bridge, waggon-way or trunk for conveying minerals from any mine, every such offender shall incur the penalties of the 4th Class.

It is a sentence of 162 words. The analogous section in the New Brunswick legislation reads as follows:

If any persons riotously and tumultuously assembled together, to the disturbance of the public peace, shall unlawfully and with force, demolish, pull down or destroy, or begin to demolish, pull down, or destroy any church, chapel, or meeting house, stable, coach-house, out house, warehouse, office, shop, mill malt house, barn, or granary, or any building or erection used in carrying on any trade or manufacture or any branch thereof, or any machinery, whether fixed or moveable, prepared for or employed in any manufacture, or in any branch thereof, any such offender shall be guilty of Felony, and shall be liable to be imprisoned for any term not exceeding fourteen years.[27]

This sentence is 37 words shorter. Although there was little or no change in content, this act made a real break with the past and radically altered the form of the statute-book, giving it the appearance of a modern legal text.

One drawback to this legislation was that it made citation difficult, since the chapter in the statute-book could easily be confused with chapters in the code. When referring to the offence of rape, for instance, a full citation would read: 'Indictable Offences Act, 1849, 14 Vict., c. 29; c. 1, s. 2, art. 10.' This was no mere technical quibble, for the English commissioners who revised Sir James Fitzjames Stephen's draft criminal code in 1878 stated unequivocally that they had changed Stephen's similar format 'in order to avoid the use of the word "chapter" as the name of a sub-division of what might itself ultimately become a chapter of the statute book.'[28]

This problem was solved by Nova Scotia. In the same year in which the New Brunswick acts were promulgated, the council and assembly of Nova Scotia resolved unanimously that the statutes of the province 'be consolidated, simplified in their language and republished in one uniform code,' and asked the lieutenant-governor to issue a commission to implement their resolution.[29] Accordingly, four lawyers were appointed, two of whom were members of the legislature.[30] They soon found that one of their major problems was that '[e]very variety of style ... is to be found in the statutes that remain in force, from the terseness and vigour which distinguish some few of the enactments, to the verbiage and interminable periods, which render it a hopeless task to find out the meaning of too many of the others'.[31]

To rectify this situation, the commissioners considered eliminating repealed statutes and parts thereof and printing the remainder in chronological order, as had been done in Upper Canada, or arranging them in a topical order, as in Lower Canada. They rejected both courses as falling 'far short of what the legislature obviously contemplated and what we ourselves desired.'

Instead, they took the Revised Statutes of Massachusetts and the Revised Statutes of New York as their models. These statutes made up the entire public statute law of each jurisdiction. They were written in a short, concise, non-technical style, and set out the law in one or two volumes in an integrated and topical layout. While the resemblance between the models and Nova Scotia's derivative is pronounced in matters of layout and style, the commissioners remarked that the laws of those two jurisdictions 'have offered us little or no assistance'; the form was foreign, the substance Nova Scotian. Working with these guidelines and with the knowledge that the legislature 'expected that the new code should present the law, in all essential particulars as it was,' they produced the code in one octavo volume in 1851. It subsumed the content of 750 repealed statutes, and contained all the public statute law of the province. A topically ordered table of contents made it easy to find any subject, and revealed that the code was divided into 4 parts, 41 titles, and 170 chapters, each of which consisted of one or more sections, and ran to 578 pages (see figure 4). In particular, Part Four, which comprised fifteen chapters, set out the whole of the statutory penal law.

While this was a notable innovation in that it was the first occasion when all substantive and procedural criminal law of a jurisdiction was integrated in one systematic treatment, the task had been made somewhat less demanding than would otherwise have been the case by liberal borrowings from the New Brunswick Acts of 1849. The parts, titles, and chapters are each numbered consecutively in arabic numerals. Each chapter is summarized by a short, descriptive headnote, and the sections within each chapter are marked off in arabic numerals beginning at 1. There are no regnal years anywhere in the volume, and no words of enactment, except for the first sentence of the work: 'Be it enacted by the Lieutenant-

PART IV.

OF THE CRIMINAL LAW AND THE ADMINISTRATION OF CRIMINAL JUSTICE.

TITLE XL.

[OF OFFENCES AGAINST THE GOVERNMENT.

CHAPTER 155.

OF TREASON.

1. Whoever shall compass or imagine the death of the queen, or of her eldest son and heir, or shall levy war against her, or adhere to her enemies giving to them aid or comfort, and shall thereof be duly convicted, shall be declared and adjudged to be a traitor, and shall suffer death and forfeiture as in cases of high treason. *Treason defined ; punishment.*

2. All acts of the imperial parliament directing the proceedings and evidence on trials for high treason in England, shall have their full force and effect, and be observed as the rule on trials for high treason in this province. *Proceedings and evidence to be as in England.*

CHAPTER 156.

OF OFFENCES RELATING TO THE ARMY AND NAVY.

Figure 4 The first code of statute law in British North America: a page from the Revised Statutes of Nova Scotia, 1851

Governor and Assembly, as follows.' The commissioners were able to introduce this innovation by virtue of a special statute enacted by the legislature in 1851 in emulation of Lord Brougham's Act of the previous year.[32] Contrary to their expressed intention, the commissioners did recommend some substantive amendments, which 'became unavoidable in the work'; these were noted in the margin of the draft bills. Unlike the contemporary situation in England, however, the commissioners, who were also members of the council or the assembly, could explain and defend their proposed changes when the code came up for debate in those chambers.

Although the code was a great improvement on what had gone before, it was not without defects. While the draftsmen did a commendable job of compression in the new style, they also preserved the traditional English form of the sections. They were still made up of one sentence with no subdivisions, and in the penal chapters one still had to read to the end of the sentence to discover the class of crime and the punishment. Much was still left to the common law: there were no definitions of important terms such as 'larceny,' 'murder,' and the like; several major offences, including sedition and piracy, remained unenumerated. This was not a satisfactory situation, since judges defined such words and concepts by reference to the common law as the need arose; and with a judge's ability to distinguish, such definitions were by no means uniform.[33]

Although the elimination of these shortcomings would have been desirable, we should not lose sight of what was accomplished. The Revised Statutes of Nova Scotia is an elegant and innovative work that made the whole of the public statute law accessible to all. It has a modern, functional appearance and a clear, concise, and uniform style which makes it relatively easy to read and comprehend. Indeed, its chapter format became the model for all subsequent Nova Scotia statutes. Finally, the legislature ensured that there would be no confusion between the chapter of the enacting statute and the chapters of the code by providing that the work was to be cited as the 'Revised Statutes,' followed by chapter and section numbers.[34]

This innovation was copied by New Brunswick in its Revised Statutes, which were enacted in 1854.[35] In the year the Nova Scotia code was published, the lieutenant-governor of New Brunswick, responding to an address from the legislature, appointed a commission of three lawyers, two of whom were members of the assembly, to 'consolidate, simplify in their language, revise and arrange in one uniform code, the

Acts of Assembly.' The commissioners followed much the same procedure as their colleagues in Nova Scotia had done. They used the same model, but achieved even greater brevity; for example, they used only forty-three words, to lay down the law concerning malicious damage to structures under the rubric 'riotously pulling down buildings': 'Any person who shall unlawfully and maliciously pull down or destroy, or begin to pull down or destroy any building, bridge, or other erection or machinery therein, shall be guilty of felony, and shall be imprisoned for a term not exceeding fourteen years.' The resulting octavo volume of 577 pages was similar to that of its sister province in appearance and content, but was slightly smaller in size. It too was divided into parts, titles, chapters and sections, and the chapters were supplied with head-notes. Substantive and procedural criminal law was systematized, and formed the fourth part of the code. Regnal years disappeared, words of enactment were omitted from all but the first paragraph, and all previous public statutes were repealed. As in Nova Scotia, the new format became the model for all subsequent statutes. It is evident that the draftsmen in both maritime provinces had achieved a compression of the law and an economy of style that could only have made Fitzjames Stephen envious. Furthermore, their bills became law twenty-five years before Stephen's draft code was read the first time.

Legislation in the Province of Canada had begun to alter the format of the statutes even before any such action was taken in the maritimes. Subparagraphs were introduced in sections of the Common Schools Act of 1843. They were identified by a large arabic numeral, and each consisted of a sentence closed by a period.[37] Section XIV, for example, had five such divisions, which, together with the introducing matter at the beginning of the section, totalled over 350 words. Although this was a clumsy method of dividing a section, it made the material much easier to read and cite than the same words in the traditional one-section, one-sentence format. There was no success, however, in bringing system to the penal statutes. In 1850, a year after Premier Wilmot's codification of the criminal law was enacted in New Brunswick, William Badgley, the MLA for Missisquoi, introduced two bills in the assembly to effect a similar codification in Canada. He told the House that the measures had been drafted from Canadian and English statutes and the codes of neighbouring states of the republic, and that his object was to have them read a second time pro forma and referred to a select committee. Its report could then be digested over the recess and so form the basis of informed debate when the bills were reintroduced in the next session.[38]

Badgley had been attorney general in the Tory administration of Henry Sherwood, and at the time he brought in his criminal law bills he was the well-informed and articulate leader of the opposition in the Reform administration of Baldwin and Lafontaine.[39] It may be that this had a great deal to do with the fate of his bills. At any rate, in debate both Lafontaine and Baldwin refused to accept Badgley's proposal on the grounds that it would commit the government to the principle of the measure. Accordingly, second reading was postponed and nothing more was heard of the legislation in that session.[40] Undaunted, Badgley introduced the bills in the next session, during the first year of the Hincks-Morin administration. This time they got through second reading and went to a select committee. Its report reviewed at length the sorry state of the criminal law in the Canadas and praised Badgley's bills. Nevertheless, the committee refused to endorse them as they stood, but recommended that a commission be appointed to revise them for subsequent consideration by the assembly. Badgley so moved and the motion was passed, but that was the last that was heard of the matter.[41]

In this period of legal ferment in the maritimes and Great Britain, the legislature again turned its attention to the format and style of the statutes, although no mention of these matters has been found in the *Debates*. In 1852 the sessional statutes were issued for the first time in a quarto volume. On the pages within, the title of an act was printed at the centre of the head of each page it occupied. The year, the regnal year, and the chapter number, all in arabic numerals, were shifted to the edges of the head of the page. Subparagraphs began to be punctuated with semicolons in 1854, which was also the first year in which enacting words were omitted from all but the first section of a chapter. In the session of 1855 a bill in the style of Brougham's Act of 1850 was passed, which laid down that the preamble to acts would be shortened, standardized, and placed at the head of each measure, after which 'the various clauses of the Statute shall follow in a concise and enunciative form.'[42]

At the beginning of the same session a petition from the municipal council of Lanark and Renfrew requesting a general revision and simplification of the law was read in the assembly.[43] It was not the first time such a request had been made; in fact, similarly worded petitions had been a feature of several preceding sessions,[44] for by this time there were on the statute-books about 4,700 acts of the provincial Parliament and its two predecessors.[45] The legislators eventually responded in 1851 by moving an address for the issue of a commission for the revision and consolidation of the statute law of the three jurisdictions, but to no avail.[46] In 1856, however, the attorney general of Upper Canada, John A. Macdonald, responded to a similar motion in the session of 1855 by appointing six lawyers 'to examine, revise, consolidate and classify the Public General Statutes of Upper Canada' and, in conjunction with commissioners to be appointed from Lower Canada, to effect a similar review and revision of the provincial statutes.[47] Six Lower Canadians were duly appointed and given similar terms of reference for their jurisdiction. Of the total of twelve commissioners, four were members of the assembly, and so would be able to advocate and explain their work when it came before the House for legislative sanction. When that occurred, it was unlikely that the legalists in the assembly would be opposed to the measures; if the editorial writer of the *Upper Canada Law Journal* in any way reflects the opinion of the members of the profession, they were just as much in favour of a thorough revision as the individuals and organizations that had begun the process with their petitions. Quoting Richard Brinsley Sheridan, the editor argued that when a bill imposing a tax is enacted and is followed by 'a bill to amend the bill that imposed the tax – a bill to explain the bill that amended the bill that imposed the tax – a bill to remedy the defects of the bill that explained the bill that amended the bill that imposed the tax; and such measures [continue] and infinitum, it is time to reduce and consolidate.'[48]

As their counterparts in the maritimes had done, the commissioners reviewed the work of codified jurisdictions in the United States, the drafts of the imperial commissioners, and the codes of Nova Scotia and New Brunswick. While the last two codes were of considerable interest to the commissioners, they pointed out that their terms of reference were different from those issued in the maritimes.[49] Inevitably, then, their work would assume a different form. They developed a logical topical order which was similar for each of the three jurisdictions, classified the acts according to the order, and consolidated the statutes pertaining to a particular topic in accordance with guidelines set by John A. Macdonald.[50] This process is described in detail in the first report of the commissioners for Upper Canada, which, accompanied by a draft of the Upper Canada revision, was submitted to the Cabinet during the session of 1858 by the chairman, James B. Macaulay.[51] However, both the report and subsequent letters from Macaulay made clear that it was by no means complete and that the manuscript of the provincial volume was still with the printer.[52] That too was not in its final form, especially in the area of the criminal law, where more work was needed to make it uniform across the province. To accomplish the work in time for the volumes to be considered in the next session (1859) the Upper Canadian commission would have to be reorganized, since all but Macaulay had returned to private practice after the completion of the current drafts.

To resolve the questions he had raised, Macaulay met with the attorney general, who suggested that Judge Gowan, who had recently drafted the Crown Attorney's Act and the Common Law Procedures Act, would be a zealous and efficient commissioner.[53] Accordingly, Macaulay requested the services of Gowan; he was appointed, and the two men got down to the task of revising and correcting the drafts.[54] They were ready for enactment early in 1859. On 4 March, Attorney General Macdonald moved first reading of bills to consolidate the Statutes of Upper Canada and of the Province of Canada, the first of which contained 1,377 and the second 1,299 pages. They were given second reading on 8 March, and sent to a select committee. One month later the committee reported the bills, as amended. On 12 April, after what must have been only a perfunctory examination, the committee of the whole House reported the bills without further amendment, and they received third reading the next day. Royal assent was given on 14 May.[55]

Considering the size and complexity of the legislation, the bills went through smoothly and expeditiously. No evidence has been found to suggest that there was any opposition to the measures. How was this done? According to that astute observer, Judge Gowan, 'Sir John Macdonald, when the vols of the Consolidated Statutes were submitted to the old Parliament of Canada, had a representative committee appointed; he told them candidly it would take a quarter of a century in such a body following the usual rules to go over and test the correctness of the matter presented – he enlarged upon the advantages of having the whole stat[ute] law better expressed and condensed into a small compass and he suggested taking up some bit, testing that and judging the rest by it – an *ex pede Herculem* appeal – and so it was done – he got his measure through.'[56] But even a political magician like Macdonald could not have performed this trick if members of the committee such as Antoine Dorion or Oliver Mowat had been inclined to oppose the legislation, as the English experience demonstrates.

For several reasons, no one was so inclined. To begin with, only the members from Upper Canada had much interest in the matter, or at least in the public and private law; in accordance with an act of 1857, a commission was already at work on the civil code of Lower Canada which, when completed, would 'embrace all the present statutes of joint application [that is, provincial statutes] except those of a criminal nature.'[57] They were timely measures, and would keep Canada abreast of developments in the maritimes and anticipate the codification of English law, which was expected at any moment.[58] Moreover, the bills were not an alien importation; they had been drafted in large part by sitting members. But perhaps the main reason for the absence of opposition was that, except for matters of non-substantive detail or the reconciling of conflicts in statutes that dealt with the same matter in different ways, there was no amendment of the law. No punishments were changed, no old rights were abrogated or new rights created. As in the maritimes, Canadians did not want change; they wanted compression and systematization. This is precisely what the commissioners gave them, as their report makes clear: '[W]e should attempt an effectual consolidation without deviating from the original text when the language is explicit and concise, and only expunging or recasting where it appears that partial alterations or greater brevity may be safely adopted without affecting the import and meaning of the original Statute.'[59]

But while they did achieve compression, there was no change in style, as another comparison of the section on riotous destruction of buildings will illustrate. Section 6 of the Malicious Damage Act of 1841 reads as follows:

And be it enacted, that if any persons, riotously and tumultuously assembled together to the disturbance of the public peace, shall unlawfully and with force demolish, pull down, or destroy, or begin to demolish, pull down, or destroy any church, chapel, or meeting house, for the exercise of any mode or form of religious worship, or any house, stable, coach-house, out-house, warehouse, office, shop, mill, malt-house, hop-oast, barn or granary, or any building or erection used in carrying on any trade or manufacture, or any branch thereof, or any machinery, whether fixed or moveable, prepared for or employed in any manufacture, or in any branch thereof, every such offender shall be guilty of felony, and being convicted thereof, shall be liable, at the discretion of the Court, to be imprisoned at hard labour in the Provincial Penitentiary for the term of his natural life, or for any term not less than two years, or to be imprisoned in any other prison or place of confinement for any term not exceeding two years.[60]

The relevant section of the Consolidated Statutes renders this as follows:

If any persons, riotously and tumultuously assembled together to the disturb-ance of the public peace, unlawfully and with force demolish, pull down, or destroy, or begin to demolish, pull down or destroy any church, chapel, or meeting house, for the exercise of any mode or form of religious worship, or any house, coach-house, warehouse, office, shop, mill, malt-house, hop-oast, barn or granary, or any building or erection used in carrying on any trade or manufacture, or any branch thereof, or any machinery, whether fixed or mov-able, prepared for or employed in any manufacture, or in any branch thereof, every such offender shall be guilty of felony, and shall be imprisoned in the Penitentiary for the term of his natural life, or for any other term not less than two years, or be imprisoned in any other prison or place of confinement for any term less than two years.[61]

Thus, the length of the original was reduced by twenty-five words. But the retention of this style also meant that definitions and several specific offences were left to the common law.

One area in which the commissioners were able to make a considerable improvement was criminal procedure. Where possible, they extracted procedural details from substantive enactments and transposed them to a more appropriate place in the volume. For example, the Malicious Damage Act of 1841 has forty-two sections. Of these the substance of ten, or nearly 25 per cent, was integrated with the procedural chapters, by now almost wholly Canadian, in the Consolidated Statutes.[62]

The work was divided into 11 titles, 12 subtitles, and 111 chapters, and had three comprehensive schedules that detailed the disposition of all of the acts consolidated in a total of 1,377 pages. As in the maritime legislation, the final division – Title Eleven – set out the criminal law, which formed a subcode of 23 chapters and 257 pages. Unlike the Nova Scotia and New Brunswick codes, it was not a continuous text. Each chapter stood alone as a separate statute, complete with title and en-acting words. For this reason, and because its provisions had not been written from first principles but were merely abridgments of former statutes, its length was more than twice that of the two maritime codes. With the publication of the Consolidated Statutes of Canada and its companion volumes for Upper Canada in 1859 and Lower Canada in 1860, the statute-book took on its modern form. These collections intro-duced the use of bold-face arabic numerals to denote sections and light-face type to mark off subparagraphs; sub-subparagraphs were identified by lower-case letters of the alphabet (see figure 5).

Joint Stock
Banks.

19. Any number of persons, not less than five, may associate themselves together as a Joint Stock Bank, to be conducted at some one place, and at such place only, in Upper Canada, or at some one place, and at such place only, in Lower Canada, such place being in either case, some City, Town or Village, upon the following terms and conditions,

Articles of Association.

that is to say : such persons shall execute articles of agreement, and if the place be in Lower Canada, such articles shall be in Notarial form, but if in Upper Canada, then the articles shall be in duplicate, under the hands and seals of the parties, and such articles in either case shall state :

1. The name under which the Bank is to be conducted, which shall be the corporate name of the Company ;

2. The place at which the Bank is to be conducted as aforesaid ;

Contents of.

3. The whole Capital Stock of the Company, which shall not be less than one hundred thousand dollars ;

4. The number of shares into which it is divided, which shall not be so great as to make each share less than forty dollars ;

5. The name and residence of every Shareholder, and the number of shares held by him ;

6. The periods at which the Company is to commence and terminate ;---13, 14 V. c. 21, s. 9.

7. The amount for which each Shareholder is to be liable, beyond twice the amount of his shares---if it be agreed that the liability shall be so extended ; and,

8. Such other provisions and clauses as may be agreed upon ;

a. With regard to the management of the affairs of the Company ;

b. The election or appointment of the Directors, Cashier or other Manager and Officers, their powers and their terms of office;

c. The transfer of shares ;

d. The division of profits ;

e. The calling in of instalments on the stock ;

f. The increasing of the stock by the admission of new Shareholders or otherwise ;

g.

Figure 5 The forerunner of the format used in modern statute-books: a page from the Consolidated Statutes of Canada, 1859

By the time of Confederation, all the British North American colonies except Prince Edward Island and British Columbia had accomplished what the chancellors of England from the time of Henry viii had never been able to achieve:[63] they had managed to consolidate and codify the public statute law of each jurisdiction and to repeal all the law that had preceded it. Part of each code was a subcode of criminal law, which ranged from the brief 18 chapters and 50 pages of the Revised Statutes of New Brunswick to the relatively ponderous 22 chapters and 257 pages of the Consolidated Statutes of Canada, which were supplemented by over 400 pages of 'provincial' provisions in the codes of Lower and Upper Canada. But the codifications had done more than reduce the bulk of the law and arrange it systematically. They had introduced, on the largest scale possible, styles of drafting which vastly increased the accessibility and readability of the law, or, indeed, of any piece of administrative writing. The codes became models for all similar writing in the community at large.

5

Preparation for Codification in Canada: The Revised Statutes of Canada

After Confederation, Sir John A. Macdonald was faced with two major tasks: that of cementing the union by demonstrating that his government could legislate effectively for the new jurisdiction, and that of engendering a sense of national unity among its people. In large part the latter aim was to be accomplished by giving them a common criminal law. To carry out these tasks, he vested himself with the authority to deal directly with the problems by assuming the combined portfolio of minister of justice and attorney general, in addition to the office of prime minister.[1] After the prorogation of the first session, in which ninety-five bills were given royal assent, it was evident that the first task had been accomplished. But there were problems with the second. Each of the contracting jurisdictions had a code of criminal statute law, but they were by no means the same in style, content, or punishments. There were a number of options open to the prime minister. He could attempt to adopt any one of the codes. That would be a fast and cheap solution, but if he attempted it he ran the risk of the legislation's getting bogged down in controversial and impassioned debate. A more equitable and practicable solution would be to issue a commission to assimilate all the provincial legislation into a federal code, a process he contemplated but rejected because of its expense (although a more compelling reason, which he left unstated, was that it would be a very lengthy process if properly executed, and time was of the essence).[2]

A third option would be to follow the advice of Judge Gowan and pursue a middle course. He could adopt Greaves's Criminal Consolidation Acts, suitably amended, as the substantive dominion penal law, and assimilate the essentially similar procedural law that had been developed by the former colonies.[3] This was the option he chose. It was both ready-made and cheap, and Parliament would find it difficult to criticize the product of Westminister. For political reasons – and these were perhaps the most compelling – it would enable him to avoid comparing the merits of the various colonial codes. As an added bonus, the dominion 'would thereby enjoy the inestimable advantage of having English decisions as authority in our courts,' a benefit that was always a prime consideration with the prime minister.[4]

To put the legislation in shape, Macdonald employed his former subordinate from Ottawa, Gustavus Wicksteed, the law clerk of the assembly, who had been given a similar appointment in the dominion government, and his private secretary, Hewitt Bernard. Work began in the second half of 1867, when the two men were also busy with a variety of other important measures.[5] They had little time for recasting Greaves's Acts if, as was likely, the prime minister intended to introduce the legislation during the first session of Parliament. Nor did they have authority to make any significant changes in the style or to effect any substantial compression, since Macdonald had set strict guidelines for the work.[6] Their bills were, as Mr Justice Taschereau said, 'taken almost textually from … the Imperial Criminal Law Consolidation Acts of 1861,'[7] except for the few additions from provincial statutes that were not included in the English acts.[8] Furthermore, no effort was made to eliminate the crimes enumerated in these enactments that were not in the colonial statutes. There were understandably, many such offences, such as killing pigeons and stealing from oyster beds, for Greaves's Acts were intended to regulate a much larger urban and commercial population.

The first session of Parliament began in November 1867, and recessed from 21 December to 14 April. Early in the new year the two draftsmen were feeling the pressure of recasting the five English acts and the several colonial procedural statutes. Accordingly, Bernard wrote to Gowan (who in the meantime had been employing his drafting talent for the Liberal government of John Sandfield Macdonald in Ontario), advising him that he and Wicksteed would 'avail ourselves of your offer [to] revise our work.'[9] They did so, and on 1 April eleven bills to assimilate the criminal law of the provinces were introduced in the Commons by John A. Macdonald and given first reading. Second reading was to have been six days later, but on that day, 7 April, D'Arcy McGee was assassinated and the House adjourned for the following week. On 6 May, three weeks after it reconvened, Macdonald 'moved the second reading of the Bill respecting offences relating to the coin. He said with reference to this and a number of Bills relating to the criminal law, that he would ask the House in a great measure to accept them on trust. They had been prepared with a great deal of care. He had also examined them carefully himself, they would be open to amendment in Committee; and in the Upper House, where he had asked the Postmaster-General to take charge of them, they would also be subjected to careful scrutiny.'[10]

The legislation was nearly a month behind schedule. If it was to get to the Senate before prorogation on 22 May, extraordinary measures would have to be taken. Such was the case: all the bills in the series were forthwith 'read a second time, considered in committee, and ordered to be read a third time tomorrow.'[11] This was short shrift for measures that amounted to more than 230 pages of text and contained well over half the substantive criminal law of the dominion, but they were indeed read a third time the next day, and passed.[12] As in 1859 the parliamentary magician had pronounced the magic words, and the legislation was through without any questions. It should be noted, however, that the Commons was composed largely of members from the Canadas, whose laws were not unlike the English statutes in their formulation. In the Senate, where the maritime element was proportionately much larger, the magic did not work.[13]

The Senate feared that if it submitted to the prime minister's pressure in such cases, it would degenerate quickly into a mere rubber-stamp for the Commons, especially in the closing days of a session, as was alleged to have been the case with the Legislative Council of Canada.[14] To formulate their protest, a special committee was formed under the chairmanship of the government leader, Senator Alexander Campbell, on 30 March. Its report, tabled on 7 May, stated that it was 'impossible for this House to discharge the duties devolving upon them unless ample opportunity is given them for the discussion of all measures subject to their consideration, and in the absence of any other remedy they recommend the extreme measure of refusing to pass important Bills brought in close at the end of the session.'[15] Notwithstanding, the criminal law bills were introduced by the same Senator Campbell on 12 May, ten days before Parliament was due to be prorogued. He told the members that although the Senate would not have time to give the bills due consideration, they had been carefully drafted, they were based on English acts which had matured for years, and the House would have to take them on trust. Further, he said, what some members thought were new offences were really not. Finally, he asserted that '[n]o matter what course we take we cannot legislate upon this subject from our own knowledge. In a matter involving so much study we must trust somebody else to prepare these bills, and it could not very well be undertaken by a committee of our own House.'[16]

It was not the most politic speech Campbell ever made, and, as we shall see, he learned a great deal from this experience. It did him no good in getting the legislation enacted, for by this time several senators had left Ottawa in anticipation of prorogation and the Liberals were temporarily in the majority. The Senate split on party lines, and the opposition rolled over the government. To begin with, Jonathan McCully, who had been a member of the commission responsible for the Revised Statutes of Nova Scotia in 1851, made the point by implication that penalties for killing pigeons in the urban areas of England or in Canadian cities, where domestic birds could be costly, made sense. They made no sense in country areas in which pigeons were a pest. Consequently, '[u]nder a clause of this bill every man who touched one of those pigeons, which were a nuisance to the neighbourhood, would have brought down upon himself this penal law.'[17] The debate went downhill from that point for the government, and Senator John Sanborn, a Quebec Liberal, finished it off with a strong speech in which he objected to the late appearance of the bills and declared himself strongly opposed to passing them in their current form. He suggested that they be revised after prorogation, printed, and distributed to legal and judicial bodies throughout the dominion, and then, in the light of their comments and criticisms, put together in an integrated code in a future session. If the bills went through as they were, he predicted, the government would eventually be swamped with both public and private bills to amend the essentially English acts. He then moved that the bills not be read a second time.[18] The motion was carried, and that was the end of the criminal law bills for 1868.

Governor General Charles Monck was incensed by the Senate's decision, and said so privately to Macdonald and, more diplomatically, in his prorogation speech.[19] This was gleefully reported to Gowan by Wicksteed, who opined that the senators 'may be wiser next session.'[20] He also told the judge that there would be plenty of time to work on the criminal legislation, the latest copies of which would be sent to Gowan for revision. The speech was also reported verbatim in several newspapers.[21] But no reporter or editorial writer commented on the rebuke, and the prolific correspondents of the day did not make it the subject of letters to the editor (or at least no letters were published in the days following prorogation). This behaviour epitomizes the attitude of the press and the general public in the nineteenth century to the criminal law. There was great interest in the application of the law, and transcripts of testimony in notorious cases often ran to more than a full newspaper page day after day;[22] but amendments or other alterations to the statute criminal law were seen to be the exclusive province of a small group of lawyers in Parliament.

During the recess there was a steady flow of suggestions from legalists and laymen, some unsolicited and some in response to requests from the Department of Justice. A few of these were incorporated in the bills the prime minister began to introduce early in the session of 1869.[23] His tactics were different from those of the previous year. The legislation itself had been changed only slightly, but, although the Commons had passed it without a murmur the previous year, he was more conciliatory this time, telling members that 'valuable suggestions had been received on the several subjects during the recess by the Government, and the alterations, which he hoped would be considered by the House as amendments, had been incorporated.' The bills were put through clause by clause; Macdonald stated the current law in England and in the provinces, so that the members could compare it with the government's proposals. Although the 'language used in such measures in the Lower Provinces might be shorter and more concise,' he had chosen 'to adhere to that before the House ... [so] that the body of the Criminal Law should be such that the Judges in the Superior Courts should have an opportunity of adjudicating upon it, as on English law. It would be of incalculable advantage that every decision of the Imperial Courts at Westminster should be law in the Dominion. On every principle of convenience and conformity of decision with that of England, he thought it well to retain the English phraseology.'[24]

Amendments were proposed and passed or failed according to the temper of the House, and Macdonald even deferred debate when it was found that a member of the opposition who had proposed to move an amendment was reported to be absent from the House.[25] It was, in short, a very different performance from the previous year's.[26]

In the Senate, Campbell emulated the prime minister's conciliatory performance. He had more need to do so, for resentment of the governor general's rebuke transcended party lines, and the senators made no secret of their displeasure.[27] However, the change in the government's attitude and the fact that the bills began to arrive in the Upper House early in May changed the mood of the members, and while McCully and Sanborn extolled the virtues of the concise maritime codes and deplored the verbosity and redundancy of the English acts, they did so without rancour. Debate proceeded in a co-operative manner, compromises were made, and amendments were won and lost by both sides of the House. Well before prorogation the criminal law consolidation bills had received third reading in the Senate and were given royal assent on 22 June.[28] These statutes, together with other penal enactments of the first and second sessions, totalled thirty-one acts covering 364 pages.[29]

The old adage that what is lost on the swings is gained on the roundabouts was certainly true of the decision to adopt Greaves's Acts as substantive Canadian criminal law. Since the speedy resolution of the problem was a matter of the highest national priority, the decision was right because it exerted a unifying influence on the new jurisdiction; and it was right because it was politically expedient to avoid invidious comparisons of former colonial penal codes. But it was wrong because the English laws brought in much that had never been law in any colony and, having been enacted for a unitary state, they contained provisions that were ultra vires the dominion Parliament.[30] They were also regressive. They brought back the style of the past. For example, the section on riotous damage to buildings was 4 words longer than the similar section from Greaves's Acts quoted above and, at 280 words, was well over 100 words longer than any similar section in any pre-Confederation colonial code.[31] In all of the five statutes, the symmetry of long, one-sentence sections is relieved only once by the inclusion of the section on kidnapping, which had been formulated by the dominion draftsmen who had employed the Canadian style of short, concise phrases and numbered subsections.[32] Furthermore, the English acts perpetuated the confusing mixture of substantive and procedural matter, which all the provinces had corrected to a greater or lesser degree in the codifications of the 1850s. The Larceny Act, for example, had 124 sections and ran to 35 pages. Of these, 45 sections totalling 8 pages were devoted to procedure.[33] But nowhere in this mass of words was it made clear what 'larceny' meant. As far back as the early fourteenth century the word had been defined as 'the treacherous taking of a corporeal moveable thing of another against the will of him to whom it belongs, by evil acquisition of possession or of the use.'[34] This is a perfectly understandable and succinct definition. It is clear that larceny comprehends the modern crimes of theft, robbery, and other cognate offences. In contrast, as Fitzjames Stephen pointed out, '[t]the arrangement of the [Larceny Act] is so strange that a person who, with no previous knowledge of the subject, attempted to find out from it what was the English law relating to the punishment of theft, and other similar offences, would be simply bewildered.'[35] Mr Justice Cave was more concise and colourful: 'Our law on the subject is a thing of shreds and patches.'[36] It is obvious that an individual who wished to read the Larceny Act with any degree of comprehension had to know and understand the common law pertaining to the subject. Some idea of what is involved can be gained from learning that Stephen thought it necessary to devote two chapters of his *Digest* to laying a foundation for 'a knowledge of the doctrines [the Larceny Act] presupposes' before he attempted to define 'theft.'[37]

Samuel R. Clarke did not take this trouble. He was a young Toronto lawyer who was called to the bar in 1870. His treatise on the criminal law as applicable to Canada, the first of its kind, was published in 1872, and was dedicated, by permission, to the prime minister for his work in assimilating the criminal laws of the colonies. But without Stephen's groundwork, Clarke's 'definition' of larceny, which is really two separate and different descriptions of the offence, is confusing and of little help to the lay reader.[38] Indeed, the thought is inescapable that the first question any intelligent person accused of larceny would ask after reading these passages is, 'Which version of larceny am I to be charged with?' So, too, with felony: the elaboration of this term takes up three pages and is supported by citations from fifteen judgments. For the analogous elaboration of 'misdemeanour,' Clarke refers the reader to two pages of *Russell on Crimes*.[39] There is no mention of treason or sedition in the text or in the index – odd omissions for a volume that purports to be a comprehensive treatise in criminal law. In truth, and notwithstanding its frequent citation of Canadian cases, Clarke's book could fairly be described as excellent proof of the need to systematize and simplify Canadian criminal law.

In the summer of 1870, a year after the passage of the criminal law bills in Ottawa, R.S. Wright received his commission from the Colonial Office to draft a criminal code for Jamaica.[40] At the same time, Judge Gowan, accompanied by his wife, left for Europe on the first long leave he had been able to take since his appointment to the bench twenty-seven years earlier. The Gowans were absent for nearly a year, during which time they met most of the senior men in the legal hierarchy of England and Ireland and in the Colonial Office. Among them were Lord Thring, the parliamentary draftsman who introduced the relatively concise and economical style of the modern British statute and who gave Gowan a copy of his *Instructions to Draftsmen*; Lord Cairns, who was between appointments as lord chancellor; Lord Dufferin, soon to be the governor general of Canada; and Lord Carnarvon, a former and future colonial secretary.[41] Lesser lights of the Colonial Office with whom he dined included Robert Herbert, the permanent under-secretary, and Sir Henry Taylor, the originator of the colonial criminal code project, who presented Gowan with copies of his paper on the subject.[42]

After learning that they had a mutual interest in codification and that the judge was an expert legislative draftsman, one of these men introduced him to R.S. Wright, probably in the early summer of 1871.[43] By this time, Wright claimed to have made considerable progress with his code, so that he and Gowan had much to discuss during the 'long talk [they] had about codification and the Criminal Law' in Wright's chambers.[44] It may also have been Wright, who was collecting relevant documents for his enterprise, who introduced Gowan to Mrs Livingstone Barton. She was the daughter of Edward Livingstone, who had codified the law of the Louisiana, and in 1871 she was in Europe seeing the French and English editions of her father's works through the printer. From her letter to Gowan offering him a copy of the French edition, it is evident that they had discussed her father's work during their meetings.[45] Thus, when Gowan embarked for Canada, he had much firsthand information on codification, and much news for Sir John A. Macdonald.

When Gowan arrived in Quebec in July 1871, Senator Sanborn's prediction was coming true. By then it was clearly evident that the substantive criminal law of the dominion was something more than the sum of borrowed English statutes and one or two excisions from the penal law of the former colonies; cracks in the 1868-9 legislation were being papered over with acts to amend acts. In the sessions of 1870 and 1871 twelve penal statutes were passed: six were amending acts. The proliferation continued under Macdonald and into the Mackenzie administration, by which time 'An Act to further amend an act' had made its appearance, and fourteen more amending statutes were in force by 1874. The penal laws now covered 445 pages, as opposed to 369 in 1869.

For once, such figures were culled not from a laborious search through the annual volumes of statutes, but from a handy reference book. In 1874 the Department of Justice put together a volume of the criminal statutes enacted since Confederation. It was in no sense a consolidation or code, but it must have been a godsend to magistrates and practitioners; although it merely reprinted the acts by regnal year, in chronological order, it had a table of contents consisting of the chapter numbers and titles of the acts, a reasonably comprehensive index, and continuous pagination.[46]

That year also saw the appearance of a much more sophisticated aid to the profession in the form of the first volume of *The Criminal Law Consolidation and Amendment Acts*, written by Mr Justice Henri-Elzéar Taschereau, a young and able member of the Quebec Superior Court.[47] Although it was a conventional treatment for the time and not unlike Greaves's similar volume of 1862 – an annotation of the statutes it reproduced – it was much easier to read and understand than the average law text, for the judge was a gifted writer with a clear, logical, and uncomplicated style. It would, however, be considered unhandy today, because it contained citations only to English decisions. But it should be remembered that Greaves's Acts had been in force in England since 1861; consequently, there was a large number of these, which, moreover, were binding on Canadian courts. These were necessary because of the paucity of authoritative Canadian judgments. The Supreme Court of Canada had not yet been formed, and judgments given in one province were not binding in another. Furthermore, as Taschereau pointed out, there was a thorough discussion of Canadian cases in S.R. Clarke's *Treatise*, and to repeat it would have been 'superfluous.'[48]

Late that year or early in 1875 Taschereau sent Greaves a copy of his work, in which he had quoted the English lawyer extensively.[49] Greaves's reply, dated 18 February 1875, is the first letter extant in the extensive Taschereau-Greaves correspondence, which continued for several years and possibly until Greaves died in 1881.[50] The judge derived considerable benefit from this exchange, which he acknowledged in the preface to his second volume, a treatise on criminal procedural law published in November 1875. Unlike Greaves, who would have had to contend with several procedure statutes and many amending measures enacted over a period of forty years if he had wished to compile a similar work, Taschereau was able to produce a clear and coherent annotation because the relevant law of the pre-Confederation colonies had been assimilated in four comprehensive statutes in the 1869 consolidations.[51] This is reflected in the annotations: copious reference is made to Canadian decisions.

Meanwhile, in 1874 the Ontario government determined to issue a revised edition of the Consolidated Statutes of Upper Canada. A commission was formed, and Oliver Mowat invited Judge Gowan to join in February 1876.[52] Gowan accepted, and from the ensuing correspondence it is evident that a close relationship developed between the two men.[53]

The Revised Statutes of Ontario, which came into effect in 1878, comprised two elegant volumes. The technical apparatus of titles and subtitles was similar to but somewhat more detailed than that of the Consolidated Statutes of 1859, and the system of chapter headnotes was borrowed from the maritime codes. It is also evident that efforts were made to make the work more clear and concise than its predecessor. This may have been due in part to Gowan, who had before him not only the Canadian models but also Wright's draft code. Wright, who had been influenced by the tightly written *Norddeutsches Strafgesetzbuch*, had completed the work in January 1874, and Gowan had been sent a copy 'for observation,'[54] probably about the same time Fitzjames Stephen agreed to review and revise it later that year.[55] Similar activity was going on in Nova Scotia and New Brunswick, where revised statutes were promulgated in 1873 and 1877 respectively.

These ongoing reforms in the provinces, and the obscurity and confusion which the proliferation of amending acts was bringing to the dominion statutes, were no doubt the primary reasons for the Mackenzie administration's decision to consolidate and codify the federal enactments. In 1877 Edward Blake, the minister of justice, moved that $8,000 be appropriated 'to meet the estimated expenses in connection with the consolidation of the Laws.'[56] He explained that the work would begin with the collection and collation of all relevant statutes, provincial and federal. Two of the junior commissioners who had worked on the Ontario revision would be employed for this laborious task.[57] Blake did not see the work through to completion, however; he resigned his portfolio on 7 June to take up the less demanding duties of president of the Privy Council. On 23 June Gowan, perhaps motivated by the item in the estimates, raised with Blake the question of codification of the criminal law and offered to lend him Wright's code.[58] Blake replied, 'I have for sometime been anxious to see the criminal law placed on a better footing, and had I remained in my late office I would have made an effort to combine to some extent codification with consolidation. But the causes which led me to leave the office finished my attempts to try to deal with the subject at present, and therefore I do not think I can usefully avail myself of your kind offer to lend me the draft in your possession.'[59] Martin L. Friedland, the legal historian who rescued Wright and his code from oblivion, demonstrates effectively that the code was 'in many, if not most, respects ... a much better Code than either James Fitzjames Stephen's Draft Code of 1878 or the Royal Commissioners' Draft Code of 1879.'[60] At a time when the Mackenzie government had both the intent to systematize the criminal law and a blueprint for a better code than that which was enacted fifteen years later, the initiative failed because Blake did not have the will to push it through to completion. The incident remains a fascinating 'might have been' in Canadian history.

After completing work on the Ontario revision late in November 1877 (for which he received a gold medal struck for the occasion), Judge Gowan and his wife left for England on another long vacation.[61] They toured the Continent during the cold winter months and returned to England in the early summer. The judge was in London when Stephen's draft code was introduced, debated, and withdrawn, and he must have followed the debate and Stephen's interjections in *The Times* with interest. Gowan himself had something to add to the discussion. He had taken copies of the Revised Statutes of Ontario to England, and it was at this time that he gave or sent them to several of his highly placed friends in the Colonial Office and the judiciary, among them Lord Carnarvon and Lord Cairns.[62] Since the lord chancellor was, ultimately, the moving force behind codification in England at this time, Cairns's comments on the Canadian work are worthy of note. After remarking that he was 'examining them with the most lively interest' because of their relevance to the current effort to 'reduce our vast body of Statutes and Common Law,' he added, 'it is most interesting to me to observe how far you have gone in advance of us in Ontario in this most exemplary work.'[63] High praise indeed from the head of the English legal system.

While Gowan was away, a feeble effort was made to move Blake's consolidation project forward. After his work on the Ontario revision was complete, Thomas Langton, Oliver Mowat's son-in-law and a future partner in his law firm, was hired to prepare schedules 'of the Acts which are to be considered preparatory to the consolidation and revision of the Dominion Statutes.'[64] To keep the project alive, Blake's successor, Rodolphe Laflamme, secured a second appropriation of $8,000. But after the general election of 1878 swept Sir John A. Macdonald back into power, the initiative was allowed to peter out under the lacklustre administration of the new minister of justice, James MacDonald of Nova Scotia.

MacDonald's appointment had been brought about by a change in the prime minister's priorities. The authority of the dominion Parliament had been established, and the standardized criminal law administered in all Canadian courts had extended its unifying effect on the provinces. Now the prime minister's principal goal was to bind together the whole of British North America by implementing his National Policy, prime elements of which were to people the northwest and to link British Columbia to the rest of Canada by rail. For this reason the prime minister also assumed the duties of minister of the interior. He gave the downgraded Justice portfolio to MacDonald, one of his less able colleagues, but a man who had rendered signal service defending the government in the dark days of the Pacific Scandal, and who was, next to Charles Tupper, the most prominent and influential Conservative in Nova Scotia.[65]

This appointment did not sit well with Gowan, who, after his return from England, had discussed the matter with the prime minister.[66] He regretted that Sir John had not again assumed the duties of minister of justice, because he felt 'more at home laying before you any matter that occurs [to me] on the subject I feel most interested in,' and 'I may be too far from the sea to meet the taste of your new minister.'[67] Then, after bringing Macdonald up to date on the progress of codification in England as reported by Lord Cairns, he suggested that like measures be introduced in the Canadian Parliament. Wicksteed and he could work up the legislation, and, if it could be done promptly, there was no reason 'we should not anticipate the legislation in England.'

Gowan was not the only one who was following the events at Westminster with close attention. The *Legal News* was interested in 'the steps taken in England toward codification,' and several pages were devoted to an analysis of the proposed legislation.[68] The opposition was curious, too. In the 1879 session Philippe Casgrain, a prominent Quebec City lawyer, was moved to ask the minister of justice if it was 'the intention of the Government to codify the criminal laws, following the example set by England in that respect.'[69] He was answered by an unequivocal no from James MacDonald. Later in the session, after the commissioners' bill had been introduced in the imperial Parliament, Gowan returned to the theme in a letter to the prime minister in which his disappointment with the justice minister's reply is evident: 'I am sorry to see that your friend does not propose to do anything in the way of codifying the criminal law.'[70] He reiterated his argument for a Canadian code, and reminded Sir John that Canadian legislation had frequently been in advance of similar measures in England. A more immediate reason was advanced by Alfred F. Savary, the county court judge from Digby, Nova Scotia, who pointed out that twelve years had elapsed since Confederation, and that consolidation of the mass of laws enacted during that period had 'obviously become a necessity.'[71]

In the Senate both the layout and the form of the statutes came under attack from both sides of the House. Senator Lawrence Power, a Liberal from Halifax who had worked on the commission that had produced the fourth edition of the Revised Statutes of Nova Scotia, argued that the dominion statutes should follow the maritime model – regnal years should be eliminated, headnotes should summarize each chapter, and a table of contents should be placed at the beginning of each sessional volume.[72] His Conservative colleague from Amherst, Senator Robert Dickey, implied that these were cosmetic changes: the 'root of the evil' was in 'the phraseology and verbiage of our Statutes.' Others intervened to support these arguments in what was obviously a non-partisan debate. The only exception was the government leader, Senator Alexander Campbell. In a tactful and graceful speech, he agreed with Power that the regnal years should go, but he made the best of Dickey's implication that change for the sake of change in the location of tables and indexes was undesirable. When he dealt with the question of the form and style used in the drafting of bills, he again advanced the argument that would appeal to the many lawyers in the chamber: 'The law may be more tersely expressed in Nova Scotia than in our Statutes, but the reason why we use the form which we follow is that it is the language used in the English Statutes, and that gives us the advantage of having the interpretation placed by the English Courts upon the laws of that country, worded in the same manner as ours are. Few things could be more valuable in interpreting the Statutes, than to have the opinions of eminent men who are constantly dealing with the same subjects which are likely to come before our judiciary here.'[73]

In closing, he told Senator Power that he would 'draw the attention of the Minister of Justice to the question put by my Hon. Friend, and take care to impress upon him the views expressed in this House.' It was a skilful performance and one which demonstrated why Campbell had been the Conservative leader in the Senate since Confederation.[74] All of this activity was taking place against a backdrop of events of fundamental and much greater importance in the development of the nation, and if the debate gave the prime minister food for thought, there is no mention of it in his correspondence.[75]

In many respects 1880 was a repeat of 1879 so far as the penal law was concerned. A question was put in the House: did the government intend to codify the criminal statutes during that session? Again, James MacDonald answered in the negative, and again Gowan urged the prime minister to anticipate the imperial legislation; to no avail.[76] But Gowan was not content to lobby Sr John alone, and sought to interest another acknowledged expert on criminal law in his endeavour – Mr Justice

Taschereau, who, in the meantime, had been promoted to the bench of the Supreme Court of Canada by the Mackenzie government 'two days before leaving office in 1878 and twenty days after its defeat at the polls.'[77]

How Gowan came to correspond with Taschereau is not clear. It may have had something to do with Taschereau's volumes on the criminal law, or Gowan may have met Charles Greaves during his recent visit to London. In any event, the first extant piece of correspondence in the exchange is a letter from Taschereau to Gowan, with which were enclosed the manuscripts Taschereau had received over the years from Greaves.[78] Gowan paraphrased these letters for his own records and returned them to Taschereau with a letter of thanks. Precisely what was in that letter is not known, but since he wrote several drafts which have survived, and since Taschereau's reply is in the Gowan Papers, a reasonable estimate of its content can be made. After thanking Taschereau for the loan of the letters and discussing briefly Greaves's achievements, Gowan got down to the topic that was of paramount importance to him. He suggested that Greaves's work showed the 'necessity for some clear authoritative definitions of the law by act of Parliament & why not in a code,' and he urged Taschereau to take up the challenge of reformulating the law: 'I would that you could be induced to prepare a consolidation of the crim law or of some part of it or better still that the govmt. would give us a code and that you could be induced to take charge of a commission to prepare it for the legislature. (You are one of the few men in the Dominion who have proved yourself equal to such a ...)'[79] To assist Taschereau in this good work Gowan enclosed a copy of Sir Henry Taylor's paper on codification in the colonies, and promised to send Wright's draft criminal code, which he had mislaid, when it came to hand.[80]

Taschereau's answer is interesting. The circumstances of his appointment show that he obviously was not a favourite of the government, and probably for this reason he did not comment directly on Gowan's suggestion. But it seems clear that he would not have been displeased if Gowan had taken the matter further: 'I entirely concur in all that you say about the necessity of a Criminal Code for our Dominion. Sir John it seems to me has only to give his fiat and we would have one. I have reason to believe that he entertains the highest opinion of you and it may be that you could induce him to render this great service to our country, and thus add to the numerous services for which Canada will always hold him as one of her noblest sons.'[81] This letter terminated the correspondence and, evidently, Gowan's initiative. While he continued to press the prime minister to codify the criminal law, he did not mention Taschereau, and there is no evidence that Taschereau raised the issue with Macdonald at that time.

But the need for some sort of reform was just as evident to the prime minister as it was to Gowan. Between 1875 and 1880 fifty additional penal laws had been enacted, of which seven were amending acts, and 115 pages had been added to the book of criminal statutes.[82] The time was not far off when this work would have to be issued in two volumes, for it contained well over five hundred pages after the session of 1880.

At this point in his tenure of office, Sir John A. Macdonald could afford to pause and catch his breath. Times were good: economic recovery was well advanced; he had won a diplomatic round with the Colonial Office and now had a high commissioner seated in England; and offers were being made to build the railroad.[83] But he cannot have been pleased with the performance of his minister of justice, whose correspondence with the prime minister is silent on the duties of his office and wholly concerned with questions of patronage.[84] That inference can be drawn from the fact that when remedial action was taken, it was the prime minister himself who initiated it.

Sometime later in the fall of 1880, he decided to take action. He would not go as far as Gowan urged, but would follow the route mapped out by Cairns – consolidation of all the public statute law, and then, possibly, codification of the criminal law. Accordingly, he earmarked $5,000 in the estimates for 1881 to begin the work of consolidation.[85] When the item was questioned by Edward Blake on 10 March, the prime minister answered him. He said that the government would follow the example of Ontario and that 'my good friend Judge Gowan might have to be brought down to keep a watchful eye on the work.'[86] No commissioners had been selected, he said, and no plans had been made: 'The Minister of Justice will apply himself to that subject after prorogation.'[87] But plans had been made and Sir John began to implement them shortly afterward. On 30 March he sent a formal letter to an old friend, James Cockburn, asking him to begin the preliminary work of consolidation.[88]

Cockburn, a Father of Confederation, a lawyer, and a staunch supporter of the prime minister, had fallen on hard times since the days when he had been the first Speaker in the dominion Parliament. He had been seriously ill since 1878, and, according to his biographer, he was virtually destitute, and subsisted on his sessional allowance as a member of Parliament.[89] All this is reflected in the personal letter Sir John sent to Cockburn with the formal letter of invitation. He made the point that when a commission was issued 'the fact of your having worked will entitle you to be paid from the time that you commenced your labours, say from the 1st April.'[90] Furthermore, the work could be done in Cockburn's home. In the meantime, the prime minister laid his plan before the Cabinet: the schedules begun by Langton should be completed prior to the appointment of a commission to revise finally and consolidate the statutes, and the 'Minister of Justice [should] be authorized to employ such assistance as may be necessary for proceeding with the work.'[91] At the same time, he secured $1,000 from the $5,000 allocation, which was doled out to Cockburn in instalments as 'disbursements re consolidation of Dominion Statutes.'[92]

At this point it looked as if, once again, Macdonald and Gowan would provide the driving force behind the work. But providence intervened. On 7 April the minister of justice informed the prime minister that Chief Justice William Young of Nova Scotia, who had been ill for some months past, had decided to retire.[93] When he did so on 4 May, the prime minister had a perfect opportunity to get rid of a political liability in Ottawa and yet retain the good will of one of the most influential Nova Scotia Conservatives. He lost no time: James MacDonald was appointed chief justice of Nova Scotia effective 20 May 1881.

His replacement in the cabinet shuffle of that date was Senator Sir Alexander Campbell, perhaps the best man Macdonald could have chosen from the talent then available in Parliament.[94] Campbell took hold at once. For example, requests from Cockburn for material for the consolidation project, which James MacDonald had not bothered to acknowledge, were dealt with by Campbell on the day they were received.[95] The prime minister also made a wise choice in appointing the man who eventually became the secretary of the commission, Alexander Ferguson, an Ottawa lawyer; he, like Cockburn, was a diligent worker. Their task was not an easy one.

They began by reviewing and extending Langton's work in preparation for the main task, which began officially on 15 November. On that day Cockburn resigned his seat in Parliament for reasons of ill health. He was simultaneously appointed commissioner at a salary of $4,000 per annum, from which was deducted the several disbursements made to him in the previous months.[96] By the terms of his commission he was empowered to review all the statutes of the former colonies, now jurisdictions within the dominion, and to 'collect therefrom all the unrepealed enactments as relate to matters now within the exclusive legislative authority of ... Parliament'; to review all dominion statutes enacted since

1867 and collect all acts still in force; and to classify this mass of material according to subject, consolidate it, and recommend what part of it should be repealed, continued in force, or otherwise disposed of.[97] In the course of this labour Cockburn examined several thousand enactments, and recommended that 1,294 be repealed.[98] He completed nine books of schedules and filled thirteen volumes containing upwards of 350 pages each with the statutes he had consolidated.[99] Elaborate indexes were prepared for all of these. The work was done in longhand; there were no typewriters.

In addition to the tasks specified in the commission, Campbell later issued supplementary instructions to Cockburn: he was to concentrate on the collection of statutes pertaining to the criminal law and to consolidate them in a bill to be introduced in Parliament in the session of 1883.[100] Campbell did not intend to press for its passage at that time, but he wanted a statement of intent that would allow members to see and comment on what was proposed. Responses and suggestions were to be integrated into a subsequent bill, which could then be passed expeditiously.[101] After a good deal of effort had been expended in this initiative, the scheme was abandoned in favour of a more ambitious proposal developed by George Wheelock Burbidge, the new deputy minister of justice.

Considering the swamp of patronage in which senior governmental appointments were usually mired during the nineteenth century, the story of Burbidge's appointment is refreshing. Born in 1847, he was a superior student and graduated from Mount Allison with a BA in 1867. After teaching school for two years, he returned and took his MA in 1870. He then studied law, and was called to the New Brunswick bar in 1872. He soon became one of its leaders, a partner in a Saint John law firm, and a supporter of the Conservative party. He was the secretary of the commission that drafted the 1877 edition of the Revised Statutes of New Brunswick; concurrently, he prepared an index of the statutes in force as of 1878, and he was the law reporter for the New Brunswick Reports from 1877 to 1882.[102] In the spring of 1882 Zebulon Lash, the deputy minister of justice who had been appointed by Edward Blake in 1876, gave notice of his resignation. Campbell evidently asked him to recommend his own replacement. Lash told him that 'Burbidge is an unusually sound man.' In a letter to the prime minister Campbell listed Burbidge's qualifications for the job. Significantly, he first mentioned that Burbidge 'was employed on the revision of the New B[runswick] Statutes.' After detailing several cases which Burbidge had litigated successfully for the Crown, he concluded: 'Lash knows well what are the qualifications most necessary and has seen Burbidge a good deal and recommends him in preference to [Connally?] for general good sense – facility with business and [readiness] of dealing with men – he thinks his knowledge of law quite equal to [Connally's?].'[103] The emphasis is on Burbidge and his professional qualifications; there is no mention of politics or patronage, or of the region of the dominion he represented. Burbidge was appointed deputy minister of justice on 23 May 1882.

It became apparent almost immediately that Cockburn and Burbidge viewed the content and purpose of the consolidation from different perspectives. Cockburn had been instructed to digest the written law, and he had done that and no more; there is no evidence to suggest that he saw the consolidation as an instrument of change. In contrast, as soon as Burbidge was appointed he began to forward to Cockburn the considerable correspondence from the legal profession and the public at large advocating amendments to the law which had originally been directed to the Department of Justice.[104] Obviously, he thought that amendments should be incorporated in the consolidation.

But it was the minister of justice, not Burbidge, whom Cockburn had to satisfy. He evidently did so, because in the following September, after 'a complete examination' of his work, Campbell informed the prime minister that the point had been reached where the details of the consolidation should be finalized and a bill prepared to give it effect. There were two ways in which this could be accomplished: Cockburn and Ferguson could prepare the draft, after which additional commissioners from Quebec and the maritimes could be appointed to review and polish the work; or the commissioners could be appointed immediately to assist in the preparation of the draft. Campbell suggested that the former plan would be the better and more economical course of action. Macdonald agreed, and instructions were issued to that effect.[105]

Cockburn and Ferguson bent to the task, but it was slow going. Consequently, no legislation was ready to be introduced in the session of 1883. Questions were asked in the Commons; as a result, Edward Blake was able to unravel the tangled skein of Cockburn's appointment.[106] Toward the end of the session it became evident that the draft would soon be ready to be examined by a full commission. Campbell therefore moved to procure a supplementary estimate to cover the anticipated expenditure and began to formulate a plan to get the job done. As it turned out, Burbidge was to be a commissioner, and he and Cockburn were to be responsible for the consolidation of the criminal statutes.[107]

Burbidge began to prepare for his task well before the issue of the commission by purchasing the latest edition of *Archbold's Criminal Procedure*.[108] But after a few days with the 1,500-page volume of undigested material, he decided to create an alternative to the mass of information that a conventional dominion consolidation would provide: he would produce an unexpurgated consolidation of the statute law as directed by the minister and, apparently working on his own, he would draft a code of combined common and statute law modelled on Fitzjames Stephen's work.

To this end Burbidge wrote to a colleague, John Courtney, the deputy minister of finance, whose brother was the secretary of the treasury in Britain:

You are aware that there is in course of preparation a consolidation of the Statutes of the Dominion which will include the Criminal Law.

In connection with the preparation of the latter branch of the work it is desirable that consideration should be given to the reforms during the late years made and suggested in England for which purpose I will need to obtain:

1 Six copies of the Criminal Code as prepared by Sir James Fitzjames Stephens [sic].

2 Two copies of the report made thereon by Lord Blackburn, Mr Justice Barrie, Lord Justice Lush and himself.

3 Six copies of each of the bills relating to the Criminal law or judicature introduced into the Commons at the present or late session of Parliament.

4 Any further information which your correspondent being on the spot may judge to be of assistance for the purpose indicated.

Would you do me the great favour of forwarding this letter to some friend of yours in London who would for your sake oblige me, and request him to have the kindness to procure what is wanted.

For any expense your friend is put to I will gladly reimburse him.[109]

The old-boy network functioned smoothly. On 9 August Burbidge gratefully acknowledged receipt of a bulky crate of documents which had been shipped to him through the Canadian high commissioner in London. After perusing this material, Burbidge realized that he would be able to derive additional information from Stephen's *Digest of the Criminal Law*. For this reason he personally ordered a copy of the 1877 edition from the publishers on 15 September.[110]

In the meantime Macdonald had issued the commission, and five commissioners, including Burbidge and Cockburn, had been appointed.

Campbell, the chairman ex officio, had divided the work among the members and decreed that it was to be done on the premises of the Department of Justice.[111] Each of the five was made responsible for the revision of a specific group of statutes. They were collectively responsible for ensuring the accuracy of the work as a whole; they accomplished this by jointly revising each section of the work completed by a member during 256 meetings of the commission, each of which lasted more than five hours.[112] Presumably, these meetings were chaired by Burbidge, since Campbell did not take part in the day-to-day work. When Cockburn died on 14 August, Burbidge became the de facto chairman of the commission and the principal adviser to the minister.

By the following spring, sixty-two non-criminal chapters of the consolidation were complete. Burbidge had also drafted a code of indictable offences, which he prevailed on Campbell to accept as a sixty-third chapter in place of the previously consolidated criminal statutes.[113] Although the code obviously was patterned on the commissioners' draft code of 1879 (which, it will be recalled, subsumed only indictable offences), there were many differences. It was considerably shorter (seven titles and thirty-six parts as opposed to eight titles and forty-five parts in the English work). Burbidge specified only four punishments instead of six: penal servitude and flogging had been omitted, and his sections were not in correspondence with those of the commissioners' draft. Moreover, wherever applicable the text and punishments specified were taken from Canadian statutes.[114]

During the session of 1884 the minister tabled this material in the Senate as a progress report.[115] He made it clear that the government had no intention of attempting to enact any of the material, two thousand copies of which were distributed not only to members of Parliament, but also to judges, lawyers, and other members of the public. Rather, his objectives were to show what had been done and to provide something tangible to read and analyse and so generate discussion during the recess. This, he hoped, would generate constructive criticism, which could be incorporated into 'a further and more accurate revision, and probably an approved one.' However, he also made it clear that while several advantages would accrue if a suitably amended version of Burbidge's draft code was enacted, '[i]t will be for Parliament, of course, to decide hereafter how far it is desirable to adopt that code, or how far it is desirable to fall back on a simple consolidation of our own statutes.'[116]

Parliament was prorogued shortly thereafter. Summer came and passed into fall. By December 1884 neither the minister nor the Justice Department had received any comment on the consolidation.[117] Nevertheless, Burbidge was able to report that the work was complete in a draft of 185 chapters and several schedules filled over 2,600 pages, and that a comprehensive report was in preparation.[118] Campbell then began to think about the tactics whereby the legislation could be enacted. Since he was in the Upper House, the most convenient and expeditious plan would have been to introduce it in the Senate, where he would have been able to steer it through the first parliamentary rapids. But this would have raised complex constitutional issues concerning the right of the Senate to initiate such legislation.[119] Moreover, the absence of any comment on the material previously distributed implied that few persons, if any, had read it; would Parliament baulk at enacting this massive measure in one session?

For help he turned to John Bourinot, the chief clerk of the Commons and an acknowledged expert on constitutional law.[120] In an exhaustive discussion of the subject, Bourinot concluded that the Senate did have the constitutional right to deal with the matter in the first instance. But he did not recommend that it do so. Instead, he suggested that Parliament follow English precedents, which would not engender opposition unnecessarily: a select committee of both Houses should be formed to review and revise the consolidation, under the chairmanship of the minister of justice, and to draft a bill to give it effect. The bill would then be introduced in the Commons.[121] Such a procedure would ensure that there would be wide-ranging discussion of and publicity for the measure, and that members of the Senate and the Commons would have full opportunity to make changes prior to the introduction of the enacting legislation. After this, consideration of the bill would very likely be pro forma, and the necessity for its consideration by a select committee of either House would be obviated. Bourinot's advice was taken. The commissioners' report and the volumes of the consolidation were tabled in the Commons and Senate at the opening of Parliament in 1885.

But before further action was taken, it became clear that Campbell had had second thoughts about Burbidge's draft code. Senator Power, the Nova Scotia codifier and opposition critic, asked whether the minister intended to proceed with a criminal codification bill as well as with the consolidation. Campbell thought not; perhaps in the next session, but maybe not then. This was a foggy answer, a placatory assurance that '[w]hat we are proposing in consolidating the statutes is to give the law as it stands,' and a signal that he intended to take no chances.[122] He knew that Burbidge's draft included not only the many changes incorporated by Stephen, but also the relevant amendments proposed by Canadian commentators. Privately, he approved of it; but he also had to recognize political realities. However much he wanted a rational, systematic treatment of the criminal law, he did not want the inevitable controversy that such a measure would create to jeopardize the work of the past several years. If he wanted to put through a massive revision of the statute law, he had to lay aside the criminal code for the time being.

On 16 March the minister moved that the House of Commons be asked to unite with the Senate to form a joint committee to examine and report on the consolidated statutes, the first motion for such a committee made in the Dominion Parliament.[123] He followed with a major speech that demonstrated his mastery of the subject and his ability to carry the House with him. It began with a complete review of the history of codification in the colonies before Confederation, including the names of the commissioners and the details of their work. He was obviously speaking from notes or a prepared script; a question was asked that required an extemporaneous response, and it was in this exchange that the minister showed himself to the best advantage. It occurred when he passed over Prince Edward Island with the remark that there had 'never been a consolidation there.' Senator George Howlan of that province challenged this statement repeatedly. Campbell attempted to bypass the obstruction diplomatically, but when he became irritated by the continued interjections he gave the senator chapter and verse on the several republications of the island statutes, and concluded that '[t]here was no consolidation in the sense that we mean.'[124] Howlan finally agreed that this was true.

Campbell went on to describe the process whereby the consolidation had been accomplished, and analysed several chapters of the work to illustrate the method that had been used to achieve condensation without introducing change. In the course of these remarks he praised the commissioners, especially Burbidge, complimented Senator Power and the new member, Senator Gowan, on their past achievements in the field, expressed his desire for their assistance with the proposed legislation, and compared the financial outlay for the dominion work favourably with that of Ontario in 1877. All in all, it was as well-planned and effective a speech as any made on the subject in the pre-Confederation legislatures or in the imperial Parliament.[125]

Unfortunately for Campbell, all of his patient work on the Revised Statutes of Canada, as the consolidation was to be titled, was negated for that year by a series of events that drew attention away from the routine work of Parliament. News of the clash between the Métis and the North-West Mounted Police at Duck Lake came a few days after his speech, and for the rest of the session he and, to an even greater extent, Burbidge were engaged in the prosecution of Louis Riel and in other ramifications of the Rebellion.[126] At the same time the prime minister, who would pilot the Revised Statutes of Canada through the Commons, was much more interested in enacting the 1885 franchise bill. Apart from these major considerations, Macdonald was also distracted from parliamentary routine by a crisis which blew up over the financing of the Canadian Pacific Railway, and by the negotiations required to bring John Thompson, then a justice of the Supreme Court of Nova Scotia, into Cabinet.[127]

Nevertheless, the joint committee was convened and began its deliberations on 27 March. A month later Macdonald introduced Bill 130, An Act Respecting the Revised Statutes of Canada, in the Commons, where it received first reading.[128] He probably made this move in the hope that there would be no obstacle to the speedy pro forma acceptance of the measure by the joint committee; if so, his hope was soon dashed. In the course of its protracted deliberations the committee recommended many detailed amendments, the enumeration of which covered six pages.[129] Macdonald knew what was going on in the committee, and he knew too that the persons who would normally deal with the matter were otherwise engaged. He also realized that, even if the measure were pressed, it would get into Parliament very late in the session, and he had no wish to repeat the experience of 1868. He therefore withdrew Bill 130 on 9 June, notwithstanding Campbell's advice to press ahead with it.[130] In the event he was proved right, because the committee report was not tabled in the Commons until 30 June, less than three weeks before prorogation.[131]

Immediately afterward, the really intense bargaining to recruit Thompson into the Cabinet began. Thompson was not eager to leave his congenial employment on the bench for Ottawa, and would do so only if he were given the Justice portfolio. When it became clear to the prime minister that there was no possibility of compromise on this issue, he unceremoniously shuffled Campbell back to his old ministry, the Post Office, and Thompson was installed as minister of justice on 26 September.[132] There were certain drawbacks to this change. So far as the Revised Statutes of Canada were concerned, about which Thompson knew nothing, it meant more work for Macdonald. For years the prime minister had maintained only a watching brief on the process; Cockburn,

Burbidge, and Campbell had done the work. Now, with Campbell resentful and Burbidge in London for Riel's appeal, Macdonald was forced – briefly – to become involved in the minutiae of the work.[133]

With Parliament in recess, and with assistance from the prime minister, Thompson was able to settle into his new job comfortably and to assume his responsibilities quickly. By the beginning of 1886 he was fully in control of his department, and was thus able to relieve Macdonald of his duties as spokesman for Justice in the Commons. However, it was one thing to be the chief executive of a department; it was quite another to pilot a bill through a chamber of well over two hundred imperfectly disciplined and often disrespectful MPs, as he quickly found out. In his maiden speech on 3 March, a week after the session began, he moved first reading of Bill 9, An Act Respecting the Revised Statutes of Canada. He gave an abbreviated version of Campbell's address in the Senate the previous year, and also stated that the statutes of 1885 had been incorporated in the text, together with the amendments suggested by the joint committee. In the course of his remarks he said: 'After the attention which the subject has received in both Houses last Session, I take it that the present Bill will be, in its progress through its chief stages, regarded as of a merely formal character; but at the same time it may be convenient for the House that I should make briefly such explanations as seem to be in point at this stage, rather than at the second reading of the Bill, in view of its probably formal disposition at that stage.'[134] It appears that the minister assumed that the Revised Statutes of Canada would receive pro forma acceptance. He was quickly disabused of this notion by Edward Blake, who pointed out that, apart from the twelve who had been members of the joint committee, no member of the Commons had had any opportunity to discuss the measure. Moreover, he wanted to know 'exactly what alterations have been made in the volume.' Thompson recovered very quickly. He claimed to have been misunderstood and said, gracefully, that of course he would be 'greatly gratified if the Bill received from the members of the House a great deal more than merely formal consideration.'[135] Quick thinking and a willingness to compromise defused what could have become an acrimonious debate, and the motion was agreed to without rancour.

However, this encounter seems not to have been sufficient warning to the minister that the opposition would not be pushed into doing something merely because he said it should be done. When he moved second reading a month later, Blake asked if it was 'the intention of the Minister that this bill shall not be referred to a select committee?' Thompson replied that 'it need not be referred to a special committee this year inasmuch as it has already been before a committee, and that committee has reported and made suggestions which will be found running through the whole volume. I certainly thought that the House in Committee of the Whole would now be prepared to deal with the matter.' Again, Blake rose to begin the process of changing Thompson's mind. He pointed out that the bill under consideration was not the same as that of the previous year; that many alterations had been made by the inclusion in the Revised Statutes of Canada of the enactments of 1885, to say nothing of those proposed by the committee; that the committee itself, of which he had been a member, had not been exhaustive in its examination; and, finally, that 'all the consolidations which have taken place in the old Province of Canada have never been passed through the House without being submitted to a select committee for revision.' Thompson attempted to defend his position. But what he said boiled down to an assertion that the members should have done their homework after the bill had been introduced, and should have come to the sitting 'prepared to call attention to any defect which might have occurred in [the 1886] revision. If hon. members are not in a position to do so today, I will defer it to a later date, but it does not seem to me to be such a work as to require a select committee.' Blake then elaborated the themes he had previously stated. He was followed by several more members of the opposition, who cited, chapter and verse, the defects of the joint committee and of the work itself.[136]

When they were finished, it must have been as clear to Thompson as it is to a reader of the *Debates* that he was in for heavy weather if he persisted in his demand that the House go into Committee of the Whole. He wanted to put through legislation that ran to over 2,600 pages; if the House took it up in a clause-by-clause examination in its present mood, there was little chance of getting it through that session, if ever. He therefore retreated and, as in his previous encounter, made a gracious speech in which he commended the members of the joint committee for the careful attention they had given the work, agreed with Blake's view of the situation, and promised to reconsider his position.[137] On the next day he moved that the bill be sent to a select committee.[138]

From all of this it seems that in his initial encounters with the House of Commons in the role of pilot of legislative vessels, Thompson could not predict where the rocks and shoals would be. But it is equally obvious that he was a phenomenally fast learner, and that if he did run aground he was able to manoeuvre back into the deep water of progress rapidly and with the minimum of divisive argument. In this respect it is instructive to compare Thompson with John Holker: the minister had learned in a few weeks what it had taken the English attorney general years to comprehend.

It was during this early learning period that Thompson first met Senator Gowan, who was then attending his second session of Parliament. Although the volume of Gowan's correspondence with the prime minister had not declined over the years, little was heard from him on the subject of codification after the appointment of Cockburn and Campbell in 1881. Evidently, he was satisfied that events were now in train which would achieve much or all of what he desired, and that his urgings and advice were no longer necessary. Moreover, he was away from Canada much of the time, enjoying a well-earned rest after his forty years on the bench.[139] But after his appointment to the Senate in January 1885, he soon found himself back in harness. A month after taking his seat he had been appointed to six committees, two of which he chaired, and two weeks later he was named a member of the joint committee on the Revised Statutes of Canada.[140] He was thus in a good position to advise Thompson on this matter after the minister's bill was introduced in the Senate.[141] In the event, his advice was unnecessary: after the initial hiatus the bill sailed briskly through the Commons and then passed the Senate without difficulty. The Revised Statutes received royal assent on 2 June 1886, and, with the integration of the acts of 1886 in the text, came into force on 1 March 1887.

Like its predecessors of the 1850s, the work was a remarkable achievement.[142] With its enactment the legislative output of more than twenty-five years was repealed and replaced by two manageable volumes, which put the statute law of the dominion in roughly the same condition as the analogous English law in 1877, after the final volumes of the English revision were published by Lord Cairns's law reform committee.[143] In particular, the enacted criminal law was concentrated between two covers and was thus in ideal form to be codified.[144] Thompson was proud of the work; he had a copy sent to David Dudley Field, the New York codifier, and personally wrote the covering letter.[145]

But the collection was not perfect: it had the defects of its predecessors, and more. As Campbell had made clear in his Senate speeches, the law had not been altered in any major provision; it had merely been rearranged. No definitions had been supplied, and no attempt had been made to integrate any of the common law. Furthermore, the joint committee had suggested that the chapters should be numbered consecutively, that the preamble and enacting formula be omitted from all but the first chapter, and that short chapter titles be substituted for the full titles of the draft.[146] That is to say, the revision should follow the format of the maritime codes, rather than the Consolidated Statutes of Canada. Thompson explained that the recommendation had been rejected in order to keep the dominion format similar to those of the majority of the provincial consolidations, which he said, also followed the old Canadian model.[147] Thus, each chapter of the Revised Statutes was a separate and distinct act, complete with preamble and words of enactment. And for reasons that were not given, the critical apparatus of clearly defined topics marked off by titles and subtitles, which was such a desirable feature of all the previous collections, was omitted altogether. As finally published, the table of contents consisted of a list of the titles of the chapters, each of which began, 'An Act respecting ...' Familiarity with the Consolidated Statutes of 1859 makes it clear that the 1886 work follows roughly the same order – constitutional matters, public departments, and so on. But this would not have been obvious to a beginner or to a layman, and in any case those divisions were beginning to lose their cohesion. The penal statutes, for example, which had formed the final part or title in all the codes of the 1850s, were now to be found in two locations in the Revised Statutes of Canada.[148]

Nevertheless, the statutory dominion criminal law had been compressed into 49 chapters of the Revised Statutes. They replaced 152 dominion acts and several colonial statutes, and substituted 444 pages for over 700. The core of the collection was still the Criminal Consolidation Acts of 1869, but they had been reworked in much the same way as the analogous chapters in the 1859 collection. For example, the Larceny Act of 1869 contained 124 sections; the same title in 1886 was reduced to 98. The deleted material, 26 sections and parts of others, was transposed to procedural chapters. However, the sections that remained were almost verbatim transcripts of the originals; the section on riotous destruction of buildings, for example, was still a single sentence that ran on for 233 words.[149]

6

The Criminal Code

In a profession that values above all else the latest authority, be it case law or statute law, the publication of the Revised Statutes of Canada created uncertainty. The 1881 volume of penal statutes, for example, was now superseded. George Burbidge moved quickly to rectify that situation by commissioning Charles H. Masters, a younger colleague from New Brunswick, to produce an updated version.[1] Masters was at that time an assistant reporter in the Supreme Court. He later became the chief reporter and a prolific author of legal texts, of which the volume of criminal statutes, published in the fall of 1887, was the first.[2] It was consecutively paginated, and included, in addition to the criminal chapters from the revised statutes, a detailed and comprehensive index and table of contents which set out the chapters in chronological order.[3] Inevitably, proliferation had set in. Eight criminal statutes enacted in the 1887 session were included as a separately paginated addendum. Moreover, their chapter numbers were those allocated to them in the sessional volume of 1887, and thus did not follow the order of the main work.

Mr Justice Taschereau's *Criminal Statute Law* had also been rendered obsolete, and he too moved quickly to replace it. Soon after the revised statutes came into effect, he informed the justice minister that he was working on a revised edition and asked that the government purchase four hundred copies so that he would not incur a financial loss through its publication.[4] Thompson diplomatically refused to make a block purchase, but did say that government libraries would need some copies, as would most ministries, and that he would encourage such purchases.[5] In any event, the second edition of *Criminal Statute Law* went on sale in February 1888.[6]

The work retained the format of the first edition: that is, it was a reprint of the statutes with a commentary appended to most sections. In other respects it was much changed. Eight hundred additional cases were cited, most of them Canadian decisions handed down since the enactment of the Criminal Consolidation Acts of 1869. The value of the work was enhanced by Taschereau's association with Charles Greaves, for several of the annotations had been written by Greaves or adapted from notes supplied by him. Reference to these and other changes was made easy by the enlarged and comprehensive index, which had been prepared by Charles Masters, who also compiled the tables of statutes and cases.[7] But the most significant change was that although Taschereau still treated only indictable offences, he had included all the relevant procedural law in a one-volume edition. In fact, he had contemplated a more comprehensive work that would have included summary conviction offences and related law, but was dissuaded from proceeding with it by his publisher because of the prohibitive cost of printing a two-volume edition.[8]

The project clearly foreshadowed a full-scale treatment of the penal law, however. During the following months Taschereau worked out the scheme in detail and presented the minister of justice with an oral proposal for a criminal code in the summer of 1889.[9] This gave Thompson food for thought. He was, like Lord Cairns, a systematizer, who throughout his career had sought to make the law sure and certain and to direct a clear, fresh current through muddy and obscure legal backwaters.[10] The idea of a code appealed to him. But he was also a highly partisan Conservative. Did he want one of the most important bills of the decade to be prepared by a Liberal appointee, Taschereau, when his friend and colleague Burbidge had already drafted such legislation?[11] Obviously not. At this point he received a letter from the judge which presented the proposition to him in a formal manner.[12] He had two alternatives: he could accept Taschereau's offer or reject it.

If he rejected it, what were Taschereau's options? The judge could draft a code; there was no doubt about that. And he could have one of his Liberal colleagues introduce it in the House of Commons, if only to embarrass the government.[13] There was ample precedent for such action, as Thompson well knew. William Wheelhouse had introduced a criminal code bill in the imperial House of Commons in 1880, on the same day Sir John Holker had brought in the government-sponsored legislation.[14] Closer to home, Malcolm Cameron, the Liberal MP for Huron West, had, annually for five years, introduced criminal evidence bills, one of which had passed all stages in the Commons and was not defeated until second reading in the Senate.[15] If Thompson refused Taschereau's offer, he would have to convince the judge that he would be wasting his time drafting legislation which the Justice Department already had in hand. This he evidently did, because, though there continued to be frequent correspondence between the two men, no more is heard of this matter until the fall of 1892.[16] This, then, was the genesis of the plan that would eventuate in the Canadian Criminal Code.

Meanwhile, on Thompson's recommendation, Burbidge had been appointed to the bench as the first justice of the Exchequer Court, which had been separated from the Supreme Court in 1887. Although he was fully occupied with organizing the court and hearing cases, Burbidge still found time to advise Thompson on matters pertaining to the Department of Justice for a considerable period after his promotion.[17] When this extracurricular activity began to diminish, he decided to put his extensive knowledge of penal statutes and codification to good use by writing a comprehensive treatment of substantive criminal law, both common and statute. To give his work added weight and authority he, like Taschereau before him, allied himself with the leading contemporary authority on English criminal law by obtaining Sir James Fitzjames Stephen's permission to follow the plan of his *Digest* of 1877.[18]

But Burbidge was much more than an editor. In large measure he quoted from the original only when Stephen, in his concise and economical way, defined an offence or a term rendered from the verbosity of the common law.[19] In fact, from a total of 629 articles, only 234, or parts thereof, are quoted verbatim from Stephen. Thus, well over 60 per cent of the work was written by Burbidge, who effected a similar condensation of the criminal law of Canada and the provinces.[20] Moreover, he improved on the original and on the bill he had drafted in 1884 by including not only indictable offences but also the summary offences of the several jurisdictions. And to his own work, as well as to Stephen's, he added notes for practitioners, supported by copious references to Canadian cases. The comprehensive index and the tables of cases and statutes cited in the volume were prepared by Charles Masters, who was himself engaged in the preparation of a companion volume of procedural law on the same model.[21] Together the two volumes would have subsumed all of the criminal law of Canada, and would thus have improved on Stephen's *Digest*, which included only indictable offences, and on Taschereau's volume, which treated only statute law. However, events overtook Masters before he was able to get his book into print.

Immediately after receiving Taschereau's formal offer to draft a criminal code on 23 October 1889, Thompson told Burbidge that he intended to codify the criminal law, and evidently gave him the impression that a bill would be introduced in the coming session.[22] Burbidge, whose *Digest* was to appear in December, asked the minister to delay the measure because of the effect it would have on the sales of his book, an appeal to which Thompson apparently lent 'an indulgent ear.' After some reflection, Burbidge wrote to the minister to apologize for his selfish request and urged him to proceed with the legislation forthwith. As was his custom, Burbidge also gave him some good advice.

One of the major flaws Burbidge had identified in the English draft bills was the provision to abolish the use of the words 'felony' and 'misdemeanour' in an attempt to get rid of the procedural distinctions between the two classes of crime. In his view, 'it would be unfortunate to lose from our law such convenient words,' and he suggested that in any Canadian legislation they be retained and redefined in terms of punishment. In short, a felony should be punished by death or imprisonment in a penitentiary, and a misdemeanour by imprisonment in a common jail for any period less than two years. This was, of course, a proposal to classify offences according to an immediately comprehensible and rational scheme similar to the systems used in the civilian codes of the Continent.[23] If the concept had been elaborated, extended to summary conviction offences, and inserted in the introductory matter of a bill, it would have constituted a satisfactory general part of a code. Although Burbidge did not put the proposal in such a direct manner, there is no doubt that he recognized the need for such a provision, explicit or not, and was attempting to influence Thompson to proceed in this direction. His effort was in vain, for there is no further mention of the matter in their correspondence. Nor was there mention of codification during the next session of Parliament, a circumstance which ensured that Burbidge's *Digest*, which received excellent reviews, sold well during 1890.[24]

Shortly after the session Senator Gowan returned from Europe, where he had been touring since the summer of 1889. As we have seen, he was displeased that no action had been taken as a result of his speech on the abolition of the grand jury, and wrote to the prime minister to voice his displeasure. Whether Macdonald sent Gowan's letter to the minister of justice or whether he spoke to him directly is not known, but Thompson was galvanized into action not only in the matter of the grand jury, but also with regard to codification. In his circular letter to the judiciary he couched the question of the grand jury within a larger framework by explaining that he wanted an expression of their opinion so that it could be incorporated in 'a bill codifying the criminal law of Canada, both as regards substantive law and procedure,' which he intended to 'lay before parliament in the near future.'[25] Before the letter was in the mail, Thompson had made provision for the drafting of a codification bill.

Sometime after their conversation in the fall of 1889, Thompson had again broached the subject of a criminal code to Burbidge and to his successor as deputy minister of justice, Robert Sedgewick.[26] They shared Thompson's enthusiasm for the project, and agreed to draft the necessary legislation in the Department of Justice, with the aid of Charles Masters, after the session of 1890.[27] This was not normal practice; it was the duty of the law clerk of the House of Commons, then Frederick McCord, to draft all public bills.[28] However, when Sedgewick relieved McCord of the responsibility for preparing a lengthy enactment, it became possible to pay Masters, a salaried civil servant, for the work he had already done on criminal procedure, presumably the subject for which he was to be responsible in the bill.[29] More important, it also ensured that the legislation was written exactly as Thompson wanted it and that the confidentiality to which Sedgewick had sworn McCord was unbroken.

By the following spring Bill 32, the Criminal Law Act of 1891, was ready to be introduced to Parliament.[30] At first sight it resembled the English draft code of 1880. Under the rubric 'Arrangement of Titles' the first six titles, which laid down the substantive law, were taken from the imperial model almost verbatim. Here the resemblance ended. The latter had only one further title, 'Procedure'; there were four in the Canadian bill, for a total of ten. Those ten were divided into 70 parts and 1,005 sections covering 331 pages. The bill was over one-third longer than the draft code of 1880 (and nearly double the length of Burbidge's draft code of 1884). The table of contents reveals that again there was a superficial resemblance between the matter covered in both works by the parts and sections of the first six titles, but almost none between the procedural divisions. However, it is not until the actual substance of the 1891 bill is analysed that it becomes apparent how much 'Canadian content' it contains.[31] In the substantive titles there are a total of 530 sections; 209 are taken verbatim or paraphrased from the English model and 321 are condensed from Canadian models or are new matter. The procedural titles contain 475 sections; 394 are Canadian and only 81 English. Thus, 715 sections, or well over 70 per cent of the dominion legislation, were drafted by Burbidge, Masters, and Sedgewick in the terse and economical style developed by Stephen. As in Burbidge's *Digest*, much of the matter quoted from imperial sources consists of definitions and terms condensed from the common law. For example, 'larceny' disappears from the statutory vocabulary and is replaced by 'theft,' which is defined as follows: 'Theft or stealing is the act of fraudulently and without colour of right taking, or fraudulently and without colour of right converting to the use of any person, anything capable of being stolen.'[32] Murder is defined, assault is defined, rape is defined, and, for the first time in any British statutory compilation, the common law offence of sedition is defined and elaborated.[33] In fact, nearly every 'Part' in the substantive titles opens with a section defining the crime dealt with in that division. To today's reader there is nothing remarkable about this legislative style – in fact, one would have difficulty conceiving of an offence that was not defined by statute. But in 1891 it was revolutionary. If the bill became law, anyone could discover exactly what elements constituted any given offence merely by reading the code. It would not be necessary, for example, to assimilate the two chapters of arcane knowledge on larceny in Stephen's *Digest* in order to understand the straightforward definition of theft quoted above. Moreover, the judge's latitude in distinguishing common law precedent in order to arrive at a definition of a crime which, in his view, suited the circumstances – in a word, his ability to exercise quasi-legislative authority – was severely circumscribed.[34]

 Another major change was the abolition of the distinction between felony and misdemeanour (section 533), a reform that had been advocated by Stephen and developed in the imperial bills. This section did not introduce any new crimes, eliminate any old ones, or alter any punishments. Murder, a felony, was still murder and was punishable by death; the forging of trade marks, a misdemeanour, was still forgery and was punishable by two years' imprisonment. Both crimes, however, were defined in Bill 32 as 'indictable offences,' and the words 'felony' and 'misdemeanour' were eliminated. The fundamental change was that the procedure for dealing with such crimes was standardized. No longer would the forger have the right to bail; no longer could he sit at the courtroom table beside his counsel when on trial. He would now be bailable on the same terms as the murderer, and he would have to stand trial in the dock.[35]

It must be emphasized that felonies and misdemeanours had been triable on indictment for centuries, and persons accused of either offence had the right to be tried by a judge and a jury. After 1892 this right was retained by persons accused of committing an indictable offence. Both before and after 1892 summary conviction offences constituted a class of crime different from indictable offences in that they were tried by a judge or a justice of the peace sitting alone. The distinction between the two was preserved by the Criminal Code, and it is incorrect to equate the pre-1892 felony with the indictable offence of today, or the pre-1892 misdemeanour with today's summary conviction offence.[36]

A particular feature of the new procedure, which must have given the minister of justice considerable satisfaction, was that it would reduce considerably the power of the grand jury. To begin with, jurors would no longer be allowed to initiate an investigation if it was suspected that an offence had been committed. That power was to be vested in justices of the peace or other magistrates, who were to be authorized to summon potential witnesses and examine them on oath (section 557). At common law the presentment of a crime (an indictment) could be made on the initiative of a grand jury, or any person could make an accusation before the jurors in the form of a bill of indictment, which they could endorse as a true bill or reject. Bill 32 (sections 636 and 637) would abrogate those rights and vest them in the bench and Crown law officers. They alone would be allowed to prefer bills of indictment to the grand jury directly or indirectly by granting permission to a person to proceed with an accusation. The only criminal function remaining to grand jurors would be to endorse or reject bills of indictment sent to them by legal officials.[37]

At first sight it appears unusual that the smaller, less sophisticated dominion should have a considerably larger body of criminal law than the mother country. The anomaly is explained by the fact that the legislation subsumed all the criminal law of the jurisdiction.[38] Its first six titles included the substantive law pertaining to indictable and summary conviction offences from both common and statute law, and so repaired the omission Lord Chief Justice Cockburn had exploited with such devastating effect to bring about the demise of the Commissioners' Bill in the imperial Parliament. All the procedural law necessary to operate the criminal justice system was laid down in the last four titles, and again all relevant common and statute law was included. Moreover, the

Canadian legislation improved on the civil law codifications, which uniformly followed the French practice of publishing the criminal law in two volumes, one for substantive rules and one for procedure. If one is not aware of this fact the Continental codes appear to be much shorter and more concise than the Canadian, but the perspective alters considerably if both volumes are taken into account. The contemporary German collections, for example, ran to a total of 876 sections, the French to 1,026.[39] With 1,005 sections (983 in the enacted code of 1892) set out topically in relatively short, concise sentences, Bill 32 fell comfortably in between the two older codes in bulk.

By any standard the bill of 1891 was a considerable work of legal scholarship. It followed the outline and format of the English models, which had been refined by several law commissions and sessions of the imperial Parliament, and included much of the work Fitzjames Stephen had accomplished in defining the rules of common law. To this was added the considerable bulk of dominion and provincial criminal law condensed, refined, and rewritten. But there were some omissions, and it was not as nearly perfect a compilation as it might have been. It did not, for example, purport to be exhaustive of the penal law, nor did it contain a provision to abrogate the common law, as the English models had. There was no mention of Burbidge's concept of a general part.

These omissions were deliberate. The minister of justice knew exactly what he needed in his bill to assure its smooth passage through Parliament, and he instructed his draftsmen accordingly. There was, for instance, no mention of the abrogation of the common law, one of the largest rocks on which the imperial bills had foundered, because there was no need for it. What most people, laymen and legal professionals alike, failed to perceive, or at least to comment on if they did, was that Thompson achieved substantially the same result notwithstanding this omission. Most of the common law pertaining to crime had been incorporated in Bill 32. Once that legislation was enacted, such provisions became statute law and, ipso facto, the common law doctrine on the subject was abrogated. In this one area alone, Thompson's legislation would cause fundamental change in the criminal justice system; and it was by no means the only alteration.[40]

All of the other changes were cloaked in the authority of a bill modelled on the imperial draft codes of the previous decade. Moreover, since the controversial measures in these bills had been thrashed out in the Lords and the Commons and discussed by the royal commissioners of 1879, Thompson could adopt their arguments to support his legislation – in particular, the abolition of the distinction between felony and misdemeanour. However, it would be one thing to follow the imperial text and argument on a measure that changed nothing but procedure; it would be quite another to attempt to pass legislation made in Canada that would retain the words 'felony' and 'misdemeanour' but redefine the terms of punishment. Each offence would have to be allocated to one or the other category, a procedure that would provide Parliament with an inexhaustible source of controversy. Reform was Thompson's objective, not interminable debate. Wisely, therefore, but perhaps reluctantly, he stuck to the English model and did not implement the sensible but impracticable suggestion of Burbidge, which would have given the Canadian code a general part.

Meanwhile, the routine of the Justice Department continued. A new volume of the criminal statutes was compiled and published to reflect the many penal enactments since the Revised Statutes of Canada had come into force in 1886.[41] Like its predecessors, this volume would not long remain current, for suggestions for further amendments were already flowing in from bench and bar in answer to Thompson's circular letter. One of the first of these was from Senator Gowan, who appears to have been surprised that the minister of justice was contemplating the introduction of a criminal code.[42] Although the volume of correspondence on legal matters between the two men had remained constant even during Gowan's recent trip to England, this was the first mention of codification in their letters and the first time Gowan had addressed the matter since his exhortations to the prime minister in the early 1880s. Thereafter it was a prime topic, and, in addition to giving Thompson exhaustive accounts of past efforts to systematize the penal law, Gowan offered advice, assistance, and encouragement until well after the enactment of the code.

Thompson was punctilious in thanking the senator for his efforts, and he often incorporated Gowan's detailed suggestions for amendment in the legislation. But he rarely followed Gowan's advice on tactics, and then only when he had previously decided on the same course of action.[43] Nor did he volunteer any information. When, for example, Gowan first learned of the project, he attempted to procure a copy of the legislation from James Adamson, the clerk of the Senate, who passed the request to Thompson. No copy was forthcoming, for, as Thompson told Adamson, the bill had not been completed and, indeed, the draftsmen had been at work for less than a month.[44] The senator did not receive a copy until six months later, well after its introduction in the

Commons. It is evident that Thompson played his cards very close to his vest and did not reveal his intentions or his plans even to close friends or colleagues such as Gowan, unless the individual in question played some part in those plans.

Soon after three o'clock on the afternoon of 12 May 1891 the minister of justice introduced Bill 32 in the Commons and moved first reading. Since members did not have a copy of legislation at this stage, it was, according to Bourinot, the duty of a bill's sponsor 'to explain clearly and succinctly its main provisions.'[45] Thompson was certainly succinct. He said: 'The object of this Bill is fully expressed by its title. It is intended to be a codification of the Criminal Law as well as of the Statutes relating to the Criminal Law of Canada, and it has been prepared principally on the model of the Imperial codification.'[46] That was all. Had there been no questions, the Speaker would have put the question and moved on to other matters. But there were questions. Sir Richard Cartwright, the fiscal critic for the opposition, wanted to know whether simple codification was in prospect or whether the minister intended to 'introduce any alterations, more or less, of the existing Criminal Law.'

SIR JOHN THOMPSON   The Bill includes a number of changes in the law.
SIR RICHARD CARTWRIGHT   Are they changes of any considerable importance, because this is a matter of general interest?
SIR JOHN THOMPSON   They are only of the nature of such amendments as will be made in the shape of a Bill to amend the Criminal Law generally. Fundamental changes such as have been discussed in the press during the last few months are not touched on by this Bill, because it is deemed better that they should form the subject of discussion during the progress of the Bill, or of other Bills which may be introduced. The scope of this Bill is confined to the codification of the laws, with ordinary and subordinate amendments.[47]

David Mills, a future minister of justice, wanted to know if it was intended to abolish the distinction between misdemeanour and felony. Thompson replied, 'it is proposed to abolish that distinction.' Louis Davies, a future chief justice of the Supreme Court, said that if there were a large number of amendments in the bill it would not be possible to enact it during the session. If such were the case, he supposed it to be the minister's intention to have the bill printed and distributed to members, but not to proceed further. Thompson agreed and said that he intended to move second reading later in the session, at which time he would state 'briefly what the amendments are … and ask the direction of the House whether it will be proceeded with further or deferred until the next session.'[48] The exchanges do not take up one column in the *Debates*, and most of the words were spoken by members of the opposition. Except for his second answer to Cartwright, Thompson was brief to the point of obscurity. Moreover, in view of the radical alterations his bill would make to the criminal justice system, that answer can only be characterized as the highest quality parliamentary doubletalk. This impression is reflected by the correspondent of the *Ottawa Evening Journal*, who titled his column 'A Dry Sitting' and began his account by saying that 'the Commons had a rather uninteresting session yesterday, there being little of importance on the order paper.'[49]

All in all, the first reading of Bill 32 is in sharp contrast with the course of events in the imperial House of Commons, where the account of the first reading of Stephen's draft code in 1878 covered twenty-three columns, while the first reading of the commissioners' bill of 1879 rambled on for thirty-seven columns, and Sir John Holker appeared positively garrulous in comparison with the taciturn Thompson.[50] Since there is good reason to believe that Thompson had read and analysed those debates in Hansard, and thus knew that Holker had invariably raised the hackles of the opposition during first reading, it is likely that his plan was to say as little as possible so as to avoid giving his critics targets to shoot at.[51]

Minutes after resuming his seat, Thompson was summoned to the prime minister's office to participate in discussions with the governor general. It was at this meeting that he became aware that Macdonald was seriously ill.[52] Thereafter he assumed many prime ministerial duties, and after Macdonald's death on 6 June he became government leader in the House of Commons. Thus, in addition to these added burdens and his own duties as minister of justice, Thompson became intimately concerned with the investigation of the Langevin-McGreevy scandal and the Mercier inquiry.[53]

For all of these reasons, and probably because it also suited his purpose, there was no second reading of Bill 32 in 1891, and members remained ignorant of the amendments it incorporated. It is not clear when the bill itself was finally printed and distributed to the members.[54] What is known for certain is that on 3 July Thompson asked the printing committee to authorize his request for two thousand copies of Bill 32 for distribution. The committee assented on 31 July and early in August the Justice Department began to mail copies to bench, bar, and leading members of the public.[55]

Unlike the virtual silence that had greeted Senator Campbell's distribution of the draft of the Revised Statutes of Canada in 1884, the response to Bill 32 was immediate and gratifying. This was hardly surprising, since it was perceived to have been written so as to be intelligible to the general public. W.F. Haskins, a Dunnville banker, epitomized this perception when he remarked that 'even village scribes and we laymen can read [Thompson's] laws understandingly.'[56] Replies began to trickle in within a week and, in a sense, the flow continues unabated.[57] Responses came from the whole spectrum of the criminal justice system. Some, such as Senator Gowan and William Boys, a lawyer from Barrie, reviewed the whole code and made innumerable suggestions for major and minor amendments.[58] Most, however, were content to comment on one or two sections. J.W. Johnson, the mayor of New Glasgow, wanted to enlarge the prohibition of cutting holes in ice and leaving them unguarded. The Department of Agriculture urged that a provision be included to prevent the abuse of immigrant girls. F.C. Cribben, the secretary of the Trades and Labour Council of Toronto, was concerned to see that the existing law regarding the exemption of trade unions from charges of conspiracy for organizing strikes had not been incorporated in the draft; he suggested that it should be. At the other end of the scale, Roger Clute, a Belleville barrister, suggested that a system of graded degrees of murder be instituted. On occasion Sedgewick asked a correspondent such as the attorney general of Ontario for advice on a specific section, and, in the case of the Reverend James Bogert of the Children's Aid Society, he went so far as to ask that proposed amendments be submitted in draft form.[59] The judiciary was well represented in the correspondence, but its recommendations tended to be concerned with procedure and technical details. However, there were no submissions from the Supreme Court bench or, in particular, from Mr Justice Taschereau. It may be that he was not on the distribution list for a copy of Bill 32. But even if he were, it would have been sent to the court long after the summer term had ended in early July and after he had left Ottawa either for his summer residence in Rivière du Loup or for one of his frequent overseas vacations.

In spite of the lack of response from the senior bench, the system of soliciting advice from the public worked well, and during the fall and winter some of the suggested amendments were incorporated in the draft. Altogether, twelve sections were deleted, thirteen new ones were added and many, such as section 132 on defrauding the government (thanks, no doubt, to the Langevin-McGreevy investigation), were enlarged or rewritten. But all the amendments concerned detail. There were no fundamental alterations, and Bill 7, the 1892 draft code, was little changed in appearance, numbering, or rubric from its predecessor.

First reading was on 8 March 1892, early in the session. Thompson was even more succinct than in 1891. He said, 'This Bill is substantially the same as that introduced last session, but it contains some improvements which have been suggested in consequence of the circulation of the Bill, and which I will explain to the House more fully on the second reading.'[60] There were no questions, and the motion passed without comment.[61] Second reading was set for 12 April. Bill 7 ran to just over three hundred pages, and by the rules of Parliament it was supposed to be distributed to the members prior to second reading so that they could inform themselves of its contents and see how it differed from the 1891 version. However, considering the subject-matter and the events of the previous year, it is likely that for most members this would be the first time they had read any version of the legislation. Therefore, if they were to make any intelligent contribution to the debate on the principle of the bill, it was vital that it be distributed as soon as possible.

On 4 April Sedgewick asked Samuel Dawson, the new Queen's Printer, when the bill would be ready for distribution. To his anger and dismay he found that, because of some administrative misunderstanding between Dawson and McCord, the law clerk, only forty-eight pages had been printed. If the remaining page proofs were returned to him promptly, Dawson said, it would take another ten days to complete the printing: that is, the complete bill would not be ready until 15 April. Thompson apparently intervened, and Dawson promised to run four presses around the clock and deliver the bill on 12 April.[62] He did not keep his promise, and when second reading was due the members still did not have copies of the legislation. Nevertheless, the minister pressed ahead. Indeed, he turned the event to his advantage, for he could tell the House only what he wanted to and as much or as little as he thought necessary. Without the legislation in their hands, the members of the opposition could not contradict or question him on issues of substance; they could discuss only what he chose to tell them, and he told them very little.

Second reading came on after evening recess. At seven-thirty Thompson rose from his seat and began the debate disarmingly by asking the House for its indulgence to allow him to proceed with the bill without its distribution having occurred. He told the members that he was still receiving 'valuable suggestions for its improvement,' and went on to outline what was in prospect. To facilitate the passage of the legislation, he intended to follow the precedent set during the passage of the revised statutes and, for the second time in Canadian parliamentary history, to move for the formation of a joint committee of the House and the Senate to consider a substantive measure. He hoped to have the bill distributed before Parliament adjourned the next day for Easter, so that the committee could study it over the recess and begin work promptly when business resumed. Thompson then went to the heart of the matter.

The objects of the Bill are very tersely expressed in one passage of the report of the Royal Commission which investigated the subject of the criminal law in England, in defining the effort at codification in a similar Bill in Great Britain in these words:

> It is a reduction of the existing law to an orderly written system, freed from needless technicalities, obscurities, and other defects which the experience of its administration has disclosed. *It aims at the reduction to a system of that kind of substantive law relating to crimes and the law of procedure, both as to indictable offences and as to summary convictions.*[63]

But what Thompson said was not completely true. The first sentence of the passage is indeed a verbatim quotation; the italicized sentence is not.[64] Nothing even remotely like it can be found in the report, which treats only indictable offences. The minister thus cloaked a major Canadian initiative – the inclusion of summary offences – with the authority of the imperial Parliament.

He also named Canada last when he enumerated the sources of the bill. These were, he said, the English draft code of 1880, Stephen's *Digest*, Burbidge's *Digest*, and Canadian statute law. He did not mention the colonial codes of the 1850s or the later Canadian attempt at codification in 1884. Instead, he extolled Westminster's efforts to codify the law over the preceding sixty years, and the 'immense help' these had been 'in simplifying and reducing into a system of this kind our law relating to criminal matters and criminal procedure.' Following this encomium, he specified the main divisions of the legislation by quoting the titles of the bill, which, it will be recalled, were copied almost verbatim from the imperial bill of 1880. Only when it became necessary to emphasize that the legislation would not abrogate the common law did he leave momentarily the protective cover of the English experience to explain that '[the] Bill aims at a codification of both common law and statutory law relating to these subjects, but ... it does not aim at completely superseding the common law, while it does aim at completely superseding the statutory law relating to crimes. In other words, the common law will still exist and be referred to, and in that respect the code, if it should be adopted, will have the elasticity which has been so much desired by those who are opposed to codification on general principles.'[65] He specified seven changes, including the substitution of 'theft' for 'larceny' as a legal term and the abolition of the distinction between felony and misdemeanour, and again bolstered his argument with copious references and quotations from the imperial commissioners' report.

At this point he eased into a discussion of the 'proposed abolition of the system of indictment by grand jury,' during which he reviewed the question exhaustively.[66] He made no bones about his being an abolitionist, but concluded by saying that, reluctantly and notwithstanding his personal preference, he would 'delay any request to Parliament to alter the law with regard to this system,' because no replacement for it had yet been developed. We know that this very issue had been a prime reason for the defeat of Thompson's administration in Nova Scotia, and that he had voiced reservations about its practicability at the federal level more than a year before. It is evident that this part of his speech was really a large bone for the opposition to chew on in place of the succulent meat which knowledge of the provisions of Bill 7 would have provided. In saying what he did, the minister was less than frank with the House: nowhere in his remarks is there mention of the extensive measures in the bill to limit the power of the grand jury.

In total, Thompson's speech covers four columns of print. The first is taken up with incidental information, the second addresses the content of Bill 7, and the last two are devoted entirely to the grand jury. Because of this very effective smoke-screen, and because of the way Thompson phrased his remarks, the perception of the House was that there was to be no fundamental alteration in the legal system – no tampering with the common law – and that he had made a large concession to the opposition on the question of the grand jury. This perception is evident in the speech of the leader of the opposition, Wilfrid Laurier, who said, in part, in his first sentence, '[A]s the purport of the Bill is what the Hon. gentleman has just explained, that it will not introduce any great changes but is to put in statutory form what has already existed by statute modified by the opinion of eminent jurists, I think it may go at once to second reading.'[67]

The remainder of his speech was devoted entirely to the grand jury. So was the speech of the only other speaker, David Mills, the opposition justice critic.[68] Predictably, the debate ended amicably. Thompson then named the other members of the Commons who were to sit with him on the joint committee, the motion was put, and the bill passed second reading. The House had agreed in principle to the enactment of Criminal Code.

Sir John Thompson's biographer tells us that the minister was not a well-read man with a love of literature, but that he did take 'immense trouble to master his facts.'[69] It is virtually certain that he did read the imperial Hansard to establish the facts of earlier attempts at codification.[70] It may be that in reading Sir Robert Peel's speeches on the passage of his criminal law bills in the 1820s Thompson assimilated Francis Bacon's precepts at second hand. If he did not, his achievement at the termination of debate on second reading is all the more impressive, because, knowingly or not, he had followed the lord chancellor's principles and, like Peel, had improved on the model. The law had been condensed and brought to a smaller compass in a rational arrangement. A joint committee would examine the bill, change what it saw fit to change, and recommend the result to Parliament. When the bill came into force all other statute law on the subject would be repealed; but Thompson, like Bacon, emphasized that he had no intention of abrogating the common law. In addition, he had addressed all the other concerns expressed by members of the imperial Parliament in the codification debates of the 1870s.

The Canadian draft code was comprehensive – that is to say, it included both indictable and summary offences. It had been drafted at minimal cost by persons answerable to a minister of the Crown, who had not only welcomed suggestions for the improvement of his bill from all sections of society, but who had actively solicited such assistance. Finally, his verbal presentation was superb. He did not attempt to philosophize or to delve into the history of codification;[71] he did not raise the members' ire by telling them that they had to take his legislation on trust; he did not say that he intended to make numerous large alterations, nor did he dwell on the few he mentioned. He told the House very little, and vested his bill with the authority of Westminster by clever phrasing and by using copious quotations to support the few factual statements he did make. In short, he gave the opposition very few targets to shoot at, except a large and tempting bull's-eye which he conjured up for their benefit.[72] Anything less like Attorney General Holker's procedure and his speeches in the imperial House is hard to imagine.[73]

In view of all this, the minister must have been chagrined, if not exceedingly displeased, when he read the speech Senator Gowan delivered in the Senate on the same day on which Thompson moved second reading in the Commons. The occasion for the speech was a motion sponsored by Sir John Abbott, the prime minister, to name the members of the Senate who would sit on the joint committee. Abbott spoke very briefly. He told the members that the draft code would be read that day in the Commons and that its sponsor would move the formation of a joint committee. He was careful to point out that the reason for this unusual procedure was to allow the Senate to 'participate in the consideration of the detail of this Bill, and so be in a position to pass it through this House without delay as it is not improbable that it may be late in the session before it gets through the other House.'[74]

His motion was merely a necessary formality, one of the many which go through 'on the nod.' In this case it did not. Senator Gowan rose and spoke for nearly as long as Thompson had in the Commons. In what he said and how he phrased it, he could have been Holker or Fitzjames Stephen speaking. He opened with complimentary remarks about the formulation of the bill, and went on:

I do think the Bill by far and away the most complete codification of the Criminal Law that has ever been submitted to any legislative body. But it involves gigantic changes. It in effect wipes away a large portion of that great depository of British law – the Common Law of England – as relates to the Criminal Law – that grand beacon-light of English jurisprudence, with its many reflectors, formed with wonderful skill and developed and brightened by the keenest intellects in many a conflict of opinion amongst England's jurists. It reduces to legislative expression many rules and principles found in the Common Law – in a word, it reduces to a code the whole floating body of the Criminal Law of Canada.[75]

It was lucky for Thompson that the bill had not been distributed; if it had been, Gowan might have stirred up a hornets' nest by giving concrete examples of the 'gigantic changes.' As it was, his auditors obviously believed that he was indulging in senatorial hyperbole, for this portion of his remarks did not elicit a response. He continued to elaborate the theme for some time and then gratuitously raised the question of which House the Bill should have been introduced in – a question that had been settled years before by Senator Campbell and John Bourinot. Gowan agreed that it should have originated in the Commons and that it should be sent to a joint committee, because 'in a deliberative body composed of men who are not experts, it is difficult to deal with technical questions of this kind.' Predictably, these sentiments did not sit well with his colleagues. Senator Henry Kaulbach of Nova Scotia, himself a lawyer and a Conservative, thought Gowan's remarks were 'rather premature' and was irritated by their purport, as he makes clear in his conclusion: 'I wish to express my disagreement with the hon. gentleman's opinion as to the fitness of the Senate for initiating a measure of this kind.'[76] This put an end to the discussion.

As a source of information on what had gone before, Gowan was unequalled; as a legislative draftsman, he was without peer; but as a parliamentary tactician, he was a booby. By making such a speech he was unwittingly sabotaging the minister's carefully laid plan.[77] Thompson must have breathed a sigh of relief when he learned that Gowan would be prevented from giving any more provocative speeches for the foreseeable future. Writing from his home in Barrie after the Easter recess, the senator informed him that Mrs Gowan was seriously ill and that he could not contemplate leaving her for the remainder of the session. (Gowan was then seventy-seven, his wife somewhat younger.)[78] This turn of events would keep him away from the Senate chamber, but still allow him to exercise his talents to their fullest extent via the mail.

When Bill 7 was finally distributed is not known. It may not have been available before the Easter recess, because the joint committee did not meet until 28 April, ten days after Parliament reconvened.[79] Not a great deal is known directly about its deliberations, since any record it might have generated was burned in the fire of 1916. But much may be inferred from the evidence that remains.

The committee was composed of thirty-one members, twenty-four from the Commons and seven from the Senate; all were lawyers.[80] Of the total, twenty-one were Conservatives and ten were Liberals. Only three of the latter were from the front benches of the opposition: Mulock from the Commons, and Power and Scott from the Senate.[81] Each session ran for a whole morning, and there were three or four sittings each week.[82] Attendance was uneven. Senator Scott, the most articulate and informed member from the opposition, did not attend any of the meetings.[83] Another fifteen members did not intervene in any of the subsequent debates, so it may be assumed that either they did not attend or, if they did, they took little or no interest in the deliberations. On at least one occasion only three men turned up: Louis Masson, a Quebec Conservative and a conscientious attendant; the minister of justice, who missed only one sitting; and Senator William Miller, the chairman.

Miller had been carefully selected for the job. He was an old acquaintance of Thompson's who was making desperate and persistent attempts to insinuate himself on to the honours list, but whose quest had so far been hampered by his drinking problem.[84] Apart from this failing, he was an able and effective individual who, having been Speaker of the Senate for a four-year term, was an expert in procedure and committee work. The minister knew before he chose him that Miller would be, as he put it, 'a very prompt and judicious chairman.'[85]

The other committee members posed no problems. A codified format was not a new or unwelcome concept to Canadian lawyers of that era, and Thompson had taken great care not to arouse any animosity or opposition to the draft code. Therefore, it is not surprising that he found the 'members who attend ... to be well disposed.'[86] And he kept them well disposed. According to Senator Power, they were given to understand that '[t]he Joint Committee was not expected to go through the various clauses of the bill, which purported to be taken from other sources, to ascertain whether or not those clauses were exact copies of the clauses of which they purported to be the copies.'[87] Power was not contradicted by any of the Conservative committee members, so it must be assumed that his account is essentially correct. By defining and following this procedure, Thompson was able to avoid controversial issues and to restrict discussion to those clauses he wanted discussed. Predictably, the bill passed smoothly through the joint committee. Between 28 April and 3 June, in just over five weeks, there were between fifteen and twenty sessions, during which some amendments were made and four short and non-specific reports were submitted to both the Commons and the Senate. The third of these, which took the work up to section 532, or the last of the substantive law, was tabled on 16 May.[88] The following day Thompson moved the Commons into the Committee of the Whole to begin clause-by-clause study of the bill.

What did the opposition know about Bill 7 at this point? Not a great deal. The first version had been distributed long after its introduction in the Commons, which had occurred with no fanfare and no explanation. At the same time the minister of justice made sure that all of the prominent individuals outside Parliament who would have an interest in the implementation of the legislation (and who might thus voice opposition) were sent a copy; their views were solicited and implemented if appropriate. Criticism was to be disarmed or diverted. The success of this ploy is attested to by the fact that there was no notice given to the bill – in fact, no mention at all – in the professional journals and that the public evinced no interest in response to the routine and uncontroversial coverage in the daily press. In Parliament, first reading of the 1892 version was also effected with minimal explanation, and second reading, or agreement in principle, had come and gone without any member's seeing the bill. Finally, the two- or three-line reports of the uncontroversial proceedings of the joint committee had been read in the humdrum atmosphere of a House settling into the routine of the business of the day.

But Bill 7 was three hundred pages long. And although its content was infinitely simpler than what it was to replace, it was by no means easily digested. Moreover, there was no indication where changes had been made to the 1891 draft. To discover what alterations had been made would have necessitated a painstaking comparison of the two versions article by article – not an easy task. A much more difficult task, however, would have been the comparison of the 1891 draft with the original sources to ascertain its differences in content and meaning. If any member of the opposition had really wanted to know how closely Bill 7 resembled its sources and what new content had been introduced, his labour would have been long and difficult. From the evidence of the debate it is clear that the opposition had not made the effort, not least because Thompson had convinced them that there had been little or no change. They had taken his assurance on trust.

When the bill went to the Committee of the Whole, however, it engaged the attention of the senior legal members from the front bench of the opposition. Now that they were able to read the details of the legislation, they began to perceive that changes had been made, and their resistance strengthened. But because they had not read the bill as a whole, and because it was being studied clause-by-clause, seriatim, their perception was blinkered. No one who spoke in the debates saw the bill as a whole, as an enactment that would make fundamental changes in the whole system of criminal law. Rather, they saw the trees but not the forest. Thompson may have anticipated this, but whether he did or not, he was happy to help the opposition keep its blinkers on.

He led off with an abbreviated form of his remarks on second reading, again giving prominence to the 'labours of the commission in Great Britain,' and added, 'I have much gratification in stating that the Bill has received very careful and very close consideration from the members of the [joint committee] who have taken a deep interest in its provisions.'[89] After this graceful compliment, the chairman read the first section and the debate began. Almost immediately Thompson moved to maintain the obscurity that shrouded the bill: 'I would submit to the committee whether it is necessary for the Chairman to read the whole Bill, or only those clauses to which the committee has reported amendments.' Laurier countered by saying that he thought they 'should hear the whole Bill read for the benefit of those members who were not on the committee.' Thompson conceded the point.

In this way a pattern was established which was followed in all subsequent debates. The chairman would read a section. 'Then,' said Thompson, the opposition would 'try to find out what it means, dispute about whether the common law is changed or not and ask a [medley?] of questions as to whether there is anything in the Bill to this or that effect etc.'[90] The principal speakers for the Liberals were David Mills and Louis Davies, supported by Laurier and William Mulock.[91] Thompson was the chief government spokesman, and he dominated the discussions. He was on his feet twenty-five times in the first debate, almost as often as the combined total of the opposition speakers. To rebut their arguments he relied first on the imperial commissioners, if they had expressed an opinion on the point at issue. If they had not, he defended the legislation on its own considerable merits. If the opposition hardened and it appeared that the Liberals would dig in their heels and drag out the discussion, he conceded the point and went on to the next section. As he told Senator Gowan, 'You may be sure I will not say "all or none" ... I believe in the proposed changes but am not dogmatic about it.'[92]

Nevertheless, he found the opposition tactics 'very trying to the temper,' and especially so when he was forced to concede fundamental provisions, a not infrequent occurrence. A typical example of such a concession was that made after the debate on section 122. The bone of contention was subsection 1, which defined a seditious intention as an intention

(a) To bring into hatred or contempt, or to excite disaffection against the person of Her Majesty, or the Government and Constitution of the United Kingdom or any part of it, or of Canada or any Province thereof, or either House of Parliament of the United Kingdom, or of Canada or any Legislature, or the administration of justice; or

(b) To excite Her Majesty's subjects to attempt to procure, otherwise than by lawful means, the alteration of any matter in the State; or

(c) To raise discontent or disaffection amongst Her Majesty's subjects; or

(d) To promote feelings of ill-will and hostility between different classes of such subjects.

David Mills argued that 'this section would alter the constitutional law as set out in the trial of Sacheverell,' and would thus make any criticisms of the Queen or her government or ministers seditious offences. Louis Davies also harked back to the Glorious Revolution, and held that the liberty of the subject was inextricably bound up with the common law, which is 'elastic and justly elastic. It is made by the prudence of the judges ... to suit the development of the people and the constitution.'[93] Thompson defended the definitions by pointing out that all those objections were met by subsection 2(b), which provided that it would not be sedition '[t]o point out errors or defects in the Government or Constitution of the United Kingdom, or of any part of it, or of Canada or any Province thereof, or in either House of Parliament of the United Kingdom or of Canada, or in any legislature, or in the administration of justice; or to excite Her Majesty's subjects to attempt to procure, by lawful means, the alteration of any matter in the State.'[94] He went on to develop this line of reasoning, but was careful to ground his argument in the observations of the imperial commissioners, his final words being: 'Lord Blackburn, Sir Charles Barry, Sir Robert Lush and Sir Fitz-James Stephens [sic] declared under their own hand that "this is as exact an application as we can make of the existing law." '

William Mulock then took the floor. He thought the section would impair freedom of speech and, in the most reasoned of the opposition speeches, gave what he considered to be examples of instances where free speech would be restricted or forbidden. But, more to the point, he said, 'I trust that the section will be so modified as to put that right beyond all question of controversy. If the Minister will not yield the point now, I give him notice that when the bill is reported I will move to cut down that clause.'[95] In fact, Thompson deleted subsection 1 in its entirety. The punishment for sedition was specified but the offence was not defined, and persons subsequently charged with sedition were subject to the exceedingly elastic definitions provided by the common law.[96]

Another disappointment for the minister was that his opponents forced him to abandon, item by item, his plan to cut down the authority of the grand jury. For example, section 560, which laid down that only magistrates were to conduct preliminary investigations, was dropped during the seventh debate of the committee. Section 642, which stipulated that no grand jury could bring in a true bill unless it was endorsing a bill of indictment sent to it by a Crown attorney, was eliminated in the eighth debate.[97] It is noteworthy, too, that in both instances Thompson made little effort to defend these provisions, and in fact was noticeably eager to drop a section when the opposition looked as though it would settle down to examine the issues in detail.

Thompson's non-confrontational technique was also very effective in smothering any public criticism that might have been created by the press. From their coverage it is obvious that parliamentary correspondents were bored to tears by the proceedings in committee, and they conveyed their ennui to their readers. Several ignored the debates entirely and concentrated on popular issues such as the redistribution bill, which redefined constituency boundaries after the census of 1891; others reported segments of the discussion verbatim (by this time copy could be taken directly from the *Debates*);[98] a few tried desperately to find some 'human interest' angle to divert their readers.

Some of their attempts to solve the problem make interesting reading. 'The House considered the criminal laws bill all day,' the *Victoria Daily Colonist* reported, and then devoted the rest of its coverage to the question of fishery regulations.[99] Even more bluntly, the correspondent of the *Ottawa Daily Mail* told his readers that '[t]he discussion upon the criminal law bill was naturally of an uninteresting character, being confined to a little band of some fourteen or fifteen lawyers, whose differences were for once not political but those of their own profession.'[100] The writer went on to discuss briefly the definition of 'newspaper,' a topic that had occupied the committee for a few moments, but the main item in his column had to do with the 'Bancroft Job,' a case where government patronage had evidently evolved into a conspiracy to defraud the public. The *Toronto Globe*'s correspondent wrote with flair, but his message was the same as his colleagues':

The committee of the whole on the new criminal dispensation gives the workers in the gallery a welcome breathing space, and they moralises [sic], sleep or retire to their apartments in No. 8, according as the fancy of the moment may lead them. How misleading is the familiar term 'committee of the whole.' Of the 215 members, eleven are following the clauses as they pass, and a substantial minority of the workers are moved by the power that inspired Sir Joshua Reynolds to paint – pure idleness. Occasionally a hobby calls forth a comment or a question. Col. Denison wants to know something about the law regarding the carrying of arms, and Mr Ives asks what kind of a pocket pistol is prohibited. Most of the members remaining in the chamber are working at their perpetual correspondence. A few groups are trading funny stories in voices that drown the feeble tones in which Sir John Thompson addresses the House.[101]

Needless to say, this sort of reportorial coverage, which epitomized the press's treatment of the debates on the Criminal Code, did little or nothing to inform the public of the totality of the legislation or of the changes its enactment would bring.

Nevertheless, during the ten sessions of the Committee of the Whole, which sat during the period from 17 May to 28 June, the "little band of lawyers" made substantial changes to Bill 7. When it was tabled in the Commons, the bill contained 1,005 sections. Two hundred eighty-six, or 28.5 per cent, were from English sources; 719 were new or from Canadian sources. The Criminal Code as finally enacted comprised 983 sections, of which 736, or 75 per cent, were new or from Canadian models. Since it is unlikely that any changes in the substantive law were made by the joint committee, most of the 150 amendments introduced before the bill was sent to the Senate were made in the House of Commons.[102] These included the deletion of 41 sections, the addition of 15 new ones, and the textual amendment and transposition of 6 more. In addition to these major and immediately noticeable alterations, many provisions, such as section 87 (concerning unlawful drilling), were completely rewritten; others, such as section 105 (on the use of air guns), were amplified and much extended; in some, such as section 332 (on the theft of animals), amendment was limited to the elimination of redundant phrases. However, the bill was not irreparably mutilated and was still recognizably the same piece of legislation. Thompson, whose philosophy was 'better half a loaf than none,' was overjoyed that no greater damage had been done, for what emerged after third reading on Tuesday, 28 June, was much more than half a loaf.[103]

In view of the number of amendments that had been made and the need to incorporate them in a clean copy for the Senate, the staff of the Department of Justice and the Queen's Printer must have burned the midnight oil again to effect the necessary changes. The bill was taken to the Upper Chamber for first reading on Monday, 4 July, where it was introduced by Prime Minister Abbott. It immediately ran into heavy weather. This was no surprise to the government members, who knew that a determined effort would be made to defeat the legislation.[104]

It was an unusual situation. This was the first time in the history of the Canadian Parliament that a bill concerning the substantive law, which had been examined and amended by a joint committee, had come before the Senate. It may have been the only time.[105] The chief opponent was the leader of the opposition, Senator Scott, who appears to have been the only senior Liberal to have seen the bill from the same perspective as Thompson. Scott was in a unique position. He was faced with a measure that had, in effect, the approval of the Senate so far as the committee stage was concerned, but that had not even been read the first time in that chamber. Moreover, as Scott pointed out, some of the changes to which the senators on the committee had agreed had been thrown out by the Commons.[106] This situation had profound constitutional implications, and, if it had been properly handled by the opposition, would have provided the opportunity for an extended debate. Since there were only six days before prorogation, and since Scott also assailed the government for bringing on the debate at such a late date and cited the precedent of 1868, it was possible that such a wrangle could have occupied the legal talent in the Senate for the remainder of the session.

But Scott had by no means finished cataloguing the errors of the government. Despite their hard work, the officials of the Justice Department, who did not normally draft legislation and follow it through the legislative process, had made a major mistake in preparing the copy Abbott introduced in the Senate.[107] They had not printed in italics the proposed alterations to the existing law or the amendments made by the joint committee and the House of Commons. Thus, without a painstaking textual comparison between the original bill and the version the senators had, it would be impossible to ascertain what changes had been made. Scott pointed this out in a biting critique of the legislation and asked Abbott to table the copy of the original bill used in the Commons debates, complete with amendments. He wound up his remarks by suggesting that the government stay second reading and instead send the bill to a committee of judges who would be required to put it in shape for introduction in the next session.[108]

Abbott, assisted by William Miller, moved quickly to beat back Scott's attack verbally and to provide the House with the material requested by Scott. The prime minister told the members that it was impossible to procure the actual bill used in the Commons debate, but that he had already asked that a copy of it be prepared for the Senate. Miller offered to give the leader of the opposition his personal copies of the original bill as amended by the joint committee.[109] Eventually, after a much longer and more wide-ranging debate than any that had taken place in the Commons, the bill passed first reading.[110]

Although the government had effectively sidetracked Scott's initial attack, he could have made much more trouble on the constitutional questions during second reading. He did not choose to do so, for he apparently saw all the issues he had so far raised merely as preliminary skirmishing, as procedural road-blocks which he had hoped would derail the government, but which were secondary to his main objections. He did not want a code: 'I am adverse to an innovation of this kind,' he said, and he objected in the strongest terms to the abrogation of the common law:

[F]or the first time in our history [Parliament] is ... going to depart in so important a subject matter as the criminal law of the old country from the usages of England and Great Britain and Ireland – usages which have grown up from time immemorial. We have a great many writers on criminal law who have compiled and crystallized from time to time decisions of learned judges, and it is upon those decisions that the law largely depends. When this code is passed a large portion of the learning and experience of ages will be laid aside. Instead of looking to the text books for definitions of important crimes – homicide and murder – to the writings of learned judges who have laid down well defined principles gathered after much labour from the decisions of centuries, we shall have to take up our code and ascertain what is the interpretation of the language used in the statutes we are now about to consider.[111]

Much more to the point, Scott had made a detailed study of at least a large portion of the bill, so that he was able to support at length and with copious examples his contention that the legislation 'alters very materially the Criminal Law of Canada.'[112] In truth, if the legislation had been explored as thoroughly in second reading in the Commons as it was at that stage in the Senate, it is doubtful if the bill, as then drafted, would have received approval in the lower House.

Senator Scott was the first member of the opposition to see Thompson's bill for what it was. He also did an excellent job of informing all who would listen exactly what its effect would be, and invited them to assist him in defeating it. Fortunately for Canada and for the minister of justice, the senator had made a fatal mistake. Although he had been appointed a member of the joint committee and so could have made his detailed objections known months earlier, he had never attended a meeting because, as he informed the House, he 'had not had the time to give to the work in committee that I should have done.'[113] He had made this astonishing admission early in the debate on first reading. His behaviour obviously lost him much of the backing he might have expected from traditionalists on the Conservative benches, and also caused his party colleagues to be less than enthusiastic in their support of him. The government weathered Scott's storm, the bill was given second reading, and the House devoted the rest of the week to considering it in the Committee of the Whole. It was given third reading and passed on Friday, 8 July; it received royal assent the following day, and was to be proclaimed in force on 1 July 1893.

The minister of justice, who had been gradually assuming more of the duties of leadership from the tiring Sir John Abbott, and who was by this time virtually the acting prime minister, left no doubt how important he considered the passage of the code to be. The governor general began his prorogation speech by telling the members that '[t]he adoption of the code of criminal law will confer a great benefit on all classes who are concerned in the administration of that branch of jurisprudence, and is an achievement which will reflect credit on the Parliament of Canada.'[114] The code did not receive the same prominence in the press, which, in most cases, merely reported the fact of its enactment. Predictably, it was ignored editorially by Liberal newspapers, but generated effusive praise in the *Victoria Daily Colonist* and *La Presse*.[115] The most thoughtful and objective of these was entitled 'Le Code Criminel' in *La Presse*. It lauded Thompson's immediate achievement, and it also forecast the long-term benefits of the legislation and, incidentally, demonstrated the truth of Jeremy Bentham's assertion that once the laws of a jurisdiction had been systematized in codified form, the process of amendment would become a frequent and simple process: 'quand à sa perfection, il aura le sort de tous les codes. A la session législative qui suivra sa promulgation commencera de suite à l'amender. Et cette envie d'amender deviendra plus tard une manie, une rage, comme cela s'est vu ici pour notre Code civil et notre code municpal: n'importe, le code restera et s'appellera du nom de celui qui en a eu la paternité en Parlement. On ne parlera plus du "Black Act" on dira maintenant le code criminel, "le code Thompson." '

In summary, the Senate was occupied for twenty-eight hours with 'le code Thompson.' This period included the debates on first and second reading and six sessions of the Committee of the Whole. During those six sessions the senators made ninety-two amendments.[116] If the time the Commons spent in debate is included, and if the Senate amendments are added to the 150 made by the joint committee and the lower House, it is clear that the bill received an exhaustive examination. It may have started out as Thompson's brain-child, and it may have been based on an English model, but by the time it was enacted it was a close approximation of what Canadians wanted as their criminal law.

This fact was demonstrated in an emphatic way a few months after prorogation. Mr Justice Taschereau was on leave when the Criminal Code became law. Shortly after his return to Ottawa for the fall term, the death of Chief Justice Ritchie threw the Supreme Court into confusion. After it had settled down, Taschereau turned his attention to the recent legislation. What he learned by word of mouth gave him cause for concern, and he asked the Justice Department for a copy of the Criminal Code. Sedgewick complied on 3 November.[117] Like Senator Scott, Taschereau soon discovered that many fundamental changes had been made, and he immediately realized their implications. To attempt to counter them before 1 July, when the code would come into force, he decided to emulate Chief Justice Cockburn's action in 1879. He examined the code meticulously and wrote a long and detailed critique, which he addressed to the minister of justice as an open letter dated 27 January 1893.[118]

Although much of what Taschereau said was cogent and to the point, his initiative was an utter failure. The conditions in Ottawa were completely different from those that obtained in London. In contrast to England, Canada was a country of vast distances and separate jurisdictions. Its inhabitants were subject to rational, written constitutions which specified the structure of the court systems and the composition of their benches. Unlike the central courts at Westminster and the Judicial Committee of the Privy Council, the Supreme Court of Canada was not supreme, and the senior provincial courts with criminal jurisdiction were unsupervised tribunals of equal and concurrent jurisdiction. Canadian legal systems were staffed with judges and lawyers who had been educated in a variety of autonomous systems different from the Inns of Court and from each other. To a greater or lesser degree their education and professional development were hampered by a dearth of institutional and private legal texts. They had to perform the duties of both solicitor and barrister, and their careers followed a different pattern from that of their English counterparts; Canadian judges came to the bench with experience dissimilar to and more varied than that of their brethren in Westminster.

The reasons that caused the divergence of the two legal systems also predisposed Canadians to view attempts to systematize the law from a perspective different from that of their English contemporaries. When the colonial legislators set out early to bring order to the statutes by arranging them in a rational, topical order contained in one compendious volume – in a word, to 'codify' the statute law, as the verb and the concept are defined in the leading works of lexicography in the western world – the results were generally met with approbation and acceptance by the legal profession and by society at large. For this reason, reaction to Taschereau's open letter criticizing what was perceived to be the latest version of such works ranged from censure to indifference.

Only three newspapers – two independent and one Liberal – commented on Taschereau's letter. Moreover, unlike the similar missive sent by Lord Chief Justice Cockburn to Sir John Holker in 1879, which had been copied in full and quoted extensively in the British press and the imperial Parliament, the judge's indictment received no more than cursory treatment in the Canadian press. The *Ottawa Evening Journal* ran the opening paragraphs and paraphrased the major portion of the text. There was very little editorial comment, and the writer took a statesmanlike stand when he concluded, 'No doubt Judge Taschereau's letter will receive careful consideration during the present session of Parliament, and if it should result in the code being referred to a commission of legal experts, the country can well stand the expense.'[119] Even more unconcerned was the *Toronto Mail*, which merely stated that Taschereau had sent an open letter to Thompson, and then linked some quoted matter from it by short phrases to give the item continuity.[120] The *Toronto Globe*'s editorial was a short but relatively objective examination of the event. It predicted that '[t]he minister of justice will probably take early action to amend the faults of which Judge Taschereau complains. He is doubtless as anxious as anyone to have the criminal code as consistent and perfect as it can be made.'[121] Little was heard from the professional press. The editorial writer for the *Legal News* must have gotten his information from the Department of Justice, since he told his readers that some of the items raised by Taschereau had indeed been considered by Parliament, and that 'other defects will be remedied by a short amending act.'[122] The only other legal editorialist to comment 'felt some natural pride in the *Canadian Criminal Code*,' and was sharply critical of Taschereau for publicly airing dirty legal linen.[123]

For once it seemed that there might be an individual response to press accounts of an event involving penal legislation which, because of its source, would have a good chance of being published in the letters-to-the-editor column. As he was prone to do, Senator Gowan took pen in hand to defend the code and castigate 'the learned judge'; there are drafts of long letters to the governor general and to the press in his papers.[124] But if clean copies were mailed, there is no trace of them in Lord Stanley's papers or in any newspapers of the period. These appear to be the only individual comments generated by the Taschereau letter that have survived. The parliamentary record is as silent as the grave on the subject (the session ran from 26 January to 1 April). Indeed, the only mention of the code in 1893 was a question in the Commons asking whether the government would issue members a copy, in addition to the regular issue of the statutes of the session, which was answered in the affirmative.[125] Thus, it is evident that in some measure Taschereau was a victim of the illusion created by the minister of justice, but to a far greater extent he was out of step with the times.

To arrive at a valid and meaningful assessment of Sir John Thompson's work, the Criminal Code of 1892 should not be analysed and its flaws catalogued with the benefit of a hundred years of hindsight. No: the code should be viewed rather from the perspective of a hundred years earlier, from 1791, the year in which the last major jurisdiction of post-revolutionary British North America was erected. Then the criminal law was cruel, obscure, and unsystematic. From that time on, the early legislatures worked to ameliorate the cruelty of the law to a greater or lesser extent. By the 1870s this amelioration had been completed, at least to the satisfaction of the great majority of Canadians, who saw the penal statutes as a just and fair safeguard of society. Conversely, the criminal justice system was still an unsystematic muddle of these enlightened but independent and disparate acts and common law rules.

It was not Sir John Thompson's purpose to change the substantive law. His aims were to change the form of the law, to bring order and clarity to criminal justice, to make its process systematic and rational, to reduce the amorphous and baffling common law to succinct and understandable principles, and to fix those principles in statute. To a great extent he succeeded, and he gave Canada the first enacted criminal code in the British empire. But of even greater importance was the fact that in so doing he had also achieved Jeremy Bentham's ideal: his legislation had changed the focus of the development of criminal law. Parliament would be that focus in the future, not the bench.

7

Epilogue

For more than a year after the Criminal Code was enacted there was no mention of it in the professional press. But judging from the scanty comment that was published eventually, it appears that the code was welcomed as a useful innovation.[1] It is also apparent, however, that practitioners had little or no idea of the changes the code had effected, and did not understand the principles on which it was based. Writing from Picton, C.H. Widdifield, for example, complained that although section 535 abolished the distinction between felony and misdemeanour, he could find no guidance on the forms of oath for jurors who were to try an indictable offence; were they to be sworn individually or as a body?[2] was the accused to stand trial in the dock, as had been the practice in a case of felony, or was he to be seated with his counsel in the well of the court, as was customary for an accused misdemeanant?

By the time N.W. Hoyles, the principal of Osgoode Hall Law School, published his article entitled 'Criminal Law of Canada' in 1902,[3] such misunderstandings had been cleared up. Hoyles's article demonstrated that Thompson's predictions had come true: he praised the convenience and utility of a systematic work which subsumed the criminal law of the dominion. Hoyles's method was to discuss the code topic by topic, and to demonstrate in each case how the system had been simplified and omissions in the previous law supplied. In case after case he cited examples to show how the code had been successful in solving the administrative and technical problems caused by the continued use of separate and unrelated statutes and the common law which still plagued the English system. One of these was an extraordinary case which had been heard in 1898 in a London police court. The accused was alleged to have employed a number of men to demolish two unoccupied houses brick-by-brick and board-by-board and cart the spoils away. 'When the owner came to see his property he was astonished to find a clear site, and to find no vestige of his houses.' He was even more astonished to find that in England at that time 'the facts [did] not constitute a criminal offence. At common law things real, or which savour of the realty, cannot be the subject of larceny. Thus trees and houses cannot be stolen, and to sever them and carry them away is merely a trespass at common law giving a civil action. By statute it is a felony to destroy a house by means of explosives, or for persons assembled riotously to destroy a house. It is also a misdemeanour for a tenant to maliciously pull down or demolish any building ... These, however, do not touch a demolition like that alleged.'[4] These facts became evident only after the suspect had been arrested and the prosecutor was attempting to formulate an appropriate charge. Eventually, the accused was indicted for an offence that was 'incidental to the principal fact of the case': he was charged under the Larceny Act of 1861, which made it a felony to cut or break any glass, woodwork, or metal fixed to a house with the intent to steal such items.[5] The English commentator remarked, 'The state of the law is somewhat ludicrous.' The same comment could have been made about Canadian law before 1893, because it was precisely the same. But, as Hoyles pointed out, if the accused had been prosecuted in Canada after the code had come into force, no similar problem would have arisen because section 303 made it an offence to steal any inanimate thing.[6]

Although Hoyles was proud of the code, he recognized that it was not perfect.[7] So too did the legislators who amply fulfilled the prediction of *La Presse* that once the legislation had come into force there would be an immediate urge to amend it, and that this practice would become a regular habit. In the years between 1893, when the code was proclaimed, and 1970, when the Law Reform Commission of Canada was established, there were only four sessions of Parliament in which bills were not introduced to change, augment, or cut down the code. Often, the draft legislation was abortive: it died on the order paper or was talked out. But if this occurred, the bill was usually reintroduced in the following session. This happened especially with private members' initiatives, of which a good example is Malcolm Cameron's annual criminal evidence bill.[8]

The first amendments to the code, aimed at correcting certain technical defects, were generated within the legislature by members of the small group of lawyers who had traditionally interested themselves in the development of penal law.[9] Their virtual monopoly in this field was coming to an end, however; as R.C. Macleod has pointed out, 'A new source of change in the law was becoming increasingly important. This was lobbying by a whole range of pressure groups. One of the theoretical advantages of codification of the law is that it provides a more visible target for the reformer. In the case of the Criminal Code, this is exactly what happened.'[10]

The results of such lobbying are evident from an examination of almost any annual statute-book. Social reformers, whose aim was usually to change existing law, were influential in securing legislation to protect females from abduction and seduction, to raise the age of consent, to regulate or abolish bawdy-houses, to suppress opium joints,[11] and to control trading stamps, lotteries, and gambling generally. Business groups were behind enactments concerning fraudulent debtors, passers of bad cheques or false bills, and automatic vending machines. Another cause for amendment, usually in the form of new law, was technological change. Regulations concerning the automobile, for example, first appeared in the code in 1910, when it was made an offence to leave the scene of an automobile accident and to drive a car without the owner's permission.[12] Since then, penal acts have been passed which involve such diverse technology as aircraft, computers, wire-tapping equipment, and a simple device used to establish the level of alcohol in an individual's blood. Diverse as these alterations were, however, they were merely changes in detail.

Writing in 1967, Alan Mewett, a law professor, said: 'Sir James Stephen would have been quite at home with the Criminal Code.'[13] His statement emphasizes the main characteristic of the work – its durability. Although the code of 1892 had defects and deficiencies, many of which Sir John Thompson was well aware, its basic structure has withstood the test of time. On the one hand, it has provided a strong foundation which has remained unaltered despite numerous changes in detail; on the other hand, the code of today is still recognizably Thompson's work, albeit amended and adapted to meet society's changing needs. There have been few changes of principle since the legislation was drafted.

Durable it is, but for that very reason the code still retains some of its original deficiencies. In particular, Stephen's failure to include a general part which explained the rationale of the code and defined essential terms and Thompson's decision to follow the English model in these respects have not yet been rectified. Therefore, terms such as 'indictable offence' and 'summary conviction offence' are still undefined, and this makes the code baffling reading for the layman.

There has been only one major consolidation and 'restructuring' of the code.[14] In retrospect it can be seen that it was brought on, in part, by a controversial change that violated the spirit and principle of English and Canadian law. By the terms of a 1919 amendment to section 97, which dealt with unlawful associations, an accused charged under that section was presumed guilty until he proved his innocence.[15] The reason given by the government for this enactment was the failure of the Parliament of 1892 to define 'sedition.' The legislation had its beginnings during the 'Red Scare' that swept through Europe and North America in the wake of the 1917 Bolshevik Revolution in Russia. It first took the form of an order in council of 28 September 1918 entitled 'Associations, Organizations, Societies or Groups Declared to Be Unlawful Associations.'[16] Among other things, it declared fourteen industrial unions and political parties, including the International Workers of the World and the Russian Social Democratic party, to be unlawful associations, and imposed penalties for printing, publishing, or offering for sale any material that advocated the use of violence to bring about a change in government.[17] One of the most draconian passages specified that 'if it be proved that the person charged since the beginning of the war repeatedly: (a) attended meetings of an unlawful association; or (b) spoke publicly in advocacy of an unlawful association; or (c) distributed literature of an unlawful association *it shall be presumed in the absence of proof to the contrary that he is a member of such unlawful association.*'[18] Since it was also provided that the order would be in force only 'while Canada is engaged in war' the provision had a short existence and expired two months later at the war's end.

With the rise in labour unrest in the last years of the war, particularly during the winter of 1918–19, the Unionist government of the day, fearful that the Bolshevik revolution would spread to Canada and that the criminal law would provide insufficient protection against the threat, decided to act.[19] On 1 May 1919 the metal and building workers went out on strike in Winnipeg: this action was the precursor of the Winnipeg General Strike. On the same day Hugh Guthrie, the solicitor general, moved to form a committee of the House to consider and report on the law of sedition and to recommend changes.[20] From later accounts it is clear that there was strong disagreement and acrimonious debate in the committee, which was almost evenly divided on the issue. Speaking for the minority, the Hon. Charles Murphy, a senior Liberal and member of the opposition, said that his supporters did not think that the Criminal Code was in need of amendment, and that even if it were, June 1919 was not the time to make the change. But the government view prevailed, and the report was adopted by a majority of one. Most of these facts became known when Guthrie, who had been the committee's chairman, moved and secured adoption of its report.[21] In essence, it was the order in council of 1918 revived and writ large: the penalty had been increased from a maximum of five to a maximum of twenty years' imprisonment, and the words 'any association' had replaced the fourteen named organizations. Presumably, the government would outlaw a party or a union as it saw fit. There was one further important item: it was recommended that section 133 of the Criminal Code, which specified what constituted 'lawful criticism' of the government, be repealed.[22]

The first reading of the bill incorporating the committee's report as section 1 was moved by the acting minister of justice, Arthur Meighen, who was an expert parliamentary tactician in the tradition of Sir John Thompson. He told the House that the 'measure has to do with amendments to the Code regarding sedition,' and then, in what must be construed as an attempt to mislead, continued, 'as recommended by the special committee of Parliament and concurred in by the House unanimously.' He was brought up sharply by Murphy, who told the members, 'I refer to his [Meighen's] observation that the report which deals with the question of seditious conspiracy was unanimously concurred in. My hon. friend was in the House and he will recollect that I pointed out at the time that a number of members of the committee took exception to the report.'[23]

But Meighen knew how to minimize his losses. He replied, 'That is correct,' and, after the minister had briefly answered another member's equally brief query, the Speaker put the question and the motion was agreed to on division. Second reading was also moved by Meighen, who now varied his tactics. He began: 'This section is taken practically word for word from the resolution concurred in by the House with regard to sedition.' Then Meighen himself immediately proposed an administrative amendment, which occupied the members until the question was called.[24] With a government majority of almost two to one, it was a foregone conclusion that the amendment would be agreed to. Third reading was pro forma, and sections 97A and 97B came into force on 1 October 1919.[25]

Another consequence of the failure to define sedition in 1892 was the outcome of the trials of the leaders of the Winnipeg General Strike in 1919. Luckily for them, they had been arrested and charged with seditious conspiracy under section 132 of the code, which carried a maximum penalty of two years' imprisonment, on 17 July, well before section 97A came into force. Authoritative commentators are agreed that there was no seditious conspiracy at Winnipeg in the summer of 1919, and that the purpose of the strike was an attempt to enforce the principle of collective bargaining.[26] Nevertheless, in the absence of a definition of sedition, Mr Justice Metcalf, the trial judge, was able to ensure that the accused were convicted and given exemplary sentences. A learned antiquarian and jurist, Metcalf achieved his aim by threading his way through a series of carefully chosen cases to arrive at a definition of seditious conspiracy that was at variance with the more liberal judicial view then prevalent.[27] In view of the judge's ability, there is little doubt that the strikers' punishment would have been much more severe if the new legislation had been on the statute-book when they were indicted, and if they had been charged under section 97A (or, as it has since come to be known, section 98).[28]

Although there were no prosecutions under section 98 for over a decade, there were repeated attempts to repeal it. From 1922 to 1935, bills for this purpose were introduced in all but four sessions of Parliament.[29] Before 1926 and after 1930 they were private members' bills; one was sponsored by Andrew McMaster, a Liberal, and the rest by James S. Woodsworth, the leader of the Independent Labour party (ILP) and later the leader of the Co-operative Commonwealth Federation (CCF).[30] All these bills were hotly debated, especially the bill of 1933. In moving second reading of that measure, Woodsworth began his speech by referring to the first charges laid under section 98, which had resulted in the conviction the previous year of eight members of the Canadian Communist party, including the leader, Tim Buck.[31] He said, in part, '[T]hese men did not commit any overt act whatever. They were not convicted of urging the use of force, nor were they convicted of using force. They were convicted of belonging to an association which was said to be affiliated with a body in Russia which did believe in the use of force; on that type of evidence they were convicted. If my understanding is correct the general spirit of British law is absolutely opposed to that kind of legislation.' In developing this theme, Woodsworth angered government members, particularly Hugh Guthrie, who was then the minister of justice, and who launched into a speech that must have run on for well over an hour. His argument is not convincing, and can be epitomized by his remark that '[s]ection 98 is not in any sense a hindrance to any right thinking person.'[32] Nevertheless, votes, not logic, decided the debate, and the bill of 1933 was defeated in the Commons, just as all the private members' initiatives had been. The bills brought in by Ernest Lapointe, the minister of justice in Mackenzie King's Cabinet during the period from 1926 to 1930, all passed the House but were defeated in the Senate, which was dominated by a Conservative majority. However, Lapointe had a measure of success in 1930, when the Senate assented to the re-enactment of section 133.

By the time the Liberal party returned to power with a large majority in the fall of 1935, the movement to repeal section 98 had attracted a great deal of favourable public attention and an impressive degree of support inside and outside Parliament. Religious groups, social reformers, labour unions and numerous MPs made no bones about their repugnance toward the legislation. All this is reflected in the long and acrimonious debate on Lapointe's bill of 1936, the passage of which finally put the quietus to section 98.[33]

The recurring themes in these proceedings were Tim Buck's conviction and the events he was involved in during his imprisonment in Kingston Penitentiary. Such allusions are sporadic and unconnected, and may puzzle the modern reader who is not familiar with the case. The facts have never been disputed, but it took a long time for them to emerge.[34] The inmates of Kingston Penitentiary had some justified grievances which they had raised with the authorities over an extended period, to no avail. On 17 October 1932 they planned a peaceful demonstration to bring their grievances forcefully to the attention of the administration. The protest turned into a riot when the warden, learning what was to occur, took provocative but ineffectual steps to prevent the demonstration. Tim Buck was involved, but was later proved to have counselled moderation and actually to have restrained other inmates from destroying property. By today's standards, it was a very modest 'riot' indeed. Nevertheless, the militia was called out, the riot put down, and the prisoners confined to their cells. Three days later, inmates in a cell-block far from Buck's began to demonstrate and to wreck their cells, whereupon the militiamen and guards opened fire 'through the peep-holes into the cells occupied by the prisoners,'[35] shooting one inmate in the lung. Although Buck's cell-block remained quiet during the disturbance, armed personnel patrolling outside the block began to shoot at it, and '[a]t least three rifle bullets and ten pellets of buck shot were fired into

Buck's cell by someone who knew that Buck was in the cell at the time.'[36] Since his was the only cell in the block that was shot at, there is little doubt that someone was trying to kill him. Fortunately, he was not harmed. Clearly, this was intolerable behaviour, and the incident revealed serious shortcomings in the penitentiary system. But it was covered up, and the facts did not begin to emerge publicly until months after the events occurred.

So far as was possible at the time, the matter was explored in an incisive and comprehensive speech by Agnes Macphail, Woodsworth's CCF colleague, during the debate on the Department of Justice estimates in 1934. She concluded by calling for an impartial investigation into Canadian penal institutions, and made it clear that she was only one of many individuals and organizations who advocated such action.[37] Macphail's speech was otherwise memorable for the fact that by making it she caused Prime Minister R.B. Bennett to delay the prorogation of Parliament. The government was not eager to hold an exhaustive discussion on the vote for the Justice Department estimates, because it was aware that Buck's case, a political bombshell, would be raised. So the item was placed last on the order paper on prorogation day in the hope that at ten or eleven o'clock, on a hot and humid summer evening with the governor general waiting in the wings, the members would be so eager to depart for their homes or summer cottages that their assent would be given as a matter of course. Agnes Macphail spoiled their plan; posterity is the benefactor, because her speech, unlike many parliamentary utterances, is most informative and a pleasure to read; more important, it gave her story extensive publicity in the press on a day when journalists would otherwise have been yawning over a prorogation address.[38] This embarrassing rebuff, together with the fact that Bennett's administration was in its last year and he wanted no more revelations, made it a foregone conclusion that Macphail's request would be ignored. But the question became a hotly debated issue in the subsequent election campaign, and Liberal candidates went on record promising such an investigation if they formed the next government.

The Liberals were returned to power with an impressive majority, and their election promise was one of the first items on the agenda. A few days after the convention of the first session of the new Parliament, Ernest Lapointe, who had been reappointed minister of justice, announced the appointment of what later became known as the Archambault Commission to inquire into and report on the penal system of Canada.[39] The commissioners ranged across Canada holding hearings and questioning witnesses, and deliberated for over two years. Their report of 4 April 1938, prepared at a time of high international tension, was a comprehensive 418-page book with eighty-eight specific recommendations. While most were made with particular reference to the penal system per se, one was gratuitous and actually outside the commission's terms of reference. When seen in the context of the investigation, however, it was logical and to the point, for the commissioners had identified many inconsistencies and omissions in the criminal law as laid down in the current swollen edition of the code, which ran to 1,151 sections. They advised the government that '[a] complete revision of the Criminal Code should be made at once.'[40] Coming from such a source, the recommendation was authoritative, but it was by no means original. In 1936 Thomas L. Church, a lawyer and a Conservative who interested himself in questions of social reform, asked Prime Minister Mackenzie King if a bill would be brought in for a complete revision of the Criminal Code, and whether the government would consider the possibility of creating a joint committee of the Senate and the Commons to study and report on law reform generally. King responded with one of his usual opaque answers, which amounted to his saying no to both questions.[41] The following year the debate on the death penalty gave Church the opportunity to elaborate on his suggestions. Essentially, he wanted a complete revision of the code, so that it would provide for the technological changes in crime that had occurred since the code's enactment. Second, he suggested that a standing committee on law reform and legal bills be set up, and, finally, he mooted the possibility of the creation of a separate law reform commission.[42] These ideas were reinforced by the recommendation of the Archambault Commission. Unfortunately for Church and like-minded reformers, the movement in Parliament toward revision and rationalization of the code was stopped dead by the declaration of war. Apart from a Conservative member's call for the re-enactment of section 98 in 1940,[43] there were few references to criminal law and few measures to amend the code during the war. Indeed, in 1942 there was no mention of crime, criminal law, or the code in the index to the *Debates*.

Outside Parliament, however, there was a significant development. At the meeting of the Canadian Bar Association in 1943, it was 'pointed out that no body existed in Canada with the proper personnel to study and prepare recommendations for amendments to the Criminal Code ... for submission to the Minister of Justice.'[44] Accordingly, a resolution was passed at the next meeting of the association to form a criminal law section of the Conference of Commissioners on Uniformity of Legislation 'to which several provinces and the Dominion appointed special representatives.'[45] As the pages of subsequent volumes of the conference's *Proceedings* show, the new section was a fruitful source of amendments to the code. It should also be noted that, in a sense, the civil law section of the conference was a forerunner of the Law Reform Commission of Canada and the various provincial law reform bodies that came into being in the 1960s and later.[46] The commissioners frequently went beyond their mandate to work for the uniformity of the law in being, and gave philosophical consideration to matters untouched by the law, but in which they saw a clear need for positive action. The result was that they frequently drafted bills, subsequently enacted, which 'dealt with subjects not [then] covered by legislation in Canada.'[47]

At war's end, the Archambault Commission's recommendation that the Criminal Code should be completely revised had been languishing in obscurity for eight years, but the need to implement it had become even more pressing. Consequently, peace brought new demands for a complete overhaul of the code from private individuals, various organizations, and laymen and lawyers from across the political spectrum. Typical of such requests was that made in 1947 by John Diefenbaker, even then famous for his criminal law practice. In part, he asserted that 'as it is now constituted the criminal code is composed of many incongruous sections, and a very considerable portion of it is no longer applicable to present-day conditions.' For these reasons he suggested that the minister of justice 'proceed with the recodification of the criminal code so as to bring it up to date, to remove many of the sections which are obsolete in effect, and also to amend the punishments.'[48] He was not alone, for later in the debate several other members intervened to support Diefenbaker's suggestions. In answer to similar propositions made in the following year, the minister of justice, James Ilsley, allowed that he hoped to take some action later in the session. He did not do so. But in January 1949 his successor, Stuart Garson, in answer to yet another question from Diefenbaker, finally announced the appointment of a royal commission, composed of judges, lawyers, and Department of Justice officials, to carry out a comprehensive restructuring and rationalization of the code.[49]

In all, the revision process lasted over five years. During that time the regular process of annual amendments by government and private members' bills continued. Most of these initiatives were routine: they were measures to regulate the clockwork, as it were. But the period was an

ominous one. Another 'Red Scare' swept across the western world, and
the tension between East and West eventually erupted in the Korean
War. Among other things, the events that occurred prior to the war's
outbreak caused a reaction on the political right characterized by demands for the re-enactment of section 98 or some similar legislation by
George Drew, the leader of the opposition, Arthur Meighen, now a
senator, and several of their supporters.[50] They did not get a sympathetic
hearing from the government benches or from the CCF, and no such
legislation was forthcoming. A private member's bill was drafted on the
model suggested by Drew and introduced later in the session, but it
was talked out by William Irvine of the CCF, who quoted extensively
and with obvious approval from Ernest Lapointe's 1936 speech on the
repeal of section 98.[51] Nevertheless, assuming he had public opinion
behind him, Drew then forced the issue in May 1950, with a motion that
'this house is of the opinion that appropriate legislation should be introduced so that communist and similar activities in Canada be made
an offence punishable under the Criminal Code.'[52] After a long and
heated debate, the motion was defeated by government and CCF votes.

Meanwhile, the revision of the Criminal Code was slowly moving
ahead. Eventually, after much prodding by the opposition, Stuart Garson tabled the report of the commission, together with a draft of the
restructured code, in April 1952. The first thing that was evident was
the reduced heft of the legislation. It had been reduced from the swollen
1,152 sections of the current edition to 753.[53] An inspection of the draft
bill's contents reveals that the commissioners had addressed several of
the problems Sir John Thompson had sidestepped. For example, the
new code would be exhaustive of the criminal law: the few remaining
common law offences were incorporated, and no person could be charged
with an offence unless that offence was specified in Canadian statute
law.[54] A cut-down version of the definition of sedition hammered out
by Lapointe and Woodsworth during the 1936 debate on section 98 was
incorporated.[55] Punishments were rationalized, and, to the extent possible, tailored to fit the crime.[56]

Notwithstanding its reduction in size, the legislation was still a massive piece of work. In contrast to the situation in 1892, the minister of
justice knew that there would be an exhaustive and informed debate on
second reading and in the committee of the whole, which would be
followed closely by questions from both lay and legally trained members
from the four parties then sitting in the House. He decided to make his
task easier by having the bill introduced in the Senate, where it was

referred to a standing committee that debated its provisions for several months and made 116 amendments.[57] After this process was completed, Garson introduced the bill in the Commons. His lengthy speech initiating the debate on second reading was reminiscent of Peel's in the 1820s rather than Thompson's. He began by detailing the commission's terms of reference, and stressed repeatedly that 'the purpose of the revision was not to effect changes in broad principles.'[58] He mentioned by name the senior persons, lay and legal, who had participated in the process, and made the point that outside opinion had been solicited and acted on. After sketching the history of criminal law, he went on to describe some of the provisions of the bill, such as that which made the substantive clauses of the legislation exhaustive of the criminal law. At the end of the debate Garson moved that the bill be sent to a special committee of the House for further study. Its members, twelve lawyers and five laymen, represented the four parties then seated in the Commons. As well as deliberating alone, the committee held open sessions to hear oral submissions from twenty or more organizations and received eight briefs submitted by other groups and individuals.[59]

After this careful and exhaustive process, Garson introduced a new bill in the next session which incorporated both the Senate amendments and those of the committee of the House. His speech on second reading was a longer and more detailed version of his previous address: the same points were made, and it was equally effective.[60] The debate began on 15 December 1953, and continued for nearly four months. Although there were occasional sticking-points, Garson had set the tone, and the discussion was carried on in a co-operative and, for the most part, non-partisan atmosphere. This was not unlike 1892, but what was very different was the number of members, especially non-lawyers, who spoke. For example, during a two-hour period during the debate on capital punishment and lotteries, ten members spoke; it is evident that each had been following the debate closely. Four were lawyers; six were laymen.[61] The bill passed third reading on 8 April 1954, and came into force the following year on 1 April 1955.

There is no question that the slim and restructured code was considerably easier to read and comprehend than its predecessor, and therefore was a boon to practitioners and the courts. But the mere fact of recodification did not freeze the criminal law in time: it continued to grow and to change. This was, of course, reflected in the code, which again started to become unwieldy and obscure with the addition of sometimes inconsistent or irrational amendments. One Criminal Code amendment bill was enacted in 1955, the year the new code came into force; two were enacted in 1956. Four were introduced and one enacted in 1957, four in 1958, and so on. As we have seen, a solution to the problem, or at least to the specific need to provide continuity and ensure that any amendment was logically consistent with the code as a whole, had been put forward by Thomas Church as far back as 1937, when he had suggested the creation of a permanent law reform commission.

This concept was neither new nor original. Such commissions had been appointed in New York in 1934, and in New Zealand in 1936, a year before Church broached the topic in the Commons.[62] Again, war turned politicians' minds to other concerns, and no more was heard of the idea until the mid-1950s, when it became the subject of debate in the pages of the *Canadian Bar Review*. Eminent legal practitioners advocated the concept of permanent, ongoing law reform, and put forward various means of achieving this end.[63] The minister of justice agreed with the concept in principle, but in effect poured cold water on the idea of implementing it. One element of his argument deserves quotation at length, because it illustrates perfectly the difficulties faced by an appointed body when it proposes reform measures to a popularly elected legislature.

No legislative body which has been elected by the people for the purpose of amending the law is going to delegate its responsibility for so doing to any organization outside of it. No legislative body is going to act upon the suggestions of any research body unless the credentials of that body for disinterestedness, competence and public interest are beyond question. Thus, the value of the plan we are discussing depends almost wholly upon the sponsors of the legislation. If the legislation proposed were the product of a systematic research effort made by some organization with an established reputation, that obviously would add greatly to the likelihood of its being accepted. But it would be unrealistic to suppose that measures, even so sponsored, which may command a large measure of legal agreement, will necessarily be accorded the same measure of political or legislative agreement by the governments and legislatures to which they are sent.[64]

In contrast to the minister's opinion, the Canadian Bar Association's prestigious Committee on Legal Research thought that the time had come 'for the development of permanent law-reform machinery in Canada,' although it preferred 'to leave the subject with a simple endorsement of the idea and a suggestion that it might well be referred to the legal research foundation to be established if our recommendation to that effect is accepted.'[65] This position was endorsed and adopted by a report of the Commissioners on Uniformity of Legislation the following year;[66] it was thus evident that by the latter part of the decade a large part of the legal profession supported the idea of some form of permanent organization to consider and draft law reform measures for submission to Parliament.

There was no response in the legislature until the mid-1960s, when the political climate induced by minority governments made the administration more amenable to positive reform. Even then, the first initiative did not come from the government. In 1966 Richard Bell, a legal critic for the opposition and a member of the Ontario Law Reform Commission since its inception in 1964,[67] introduced a private members' bill to establish a law reform commission. The bill did not get beyond first reading.[68] Undaunted, Bell introduced the measure in the 1967 session, with the same result.[69] But this time he followed up his bill with a question to Pierre Trudeau, the minister of justice: had there been any representation from the Canadian Bar Association (CBA) or from any other organization advocating the establishment of a Canadian law reform commission? Yes, replied the minister; as a result of a resolution passed at its annual meeting in 1966, the CBA had suggested the formation of such a body, as had the faculty of law of the University of Saskatchewan. Other representations had also been made.[70] It thus became evident that there was substantial support for such a measure among influential groups in society. Bell lost his seat in the general election that followed this session, but the Conservatives did not lose the initiative, because Bell's bill, now sponsored by another opposition lawyer, Stanley Schumacher, was again read in the opening session of the new Parliament. As before, it did not get beyond first reading.[71] However, considerable additional pressure for a law reform commission was exerted by the findings of the Canadian Committee on Corrections, popularly known as the Ouimet Committee,[72] whose influence has been thoroughly explored in the legal literature.[73] This prodded the government to act. In 1970, the year after the Ouimet Committee's final report, legislation to create a law reform commission was introduced by the minister of justice, John Turner. As he explained, it was well conceived. In addition to the recommendations of the Ouimet Committee and the Justice Department, an extensive study had been made of the Ontario, English, Scottish and New York law reform commissions, and he himself had had talks with the chairmen of these institutions. His bill was the result.[74]

The legislation was enacted in 1970 and implemented the following year. It provided for a full-time deliberative staff of four and two part-time members; of the total, two were to be laymen and the remainder judges or lawyers. Appointments, which would be for a term of seven years for the full-time personnel and three for the part-time members, would be staggered to ensure continuity. The commissioners would be independent of parliamentary direction, and any reports made by the commission were to be tabled in the House of Commons. In brief, the commissioners' mandate was to study and keep under review all statute law, and to make recommendations for its improvement.[75] After settling in, the commissioners published their first report in 1976. Since then they have produced a large body of literature on all aspects of the law – 32 reports, 56 working papers, and over 70 study papers, which can be found on the shelves of professional, public, and university libraries, where those concerning penal law often sit cheek by jowl with the latest edition of the Criminal Code.[76] However, since several of the commission's final reports have been enacted by Parliament, it may well be that the days of Sir John Thompson's variant of codification are numbered. In a laudable effort, the three latest Law Reform Commission reports, for which much of the previous work was a necessary preliminary, constitute the blueprint for a new initiative in Canadian legislation. The two volumes of *Recodifying the Criminal Law* are the draft of the general part and the substantive law of a code, while *Our Criminal Procedure* discusses the philosophical foundation of a forthcoming volume to codify the law of procedure, which will complete the draft code.[77] Unlike the 1954 restructuring of the 1892 code, the new work will be written from first principles generated from 'a deep philosophical probe of criminal law.'[78] Thus, for example, 'indictable' and 'summary' offences will be replaced by 'crime,' which is defined in standard English in the general part.[79]

When the Criminal Code came into force a century ago, it made the criminal law accessible to society as a whole. Increasingly, the public took advantage of that accessibility and interested itself in reform – progressive for the most part, but occasionally regressive. Legislators were influenced to implement such reform in annual legislation, which introduced inconsistencies in the code and made it bulky and unwieldy. The restructuring of 1954 reduced the bulk and removed many of the inconsistencies as well as most of the anomalies incorporated by default or accident in the 1892 legislation. With the creation of the Law Reform

Commission, a permanent organization was established which has been a fruitful source of ideas for progressive change in the criminal law, and has pointed the way to a new model code. Additionally, it has brought continuity to the process of limiting the growth of the present code and in keeping it logically consistent. But the results of their labours do not constitute a foregone conclusion. The commissioners can ponder the law; they can conceive and draft programs of progressive reform; and they can put forward those programs for implementation by Parliament. But politicians march to a different drummer: such measures may be enacted into law in their draft form, but historical legislative experience, from Bacon's to Thompson's, augurs for them the more likely fate of either extensive amendment or ultimate rejection, as government policy or public opinion demands.

Appendix

TABLE 1
Capital felonies in British North America 1829–1841[1]

Felony	Nova Scotia	Lower Canada[2]	Prince Edward Island	New Brunswick	Upper Canada[3]	Canada (Province)
Treason	X		X	X	X	X
Murder	X[4]		X[4]	X[4]	X	X[4]
Attempted murder	X		X			X
Rescuing persons convicted of murder					X	
Rape	X		X	X	X	X
Buggery			X	X	X	X
Carnal knowledge of female under ten	X		X	X	X	X
Robbery with violence	X					X
Robbery			X	X	X	
Burglary with violence	X					X
Burglary			X	X	X	
Showing lights to wreck vessel			X			X
Destruction of a ship			X			
Procuring miscarriage				X		
Refusing to disperse after reading of Riot Act					X	
Arson:						
of a ship			X	X	X	X
of a building			X	X	X	X
Total	7		12	10	11	11

1 Enabling Legislation: Nova Scotia: 1841, 4 Vict., cc. 5, 6, 9; Prince Edward Island: 1829, 10 Geo. IV, c. 11; 1836, 6 Will. IV, c. 22; New Brunswick: 1829, 9 & 10 Geo. IV, c. 21; 1831, 1 Will. IV, cc. 4, 5; Upper Canada: 1833, 3 Will. IV, c. 3; Canada (Province): 1841, 4 & 5 Vict., cc. 25, 26, 27. Capital felonies were those for which the mandatory punishment was that the convicted person 'shall suffer death as a felon.'
2 Neither Quebec nor Lower Canada enacted legislation similar to that listed in this appendix. Rather, on four occasions, the punishment section of an English statute which specified the death penalty was repealed, and banishment from the province was substituted therefor. See 1812, 52 Geo. III, c. 3 (LC); 1824, 4 Geo. IV, cc. 4, 5, 6 (LC).
3 Accessories before the fact to all capital felonies were liable to the same punishment as the principal: 1833, 3 Will. IV, c. 3, s. 12 (UC).
4 Accessories before the fact of murder were liable to the same punishment as the principal.

TABLE 2
Capital felonies in British North America at Confederation[1]

Felony	Nova Scotia	Prince Edward Island	New Brunswick	Canada (Province)	British Columbia[2]
Treason	X	X	X	X	X
Murder	X	X	X	X	X
Attempted murder				X	X
Rape		X	X	X	
Buggery		X	X	X	X
Carnal knowledge of female under ten		X	X	X	
Robbery with violence			X	X	X
Robbery		X			
Burglary with violence			X	X	X
Burglary		X			
Exhibiting lights to wreck vessel		X	X	X	
Destruction of a ship		X			
Piracy					X
Arson:					
of a ship		X	X	X	
of a building		X	X	X	X
Total	2	11	10	11	8

1 Enabling legislation: Nova Scotia: RSNS 1851, cc 155–62; Prince Edward Island: 1869, 32 Vict., c. 19; New Brunswick: 1849, 12 Vict., c. 29; RSNB 1854, cc 149–53; Canada (Province): CSC 1859, cc 90, 91; British Columbia: Proclamation of Governor of British Columbia, 19 November 1858.
2 See HECL IV, 330.

TABLE 3

Capital felonies and offences in the Dominion of Canada 1867–1892

Enabling Legislation	Offence	Punishment
Criminal Law Consolidation Acts 1868–1869		
1868, 31 Vict., c. 69, ss. 2, 3	treason	death
1869, 32 & 33 Vict., c. 20		
s. 1.	murder	death
s. 10	attempted murder	death
s. 49	rape	death
s. 51	carnal knowledge of a female under ten	death
Acts to ameliorate the severity of the law		
1873, 36 Vict., cc. 50, 51	rape	death, life imprisonment, or any term of imprisonment not less than seven years
1877, 40 Vict., c. 28		
s. 1	attempted murder	life imprisonment
s. 2	carnal knowledge of a female under ten	life imprisonment
Capital Felonies, RSC 1886		
c. 140, s. 1	treason	death
c. 162, s. 2	murder	death
c. 162, s. 37	rape	death, life imprisonment, or any term of imprisonment not less than seven years
Capital Offences, Criminal Code, 1892, 55 Vict., c. 29		
s. 65	treason	death
s. 231	murder	death
s. 127	piracy	death or life imprisonment
s. 267	rape	death or life imprisonment

TABLE 4
Regulations for the qualification of lawyers in British North America at Confederation[1]

	Nova Scotia	Lower Canada	Prince Edward Island	New Brunswick	Upper Canada	British Columbia
Clerkship admission examination	n 2	n 5	n 7	n 10	n 13	n 17
Requirement to keep legal terms					n 14	
Attorney admission examination	n 3	n 5	n 8	n 11	n 15	
Barrister admission examination	n 4	n 6	n 9	n 12	n 16	
Years of service for attorney:						
with BCL degree		3				
other degree	4	4	4	3	3	
non-graduate	5	5	5	4	5	
Years of service for barrister:						
with degree					3	
non-graduate					5	
Mandatory years of service before call as barrister:						
graduate			1	1		
non-graduate			1	2		
Total years of service:						
graduates	4	3 or 4	5	4	3	
non-graduates	5	5	6	6	5	

1 Enabling legislation: Nova Scotia: RSNS 1864, c. 130; Lower Canada: RSLC 1861, c. 72; Prince Edward Island: 1848, 11 Vict. c. 31; New Brunswick: 1863, 26 Vict., c. 23; Upper Canada: RSUC 1859, cc. 92, 93, 94; British Columbia: 1863, 26 & 27 Vict., statute 8.

2 The bench of the Supreme Court prepared the examination and published rules for its administration.

3 The bench of the Supreme Court and two barristers prepared and conducted the examinations.

4 Candidates were admitted as barrister and attorney simultaneously, and barristers were also counsel, advocates, proctors, and solicitors, depending on the court they practised in.

5 Examinations were prepared and administered by the Bar Society of Lower Canada.

6 Candidates were admitted as advocate, barrister, attorney, and solicitor simultaneously.

7 The examination was prepared and administered by three barristers.

8 The examination was prepared and administered by the chief justice and one puisne justice, the attorney general, the solicitor general, and the senior barrister.

9 There was no examination, but there was a mandatory one-year term of service as an attorney prior to call.

10 Candidates were examined by members of the bar under the direction of the bench of the Supreme Court.
11 The bench of the Supreme Court and four barristers prepared and administered examinations.
12 There was no examination, but there was a mandatory term of service as attorney to be served prior to call.
13 A candidate was required to pass the Law Society's examination prior to his being enrolled on its books.
14 Intending attorneys and solicitors had to keep two terms, barristers four.
15 Attorneys' examinations were set and administered by the Law Society.
16 There was no examination; the intending barrister was required to be enrolled on the Law Society's books for the requisite number of years.
17 Candidates for admission to the bar as attorney or barrister were required to produce evidence of their having been called elsewhere.

TABLE 5

Number of lawyers in dominion Parliaments from 1867–1891

Election year	Number of members	Number of members who were lawyers	Percentage of the total
1867	181	47	26
1872	200	60	30
1874	206	53	26
1878	206	52	25
1882	210	54	26
1887	215	63	29
1891	215	70	33

SOURCE: J.K. Johnson (ed.) *The Canadian Dictionary of Parliament 1867–1967* (Ottawa: PAC 1968)

Bibliographical Note

Finding Canadian sources is the most difficult task in researching and writing about the origin and development of law in Canada. It was this fact that galvanized Peter Maddaugh to publish his *Bibliography of Canadian Legal History* (Toronto: York University Law Library) in 1972. There are seventy-seven pages in the work and 845 citations. Only 28 come under the rubric 'Criminal Law,' and 14 of these were written by one man, William R. Riddell.

It is fortunate indeed for the beginning legal historian that the roots of both the penal law and the 1892 Criminal Code penetrate deeply the English experience. This was well documented in 1883 by James Fitzjames Stephen in his *History of the Criminal Law of England* (London: Macmillan) and amplified and amended by the work of later legal historians, such as Rupert Cross's 'The Reports of the Criminal Law Commissioners (1833–1848) and the Abortive Bills of 1853' in P. R. Glazebrooke (ed.) *Reshaping the Criminal Law* (London: n.p. 1948), and A.H. Manchester's 'Simplifying the Sources of the Law,' in (1973) 2 *Anglo-American Law Review* 394–413, 527–50. The difficulty of enacting codified legislation in the imperial Parliament during the nineteenth century is explained by Charles Greaves in *Criminal Law Consolidation and Amendment Acts* (London: Sweet and Maxwell 1865), and the details of the law eventually consolidated by Greaves's Acts are set out in Leon Radzinowicz's *History of English Criminal Law* (New York: Macmillan 1948–68). In turn, the penal law is placed in perspective in the context of the English legal experience by William Holdsworth's massive and detailed *History of English Law* 7th ed. (London: Methuen 1966) and, more briefly, in Theodore Plucknett's *Concise History of the Common Law* 5th ed. (London: Butterworth 1956).

Unfortunately, Canada has nothing to compare with Plucknett's *Concise History* or Lawrence Friedman's *History of American Law* (New York: Simon and Schuster 1973) and it seems that a history of Canadian law has never been published. Nor has much systematic work been done in this respect at the provincial level, with a few exceptions. Beamish Murdoch's seminal *Epitome of the Laws of Nova Scotia* (Halifax: Joseph Howe), published in 1832, details the beginnings of the legal system in that province. A similar treatment of the early Quebec experience is Hilda Neatby's brilliant study *The Administration of Justice Under the Quebec Act* (Minneapolis: University of Minnesota Press 1937). Four general histories of Quebec's provincial law have been issued during the past century, the most recent being the seventh edition of André Morel's legalistic cut-and-paste *Histoire du droit* (Montréal: Les Presses de l'Université de Montréal), which came out in 1981. Joseph Lawrence's rambling, unorganized, but informative *Judges of New Brunswick* (Saint John: n.p.) was published between 1905 and 1907; and much of the early history of the legal system in Upper Canada and Ontario is set out in the badly edited but equally informative books of William R. Riddell: *The Bar and Courts of Upper Canada or Ontario* (Toronto: Macmillan 1928) and *The Legal Profession in Upper Canada* (Toronto: Law Society of Upper Canada 1916). In a class by itself is Dale and Lee Gibson's authoritative *Substantial Justice* (Winnipeg: Peguis Publishers 1972) which recounts the Manitoba experience to 1972.

Even less historical work has been done on the criminal law, and certainly nothing to compare with Fitzjames Stephen's volumes. For over eighty years after the enactment of the code the only systematic works with historical content were articles that concentrated on the content and applicability of the law rather than on the reasons that caused it to be enacted by the legislature or enunciated by the bench. These were written by lawyers and were published mainly in legal journals. They include J.D. Cameron's 'Codes and Codification' in (1917) 37 *Canadian Law Times* 177–97; George Crouse's 'Critique of Canadian Criminal Legislation' in (1934) 9 *Canadian Bar Review* 545–78, 601–33; and John Power's 'The Criminal Code of Canada' (LLD thesis, Laval University 1928). A more recent account is Graham Parker's readable but superficial 'Origins of the Canadian Criminal Code' in the first volume of David

Flaherty's *Essays in the History of Canadian Law* (Toronto: The Osgoode Society 1981). In a class by itself is the Law Reform Commission's controversial study of 1976, *Towards a Codification of Canadian Criminal Law* (Ottawa: Information Canada).

The origins of the criminal law do not seem to be of interest to the majority of lawyers, and their journals reflect this attitude. Information can be gleaned from them only by patient study of annual indexes, and the nuggets are few and far between. The exception to this rule is the *Upper Canada Law Journal* (1855–67) and the early volumes of its successor, the *Canada Law Journal* (1868–1922). In large measure the articles and editorials in these issues flowed from the pen of Judge James R. Gowan, who was the *Journal's* financial backer and who used it to publicize anonymously his manifold interests, prime among which was the criminal law. Other legal journals, which have long since ceased publication but in which the occasional item of interest may be found, are *Upper Canada Jurist* (1844–8), *Revue de Législation et de Jurisprudence* (1846–8), *Lower Canada Law Journal* (1865–8), *Legal News* (1878–94), *Revue Légal* (1869–92), *Revue Critique de Legislation et de Jurisprudence du Canada* (1871–5), *La Thémis* (1879–84), and *Canadian Law Times* (1881–1922).

If lawyers generally were uninterested and uninformed about the development of the criminal law and the changes effected by the code, the public was even more so, and its indifference was mirrored by the press. There were at least four techniques by which parliamentary news could be covered: verbatim accounts of debates; reportorial condensation supported by verbatim quotation; reportorial comment; and editorials. Often, when the subject was controversial and debate was acrimonious and lengthy, journalistic efforts were supplemented by letters to the editor. In general, when the subject-matter was the criminal law per se, the second and third methods were employed, usually very sparsely. In fact, after a prolonged examination of newspapers during which not one letter to the editor on the subject was discovered, it is my opinion that in most papers, coverage of the evolution of criminal law and the code was used as a filler when no more readable news was available. And this was particularly the case as the distance from Ottawa increased. In newspapers on the east and west coasts and the prairies, where telegraph costs were substantial, local events often took precedence over all but the most important parliamentary news. When the longer and more discursive written accounts from parliamentary correspondents of such newspapers arrived by post, days after the events reported, much of the news was stale and was used only if the local scene was quiet. Thus, if one did not read the Ottawa or Toronto papers, it was all but impossible to form a coherent picture of the progress of legislation having to do with criminal law. Even in cities where there was sustained coverage, one could not be certain of getting the facts, because most papers were party organs. Therefore, the Liberal journals concentrated on flaws in government legislation, while the Tory press praised it; and both preferred to concentrate on the personalities involved in the debate rather than on its substance. Even so, it must be admitted that the best coverage of the evolution of the code was given by the *Toronto Globe*, a Liberal party organ, and the Tory *Toronto Mail*; that of the *Globe* was the most complete and the least subjective. Useful books on the subject are Paul Rutherford's *A Victorian Authority: the Daily Press in Late Nineteenth Century Canada* (Toronto: University of Toronto Press 1982) and W.H. Kesterton's *A History of Journalism in Canada* (Toronto: McClelland and Stewart 1967).

Of course, books on the criminal law were published. They can be divided into two classes: books of practice and annotated volumes of the enacted law. The first in the field after 1867 and a typical example of the former is Samuel Clarke's *Treatise on the Criminal Law of Canada*, 1st ed. (Toronto: Carswell 1872). *A Digest of the Criminal Law of Canada* (Toronto: Carswell 1890) by George Burbidge is the best-written and most informative volume of this type. Such works are the norm in common law jurisdictions; arranged topically, they integrate both statute and common law in a discursive commentary. Mr Justice Taschereau's *Criminal Law Consolidation and Amendment Acts* vol. 1, 1st ed. (Montreal: Lovell) of 1874 is an example of the annotation, and follows the civil law tradition. The law is set out as enacted and each section is accompanied by a commentary that includes citations to the latest decisions of the courts. Both types of book serve the same purpose: to give the user the authoritative version of the law at the date of publication. But Taschereau set the style for Canada, and most succeeding commentators have followed his pattern, particularly after the enactment of the Criminal Code, which itself was drafted topically on the plan of a civil law enactment. In fact, Taschereau was the first to annotate the new statute in his 1893 *Criminal Code of the Dominion of Canada* (Toronto: Carswell), and was closely followed by James Crankshaw's *Criminal Code of Canada* (Montreal: Whiteford and Theoret) in 1894. Both volumes are prefaced by useful and informative essays.

Unfortunately, none of the protagonists in the development of Canadian criminal law left an autobiographical record, although some of them, such as Burbidge and Gowan, were gifted writers. Nor, generally, have they been well served in this respect by their biographers, who tend to omit any mention of the criminal law, to mention it in passing, or to enumerate the achievements of their subjects without the connecting tissue of analysis. For example, there is no mention in Creighton's *John A. Macdonald: The Old Chieftain* (Toronto: Macmillan 1965) of the 1859 Consolidated Statutes of Canada or of the Criminal Consolidation Acts of 1868–9. John Castell Hopkins does devote two pages to the Criminal Code in *Life and Work of the Rt. Hon. Sir John Thompson* (Toronto: United Publishing 1895), but his treatment, though well written, is superficial and uncritical. In *Life of Hon. James R. Gowan* (Toronto: University Press 1911) Henry Ardagh details most of the salient facts of the senator's career, but his is a lifeless account in which fact follows fact in chronological order. Exceptions to these traditions are Peter Waite's *The Man From Halifax* (Toronto: University of Toronto Press 1985), in which he gives a brief but penetrating overview of the events of 1891–2 that led to the passage of the code, and Mark Fisher's well-researched dissertation 'Sir James Robert Gowan' (University of New Brunswick 1971), which sets out many of Gowan's accomplishments in an interesting and integrated account.

At least Macdonald, Thompson, and Gowan had biographers. Sir Alexander Campbell, George Burbidge, James Sedgewick, and Charles Masters were not so fortunate. Nor did the latter three leave any papers that can be traced, excepting official correspondence in departmental records. But the Public Archives of Canada (PAC) holds Campbell's papers as well as those of Sir John A. Macdonald, Sir James Gowan, Sir John Thompson, and William Miller. Edward Blake's records are lodged in the Provincial Archives of Ontario, as is another collection of Gowan's letters, the James Small and James Gowan Papers. Sir James Fitzjames Stephen's collection is in the archives of Cambridge University Library.

In many instances the most informative sources are government records. These are found in a variety of locations. Reports of the commissioners who codified the Nova Scotia and New Brunswick statutes are printed as prefaces in the *Revised Statutes of Nova Scotia* (Halifax 1851), and *Revised Statutes of New Brunswick* (Fredericton 1854). This was usually the practice in Upper and Lower Canada after Union; but in some editions of the various consolidations and revisions the reports are omitted. If this is the case, the relevant reports are reproduced as appendices to the *Journal* of the Legislative Assembly. Invaluable guides to all of this material are the three volumes of Olga Bishop: *Publications of the Governments of Nova Scotia, Prince Edward Island, New Brunswick 1758–1952*

(Ottawa: National Library 1957), *Publications of the Province of Upper Canada and of Great Britain* (Toronto: Queen's Printer 1954), and *Publications of the Government of the Province of Canada* (Ottawa: National Library 1963). After 1867 a great deal of information can be found in the *Debates* and *Journals* of Commons and Senate, and in the sessional papers of Parliament. However, for various reasons, not all sessional papers were published. In such cases it is a worthwhile exercise to review the legal journals of the period, because it was sometimes the case that a government official would edit an unpublished paper for private publication if it was of interest to the legal profession. This was the case, for example, with the reports of the commissioners who drafted the Revised Statutes of Canada in the early 1880s, which were eventually published in (1887) 10 *Legal News* 187–92 and (1888) 11, 57–9.

Much of the English experience is recorded in Hansard and the Command and Sessional Papers of the imperial Parliament. A complete set of these volumes is held in the House of Lords' library, but in very few other locations. Most North American libraries do not have this collection, so that the researcher must work with Readex Microprint cards, which makes for very laborious and time-consuming research. But there is one shortcut: the Irish University Press series of *British Parliamentary Papers* (Shannon, Ireland 1968–72) reproduces facsimile editions of all legislative documents on codification and consolidations in the six volumes entitled 'Legal Administration: Criminal Law.'

Soon after Confederation the Department of Justice became the gathering-point for all proposals to reform or otherwise change the criminal law, and the bills of 1891 and 1892 were drafted within its precincts. Thus one would suppose that the logical place to seek information would be the departmental files. Logical it may be; practically, there are difficulties. From the earliest days of its existence the Department of Justice maintained an efficient and comprehensive record system consisting of an annual mail register, file index, files, and letterbooks in which answers to incoming mail and mail generated by the department were recorded. What remains of the system is confusing. The mail registers (RG13, A2) have been deposited in the PAC, as have the indexes (RG13, A1), letterbooks (RG13, A3) and some of the files (RG13, A1). But the file numbers of those so deposited bear no resemblance to the numbers they were allocated in the mail registers. Twice before the documents were transferred to the PAC, the Justice Department consolidated the files and assigned new numbers to the consolidations. The system or rationale that governed the consolidations has not been discovered, nor has a record of the new numbers. While many of the documents in the consolidated files can be traced by reviewing the mail register and the letterbook for the relevant date, not all of the files were sent to the PAC. Presumably, some were destroyed during the consolidations, and many files, some dating back over a hundred years, were retained by the Department of Justice. Thus, a researcher who locates a desired item in the mail register may not find it in the consolidated files held in the PAC. If this is the case, it may have been destroyed or it may be in the archives of the Justice Department. While the holdings of the PAC are open to the public those of the Department of Justice are not, and permission to view its old files is difficult to obtain and may take years to be granted. The problem is that the department does not have personnel to fetch and carry files to accommodate a researcher engaged in a hunting expedition for documents which may or may not exist, nor does it have facilities comparable to those at the PAC where such documents may be examined. A request for permission to view departmental records must specify by file number which items are to be examined. Since the only file numbers that can be supplied are those from the mail registers or letterbooks, and since these do not correspond to the numbers of the consolidated files in the department, an impasse is quickly reached which only unrelenting persistence on the part of the researcher can overcome. Needless to say, the majority of the documents pertaining to the 1892 code are still held by the department (in particular, files 65/92 and 63/94).

Notes

ABBREVIATIONS

CC   Desmond H. Brown 'The Canadian Criminal Code 1892: A
            Comparative Study in Codification' (PHD thesis, University of
            Alberta 1986)

DCB   George W. Brown et al. (eds) *Dictionary of Canadian Biography*
            (Toronto: University of Toronto Press 1966–86)

DNB   Leslie Stephen and Sydney Lee (eds) *Dictionary of National
            Biography* (London: Smith, Elder 1908)

HCL   James Fitzjames Stephen *A History of the Criminal Law of England*
            (London: Macmillan 1883)

HECL   Leon Radzinowicz *A History of English Criminal Law* (New York:
            Macmillan 1948–68)

HEL   William S. Holdsworth *A History of English Law* 7th ed. (London:
            Methuen 1966)

MDCB   W. Stewart Wallace (ed.) *The Macmillan Dictionary of Biography*
            3rd ed. (Toronto: Macmillan 1963)

PAC   Public Archives of Canada

Parl. Papers Great Britain, Parliament *Parliamentary Papers*

SOR   Great Britain, House of Commons, Statutes of the Realm 1810–
            22 (reprinted London: Dawson 1963)

INTRODUCTION

1 *Parl. Papers* Commission, 1883, xxvi, 105
2 Great Britain, Parliament, Hansard, 23 February 1880, cols. 1236–7 (here-inafter Hansard)
3 By 1855 £49,716 had been expended on the several commissions. It is not likely that the expenditure over the next twenty-five years was less than this amount: *Parl. Papers* criminal and statute law commissions, 1854–55 [210] xliii, 403–6.

CHAPTER 1 DEFINITIONS AND DESCRIPTIONS

1 Cited in *Oxford English Dictionary* (hereinafter *OED*). Although 'codify' was a new word, it was not without precedent. 'Sanctify' and 'fortify' are older cognates of the term in the sense that they comprise an English derivative of a Latin root together with the suffix 'fy' from the Latin *facere*, to make. In the case of 'codify,' 'code,' from *codex* (a book of laws), was joined to '-fy': ibid.
2 John Bowring (ed.) *The Works of Jeremy Bentham* vol. 3 (1843; reprinted New York: Russell and Russell 1962) 155–210
3 'Codify' is not defined in any of the six English law dictionaries available to me.
4 Bowring *Works* vol. 4, 451; *OED*
5 Bowring *Works* vol. 3, 205
6 Ibid. vol. 1, 54
7 Ibid. vol. 3, 205
8 Ibid. vol. 2, 539; vol. 3, 158; *OED*
9 For example, Bentham contemplated codes of civil, criminal, maritime, military, and economic law. For a complete list see Bowring *Works* vol. 3, 156.
10 Ibid. 205
11 Ibid. 209–10
12 For example, if a statute imposed one penalty for a specific offence and a later enactment imposed another, the draftsman of a code that combined the two would either make a decision himself or point out the conflict to the legislature for its decision. His course of action would depend on his terms of reference. See the informative discussion on this point in Charles S. Greaves *Criminal Law Consolidation and Amendment Acts* (London: Sweet and Maxwell 1862) xii.

13 MacKenzie D. Chalmers 'An Experiment in Codification' (1886) 6 *Law Quarterly Review* 125
14 Ibid. 126
15 Ibid.
16 Ibid.
17 *Jowitt's Dictionary of English Law* 2d ed. 'Codify' and its derivatives are to be distinguished from 'consolidation' and 'statute law revision.' Unfortunately, law lexicons do not give abstract legal definitions of these expressions, but rather combine them with other terms; the result is a description at length, rather than a definition. However, the work has been done for the legal lexicographers by Mr Justice Scarman, who has given both of the terms concise and authoritative definitions. He renders consolidation as 'the technique whereby existing statute law on a given topic is reduced from many statutes into one,' while statute law revision 'is a process whereby obsolete and unnecessary enactments are removed from the statute book.' Leslie Scarman *A Code of English Law* (Hull, UK: University of Hull 1966) 5. See also *OED*, which traces the historical development of the word 'consolidation' as defined by Scarman.
18 For a detailed description of this process see CC 27–56.
19 *Grand Larousse de la langue française* (1972)
20 Mary P. Mack *Jeremy Bentham* (London: Heinemann 1962) 361, 407–29. See also Elie Halévy *The Growth of Philosophic Radicalism* translated by Mary Morris (Boston: Beacon Press 1955) 165–73.
21 Bowring *Works* vol. 1, xiv
22 Ibid. vol. 3, 156
23 Ibid. vol. 4, 436
24 The derivation of 'codify' and 'codification' is 'probably from modern French'; *OED*.
25 There is no entry for 'codifier' in any available French legal dictionary.
26 *The Continental Legal History Series* vol. 1: *A General Survey of Continental Legal History* (1912; reprinted New York: A.M. Kelly 1968) 448 (hereinafter *General Survey*). See also *The German Civil Code* translated by Ian S. Forrester (South Hackensack, NJ: Rothman 1975) xii–xiv.
27 *General Survey* 448
28 *Duden: Das große Wörterbuch der deutschen Sprache in sechs Bänden* (1976)
29 Like English and French law dictionaries, no available German law dictionary defines the verb.
30 William Smith *Dictionary of Greek and Roman Antiquities* (London 1856) 301; John H. Wigmore *A Panorama of the World's Legal Systems* (Washington,

DC: Washington Law Book Co. 1936) 17. For a discussion of the development of ancient codes, see CC 17–24.

31 It is to be noted that these definitions express, in general terms, what
enacted codes are in fact, rather than what they might be or should be.
In a most able exposition (*The Science of Law* [New York: 1878] 365–
95), Sheldon Amos, professor of jurisprudence at London University,
examines the basic principles on which codes should be constructed, the
theoretical forms they might take, and the practical difficulties that
have limited them to the less than perfect forms they have assumed in
various jurisdictions. See also Courtenay Ilbert *Legislative Forms and
Methods* (Oxford: Clarendon Press 1901) 122–9 for British theory and practice; and Roscoe Pound *Jurisprudence* vol. 3 (St Paul, Minn.: West Publishing 1959) 725–32 for an abbreviated discussion of the theoretical aspects
of codification. For a thought-provoking discussion of the general principles on which criminal law reform in Canada should be based, and a
controversial outline for a fundamental revision of the Criminal Code, see
Law Reform Commission of Canada *Towards a Codification of Canadian
Criminal Law* (Ottawa: Information Canada 1976).

32 If an attempt were made to draft a definition of 'code' which included all
the main variants of the concept, it would be so long and tortuous as
to be virtually unintelligible. To get some idea of what would be involved
in such a definition, see Bruce Donald 'Codification in Common Law
Systems' (1973) 47 *Australian Law Journal* 160–77. In his interesting and
informative but sometimes confusing essay, Donald divides codes into two
main groups under which are a total of seven subgroups. One begins
to appreciate the difficulties of definition when it is found that his two
main classifications are entitled 'Codification of all rules of law pertaining
to a given subject, regardless of original source' and 'Codification of
laws from the same original source.'

33 *Jowitt's Dictionary* s.v. 'code'

34 S.P. Sçott (trans.) *The Civil Law* vol. 12 (1932; reprinted New York: AMS
Press 1973) 5

35 *General Survey* 285; Frederick H. Lawson *A Common Lawyer Looks at the
Civil Law* (Ann Arbor, Mich.: University of Michigan Law School 1953) 11,
54, 75. Although the arrangement of an ancient code may seem unsystematic and irrational to the modern reader, it was a logical and reasonable
order for the people who actually used it. See Sir Henry Maine 'Ancient
Ideas Respecting the Arrangement of Codes' (May 1879) 25 *Fortnightly
Review* 764–8.

36 *General Survey* 284, 287

37 Lawson *Common Lawyer* 54
38 Marc Ancel 'Introduction' in G.O. Mueller (ed.) *The French Penal Code* (London: Sweet and Maxwell 1960) 11; Horst Schroeder 'Introduction' in G.O. Mueller (ed.) *The German Penal Code* (London: Sweet and Maxwell, 1961) 1
39 The 'general' part lays down the principles on which the code is based. It contains such information as the classification of criminal acts – violations, misdemeanours, felonies, and other relevant detail – definitions of punishments, elements of an offence, and limits of jurisdiction in terms of time and space. The 'special' part defines acts that are held to be criminal, delineates the classification of each offence, and lays down the range of punishment for the offence. For detail see cc 43–4.
40 *General Survey* 446
41 Canada, Parliament, House of Commons *Debates* 12 April 1892, col. 1312 (hereinafter House of Commons *Debates*)
42 Ibid.
43 (1917) 37 *Canadian Law Times* 195
44 *Towards a Codification* 28, 33 (see note 31 above). For a recent articulation of this view, but in a rather obscure formulation, see Graham Parker 'The Origins of the Canadian Criminal Code' in David H. Flaherty (ed.) *Essays in the History of Canadian Law* vol. 1 (Toronto: The Osgoode Society 1981) 249.
45 Canada, Parliament, Senate *Debates* 16 April 1892, 156 (hereinafter Senate *Debates*)
46 Lawson makes no distinction between the 'comprehensive criminal codes' of the common law countries and the codified enactments of states in the civil law tradition (see the discussion in his *Common Lawyer* at 52–4). Likewise, Williams does not distinguish between the criminal codes of common and civil law jurisdictions. He also comments favourably on the Canadian code and its comprehensive coverage of the criminal law, and on the fact that it simplified further reform, such as the major restructuring of the code in 1954: *Criminal Law* 2d ed. (London: Stevens and Sons 1961) 443.

CHAPTER 2 ATTEMPTS TO CODIFY ENGLISH CRIMINAL LAW

1 For detail on the evolution of the English statute, see cc 64–70.
2 Pitt was speaking in the debate on the Nore Mutiny of 1789. William Cobbett *The Parliamentary History of England* vol. 23 (1806–20; reprinted New York: Johnson Reprint 1966) col. 807.

3 Computed from data in S.G. Edgar (ed.) *Chronological Table of the Statutes* (London: HMSO 1974); see also Claud Mullins *In Quest of Justice* (London: John Murray 1931) 132.

4 Hansard, 9 March 1826, col. 1220

5 In 1794 there were about 150 volumes of reports, which recorded the facts and judgments of several thousand cases. By 1867 there were 1,300 volumes, and the number of cases reported was approximately 100,000: Mullins *Justice* 108.

6 For details see CC 96, 104–6.

7 See, for example, Great Britain, Parliament, House of Commons, *Journal* vol. I, 43, 44, 153. Strictly speaking, the 'penal laws' comprised a body of legislation, enacted from the fourteenth to the nineteenth century, which was designed to discriminate against and oppress Catholics. Penalties ranged from fine and imprisonment to death. From the sixteenth century, at least, usage of the term has been loose, and 'penal law' has often been used as a synonym for 'criminal law.' See Stanley Bindoff 'The Making of the Statute of Artificers' in *Elizabethan Government and Society* (London: Athlone Press 1961) 85–7; *HEL* vol. 6, 661, vol. 12, 344; and *Jowitt's Dictionary of English Law.*

8 CC 96–117

9 Justinian's plan and the resulting legislation are outlined ibid. 22–4.

10 James Spedding (ed.) *The Letters and Life of Francis Bacon* vol. 6 (London: Longmans, Green 1861–74) 71. Bacon also proposed to prepare manuals for the study of the law on the plan of Justinian's *Institutiones*: ibid. 70. See CC 106–9 for detail on Bacon's earlier proposals to bring order to English law.

11 Legal practitioners not only formed the largest professional group in the House of Commons from the fourteenth century on, but also, by virtue of their having been bred to the law in an Inn of Court before being allowed to practise, they formed the most intellectually cohesive group. They stood in sharp contrast to occupational groups such as merchants or royal officials who, though bound by common interests, were unlikely to have developed the close ties and attitudes of mind engendered in individuals who had shared a rigorous and technical education. Moreover, while available data show that such men made up between 15 per cent and 17 per cent of the membership in the parliaments of the period, the same sources also confirm the startling rise in the total number of legislators educated at the Inns of Court. In 1529 the figure, including active practitioners, was 66 out of a membership of 310, or 21 per cent; in 1584 this figure had risen to 40 per cent or 187 out of 468; by 1640 well over half the members were Inns of Court men – 61 per cent, or 310

out of a total of 507. In the context of this argument, the significance of
these numbers is that many if not all of these men would view proposed
changes to the legal system from the common perspective of the active
practitioners and consequently would tend to present a uniform front
against such proposals. For detailed statistics see CC appendix 1.

12 For details see CC 120–4.

13 *Dei Delitti e delle Pene* passed through six editions within eighteen months;
it was translated into English in 1768 and into French in 1776.

14 William Blackstone *Commentaries on the Laws of England* 1st ed. (1769;
reprinted Chicago: University of Chicago Press 1979)

15 Bowring *Works* vol. 4, 1–35. It may seem odd to see Blackstone's name
bracketed with Bentham's as a reformer, but when one looks carefully at
Public Wrongs, it is apparent that his strictures on the criminal law as
it existed were pointed and wide-ranging: for example, see page 349,
where he criticizes the rule that forbids counsel to act for a person accused
of felony, or page 381, where the punishments of escheat and forfeiture
are condemned. Moreover, it is to be remembered that the same remarks
were an integral part of the lectures he delivered at Oxford over a
fifteen-year period (1753–67) to many of the future leaders of the nation.
Bentham, of course, was an auditor of Blackstone; see his account of
the lectures and the audience in Bowring *Works* vol. 10, 45. See also Radzinowicz's remarks on this subject in *HECL* vol. 1, 345–8; and
Holdsworth's comments in *HEL* vol. 11, 579.

16 SOR I, vii

17 For commentary and criticism see Henry G. Richardson and George
O. Sayles 'The Early Statutes' (Oct. 1934) *Law Quarterly Review* 200, 540ff;
HEL vol. 4, 310–12; Percy Winfield *The Chief Sources of English Legal
History* (New York: Burt Franklin 1925) 92–5.

18 *HEL* vol. 11, 428

19 1825, 6 Geo. IV, cc. 104, 106–15. For details see Ilbert *Legislative Methods*
50.

20 Ilbert *Legislative Methods* 60–1

21 Hansard, 9 March 1826, col. 1218

22 Ibid.

23 For an extensive coverage of the period, complete with biographical
sketches, see *HECL* vol. 1, 301–449, 497–607.

24 *Parl. Papers* Report from the Select Committee on Criminal Laws, 1819
(585) VIII, 3

25 *Parl. Papers* Report from the Select Committee on the Criminal Law of
England, 1824 (205) IV, 3

26 In all, twenty-three members are recorded as having spoken in 1827 in

this and subsequent debates on criminal law consolidation. All approved the bills in principle and most were laudatory. Hansard, 9 March 1826, cols. 1240–4; 22 February 1827, cols. 642–6; 13 March 1827, cols. 1161–2; 18 May 1827, cols. 937–9.

27 For example, it was not an offence to rob a furnished house which one had rented, whereas it was 'a very serious offence to rob a ready-furnished lodging.' Peel's bill covered both cases: Hansard, 9 March 1826, col. 1223.

28 There were twenty or more acts 'relating to the preservation of [several species] of trees from theft or wilful injury.' Peel proposed to protect all trees with a general statement of the principle: ibid. col. 1220.

29 Ibid., col. 1225. It should be noted that in this period the essential distinction between felony and misdemeanour began to be blurred – that is, when a penalty less than death was substituted as the punishment for committing a felony, while the crime itself was not reclassified as a misdemeanour or lesser offence.

30 Hansard, 13 June 1827, col. 1261

31 Peel was prescient in this respect, for, as Lord Chancellor Jowitt pointed out, 'Parliament was rightly jealous of any attempt to make even the smallest amendment without its knowledge and consent.' Thus, efforts to consolidate the law came to a halt for several years after the Commons discovered that minor amendments that had not been published to the members had been made to the Post Office Consolidation Bill of 1897: W.A. Jowitt Statute Law Revision and Consolidation (Birmingham: University of Birmingham 1951) 10, 16.

32 Hansard, 9 March 1826, col. 1238

33 Ibid. col. 1244. In the next session Peel asked the members not to give a blind opinion: '[O]n the contrary, he wished and expected that the honourable gentlemen would reserve to themselves the power of ex-pressing an opinion on a subject of such vital importance.' Ibid. 22 February 1827, col. 634.

34 Ibid. 9 March 1826, col. 1216

35 Of the thirteen founding states, only five had not systematized their enacted law by 1826. In Massachusetts, for example, at least ten revisions had been issued, the earliest dating from 1641 and the latest from 1823. This last work, the General Laws of Massachusetts, in two volumes, had been edited and rewritten and was arranged topically with a compre-hensive index (Howard Stebbins 'Outline of Massachusetts Statute Law Publications' (1927) 20 Law Library Journal 72–7). Not long after Peel spoke, New York legislators enacted a major revision of the statute law which

had been in preparation since 1824 and which superseded three previous revisions of 1789, 1800, and 1813. The revised edition of 1828 came out in three volumes, and, as in Massachusetts, had been rewritten following a topical arrangement (*McKinney's Consolidated Laws of New York* [St Paul, Minn.: West Publishing 1971] vii–ix). Apart from the numerous articles on codification in current journals (for citations to such articles see *HECL* vol. 1, 577), a direct source of information for Peel on codification was Anthony Hammond, whom he employed to draft consolidating legislation. Hammond, who was one of the experts consulted by the New York commissioners, had published several works on codification, including several draft codes, and had written virtually all of the report of the Criminal Law Commission of 1824, in which there were copious references to the enacted codes of the civil law jurisdictions of the Continent and Louisiana.

36 Hansard, 9 March 1826, col. 1237
37 Gerrit Judd *Members of Parliament 1734–1832* (New Haven: Yale University Press 1955) 88
38 Hansard, 9 March 1826, col. 1239
39 Ibid. col. 1239; see also cols. 1217, 1240; 22 February 1827, col. 633; 13 March 1827, col. 1155.
40 Ibid. 9 March 1826, col. 1239
41 See, for example, Hansard, 22 February 1827, cols. 632–42; 13 March 1827, cols. 1155–62; 18 May 1827, cols. 934–7.
42 Perhaps the most famous of the modern codifications, the Code Napoléon or, more correctly, the Code civil, was drafted over a period of four years (1800–1804) by a committee of conservative judges and lawyers convened by Napoleon during a relatively calm period during those troubled times. The draft 'consisted of thirty-six laws; these were voted and put into force, one after another, from March, 1803, to March, 1804' (*General Survey* 283). Finally, they were all incorporated in the Civil Code of the French, which was enacted as law on 21 March 1804; ibid. 284.
43 Concerning procedure, 1826, 7 Geo. IV, c. 64; 1827, 7 & 8 Geo. IV, c. 28; larceny, 1827, 7 & 8 Geo. IV, c. 29; malicious damage to property, 1827, 7 & 8 Geo. IV, c. 30; offences against the person, 1828, 9 Geo. IV, c. 31; concerning forgery, 1830, 1 Will. IV, c. 66. Over two hundred statutes were repealed by these acts and by the Statute Law Revision Act, 1827, 7 & 8 Geo. IV, c. 27.
44 From the fourteenth century on, if a statute was divided into two or more parts, each consisted of one sentence and became a section of the

chapter. A long, rambling form of enacting words was always included in the first section. But the first phrase of those words, 'be it enacted' or words of similar import, was the first phrase of every succeeding section, in order to extend the coverage of the formula to their provisions. For a variety of reasons the texts became 'long, full of enumerations, exceptions, provisions, saving clauses and the like': Theodore F. Plucknett *A Concise History of the Common Law* 5th ed. (London: Butterworth 1956) 421–3. But they could not be punctuated by a period, unless the period was followed by enacting words, because the coverage of the formula terminated with the period. By the eighteenth century a statute consisted of one or more interminably long sentences without any internal subdivisions such as subsections or independent clauses. A typical example is section 1 of the Quebec Act (1774, 14 Geo. III, c. 31), a sentence of 597 words. For a discussion of the evolution of the English statute see cc 64–8.

45 Section 8 replaced 1714, 1 Geo. I, stat. 2, c. 5, ss. 4, 6; 1739, 13 Geo. II, c. 21; 1801, 41 Geo. III, c. 24; 1816, 56 Geo. III, c. 125. See Statute Law Revision Act, 1827, 7 & 8 Geo. IV, c. 27, for details.

46 See the excerpts from his speeches quoted in *HECL* vol. 1, 569, n. 7.

47 Hansard, 9 March 1826, col. 1239

48 Bowring *Works* vol. 10, 471, 574–6; vol. 11, 33, 36, 61–2; *DNB* vol. 3, 1356–66; Nicholas Underhill *The Lord Chancellor* (Lavenham, Suffolk: Terence Dalton 1978) 173–7; John Eardley-Wilmot *Lord Brougham's Acts and Bills* (London: Longman, Brown, Green 1857) xiii–xvii; *HECL* vol. 1, 355

49 *Parl. Papers* First Report on Criminal Law, 1834 (537) XXVI, 3

50 Ibid.

51 Rupert Cross 'The Reports of the Criminal Law Commissioners (1833–1849) and the Abortive Bills of 1853' in P.R. Glazebrooke (ed.) *Reshaping the Criminal Law* (London: n.p. 1948) 8. Cross gives biographical sketches of the commissioners and discusses the legal innovations recommended by the several reports. For an informed contemporary view of the subject, see Greaves *Consolidation Acts*, vii–ix.

52 Hansard, 29 March 1844, col. 1599

53 For example, the first five words were omitted from the wording of the first phrase of the quoted clause of Peel's malicious damage to property act, and the punishment of death was mitigated to transportation in accordance with the provisions of 1827, 7 & 8 Geo. IV, c. 30, s. 8, and 1841, 4 & 5 Vict. c. 56, s. 2. Otherwise, the text was unaltered: *Parl. Papers* Seventh Report on Criminal Law, 1843 [448] XIX, 173.

54 *Parl. Papers* Seventh Report on Criminal Law, 1843 [448] XIX, ii, 113–283

55 *Parl. Papers* First Report on Criminal Law, 1834 (537) xxvi, 5
56 *Parl. Papers* Seventh Report on Criminal Law, 1843 [448] xix, 12
57 Hansard, 29 March 1844, cols. 1598–9
58 Ibid. 13 May 1844, cols. 1005–15
59 *Parl. Papers* Fourth Report on Criminal Law, 1848 [940] xxvii, 70; Fifth Report on Criminal Law, 1849 [1100] xxi
60 Tumultuous petitioning, 1661, 13 Chas. ii, stat. i, c. 5. For details see Ernest L. Woodward *The Age of Reform, 1815–1870* (Oxford: Clarendon Press 1954) 139, and *HEL* vol. 6, 167.
61 Hansard, 22 June 1848, col. 991
62 Ibid. col. 992
63 Greaves *Consolidation Acts* ix–xii; review of 'Copies of the Lord Chancellor's Letters to the Judges on the Criminal Law Bills of the Last Session, and Copies of Their Answers Thereto' (1854) 99 *Edinburgh Review* 573–4
64 *Parl. Papers* Copies of the Lord Chancellor's Letters to the Judges and of Their Answers respecting the Criminal Law Bills of Last Session, 1854 [303] liii, 392
65 Ibid. 399; see also 394, 395, 396, and 397. For witty and penetrating criticism of the judges' views, see the review cited in note 63 above, and Cross 'Abortive Bills,' 9.
66 Greaves *Consolidation Acts* xii, xx–xxii; Cross 'Abortive Bills' 10
67 Hansard, 14 February 1861, cols. 439–44
68 Greaves *Consolidation Acts* xxiii
69 Ibid. xii
70 Lord Brougham's Act, or An Act for Shortening the Language Used in Acts of Parliament, 1850, 13 & 14 Vict., c. 21, s. 2., abolished the practice of icluding words of enactment in every section.
71 1861, 24 & 25 Vict., c. 97, s. 11. The text is reproduced on page 25. The repealed statutes were 1827, 7 & 8 Geo. iv, c. 30, s. 8; 1841, 4 & 5 Vict., c. 56, s. 2; 1860, 23 & 24 Vict., c. 29.
72 Stebbins 'Massachusetts Statute Publications' 76–8
73 George Martin *Causes and Conflicts* (Boston: Houghton and Mifflin 1970) 146
74 Ibid. 154
75 A.C. Patra 'Historical Introduction to the Indian Penal Code' in *Essays on the Indian Penal Code* (Bombay: N.M. Tripathi 1962) 35, 37. See also *HCL* vol. 3, 302–3, who explained Macaulay's method in detail, including the use of concrete examples to explain and demonstrate the substantive matter.
76 The Indian system can be employed, said Stephen, 'only where the

legislative body can afford to speak its mind with emphatic clearness, and is small enough and powerful enough to have a distinct collective will and to carry it *without being hampered by popular discussion'* (my emphasis): HCL vol. 3, 304; see also 302.

77 Patra *Indian Code* 34, 42; see also HCL vol. 3, 300, where Stephen makes the same points but views the situation from a far different perspective.

78 1861, 24 & 25 Vict., c. 67, ss. 2, 10. For a brief but lucid description of the system in operation see Leslie Stephen *The Life of Sir James Fitzjames Stephen* (London: Smith, Elder 1895) 249–52.

79 Stephen's mother was a lifelong diarist, and his brother Leslie was the famous literary critic and editor of the *Dictionary of National Biography*. Many of the individuals whose names found a place in the pages of the *DNB* were frequent visitors at the Stephen home: Stephen *Life* 60–1 et passim.

80 He had seven children when he left for India. His mediocre performance at the bar, which, combined with his literary earnings, brought in three to four thousand pounds per annum in his best years, is tactfully outlined by his brother (Stephen *Life* 144–8) and stated bluntly by Leon Radzinowicz: '[H]e never became an eminent, or even a successful barrister.' *Sir James Fitzjames Stephen* (London: Bernard Quaritch 1957) 7.

81 See the bibliography of several hundred items appended to Radzinowicz *Stephen* 49–62. This does not include his editorial output.

82 One of the 'most potent influences on his mind was Bentham,' from whom 'he derived the conviction that all law might, and should, be embodied in a series of brief propositions, logically arranged.' Courtenay Ilbert 'Sir James Stephen as a Legislator' (1894) 39 *Law Quarterly Review* 223. See also Stephen *Life* 123, 204, 207, 210.

83 Stephen *Life* 222–5, 284–8: James Colaiaco *James Fitzjames Stephen and the Crisis of Victorian Thought* (London: Macmillan 1983) 8–9

84 Ilbert 'Stephen as a Legislator' 224

85 Radzinowicz *Stephen* 54–5

86 In 1868 Stephen had been engaged to replace temporarily one of the circuit judges; he remarked that it was 'the very easiest work I ever did' (Stephen *Life* 232). He found a similar appointment in 1873 'thoroughly congenial' (Ibid. 343), and during a third term in 1878, he said, 'I have been trying cases and prisoners just like a real judge and I like it very much' (Stephen to Lord Lytton, viceroy of India, 19 July 1877: Stephen Papers, Cambridge University Library, Add. MSS 7349, 14/1, hereinafter Stephen Papers, followed by the numerical designator of the section of the collection.) In his efforts to secure a permanent appointment, Stephen applied for the position of recorder of London at a salary of £3,000

per annum (Stephen to Lytton, 30 January, 15 February 1878, ibid.); he lobbied influential friends such as Lytton and Lord Salisbury, secretary of state for India (Stephen to Lytton, 2 and 23 August 1877, ibid.); and he told Lytton that he had bargained for a judgeship with Lord Chancellor Cairns over the question of his (Stephen's) participation on the Criminal Code Commission of 1878 (8 July 1878, ibid.). The appointment was well worth bargaining for: the salary of a high court judge was £5,000 in contrast to his smaller and uncertain remuneration from the bar and journalism (Stephen to Lytton, 30 October 1878, ibid.). After his elevation to the bench, he wrote to his sister-in-law on 4 January 1879: 'My dearest Emily, I write to tell you that I am out of all my troubles. Cleasby [Justice of the High Court, QBD] has unexpectedly resigned, and I am to succeed him ... One great battle is won, and one great object attained; and now I am free to turn my mind to objects which have long occupied a great part of it, so far as my leisure will allow ... ' (quoted in Stephen *Life* 40). In a letter to Lytton a few days later he said, 'I hope [when] you get this that I shall not only be a judge, but shall be acting as such, instead of codifying which though it has a glamorous kind of sound is in my opinion about the hardest, the most worrying and the dullest work a poor human creature can be put to do' (7 February 1878, Stephen Papers, 14/1).

87 Stephen *Life* 306, 341. Stephen's work paid dividends, however, for its substance was reproduced in his *Digest of the Law of Evidence* (London: Macmillan 1874), which went through eight editions.

88 Radzinowicz *Stephen* 51; Stephen *Life* 304–6. For the interesting and informative story of the Jamaican code, see Martin L. Friedland 'R.S. Wright's Model Criminal Code: A Forgotten Chapter in the History of the Criminal Law' (1981) 1 *Oxford Journal of Legal Studies* 307–46.

89 James Fitzjames Stephen *A Digest of the Criminal Law* 1st ed. (London: Macmillan 1877)

90 Some idea of the compression achieved by Stephen is given by comparing the *Digest*'s 411 pages to Greaves's *Consolidation Acts*, which covered only half of the substantive law and which Greaves issued in a volume of similar size containing 453 pages.

91 James Fitzjames Stephen 'A Penal Code' (1877) 21 *The Fortnightly Review* 367–9. All quotations cited are from this article. For a technical and elaborated discussion of Stephen's method, see the preface to the first edition of his *Digest*, xx–xxiii.

92 Stephen *Digest* art. 218, at 138. For a discussion of the method Stephen employed to coin such definitions, see xiii.

93 Stephen 'Penal Code' 362, n. 1

94 'Codification of the Criminal Law,' *The Times* 8 February 1877; 'Codification of the Criminal Law' *Law Times* 10 February 1877

95 See, for example, the note of thanks for a copy of the *Digest* from the colonial secretary, Lord Carnarvon, 17 May 1877: Stephen Papers, 15/36. Much of this section of the papers is a collection of such letters of acknowledgment.

96 All the references to Holker are from his biography in *DNB* vol. 9, 1027–8.

97 Holker to Stephen, 16 January 1875, Stephen Papers, 14/1

98 Quoted in Stephen *Life* 380

99 Stephen to Holker, 20 January 1877, Lord Chancellor's Office File, 1/42, Public Records Office, Kew Gardens (hereinafter LCO 1/42)

100 Holker to Cairns, 5 March 1877, ibid.

101 *DNB* vol. 3, 672; Underhill *Lord Chancellor* 182. According to Stephen, who had dealings with Cairns over an extended period, the lord chancellor was 'a regular Commander of the Impenetrable Corps': Stephen to Lytton, 8 July 1878, Stephen Papers, 14/1.

102 Ilbert *Legislative Methods* 63–70; Underhill *Lord Chancellor* 182

103 Among other functions, the committee advised the lord chancellor on consolidation measures. Courtenay Ilbert lists the names and appointments of the first members of this committee, which still functions: *Legislative Methods* 63–4.

104 10 April 1877, LCO 1/42

105 Ilbert *Legislative Methods* 69; Friedland 'Wright's Code' 307–9

106 Stephen to Cairns, 10 May 1877, LCO 1/42

107 Stephen to Cairns, 26 May 1877, ibid.

108 Holker to Cairns, 1 June 1877, ibid.

109 Reilly to Cairns, 20 July 1877, ibid.

110 Stephen to Lytton, 2 August 1877, Stephen Papers, 14/1

111 Treasury to Cairns, November 1877; 12 July 1878, LCO 1/42

112 Parts I to VI of the draft code are substantive provisions, that is, the penal code; part VII consists of the code of procedure; schedule II, the third bill, would have repealed over a hundred acts or parts thereof.

113 *Parl. Papers* Criminal Code (Indictable Offences) Bill, s. 5, 1878 (178) II, 5–240; hereinafter, Draft Code 1878

114 The phrase is James Fitzjames Stephen's, who used it in his eloquent and incisive testimony before the Select Committee on the Homicide Bill, *Parl. Papers* Report, 1874 (315) IX, 45–8.

115 W.R. Cornish, Jennifer Hart, A.H. Manchester, and J. Stevenson (eds) *Crime and Law in Nineteenth-Century Britain* (Dublin: Irish University Press 1978) 50

116 Stephen told Lytton that he had just completed his draft code, and continued, 'I think Cairns ought to take a favourable view of my fitness for enforcing the criminal law as he has let me codify it': Stephen to Lytton, 11 October 1877, Stephen Papers, 14/1. The final draft contained 7 parts, 46 chapters, and 425 sections. *Parl. Papers* Criminal Code (Indictable Offences) Bill, 1878 (178), II, 5–240.

117 The arrangement of the index of the 1878 draft code follows exactly that of the *Digest*, except that after the substantive matter a chapter of procedure has been added. The chapters and sections of the draft code and the chapters and articles of the *Digest* follow in approximately the same order, and the content of many sections in the draft code is taken verbatim from the *Digest*. Compare, for example, section 52 of the draft code and article 88 of the *Digest* on unlawful oaths.

118 For example, see Ancel *Penal Code* 15–34.

119 Draft Code 1878, s. 286. For a succinct summary of the many changes, see the list published in *The Times*, 27 June 1878.

120 From the thirteenth century on, a convicted felon's mandatory punishment was forfeiture and death, whereas, in the main, only fines and imprisonment were visited upon the misdemeanant. Moreover, it came to be the rule that although the 'prisoner at the bar' was, in modern terms, required to be in the dock for the whole of his trial, the defendant in a case of misdemeanour was allowed to sit at the table of the court and had many other privileges not accorded the accused felon. While the punishment for many hundreds of felonies had been reduced to less than death during the first half of the nineteenth century, the offences had not been redesignated as misdemeanours or lesser offences. Thus, the anomalous situation existed whereby the felon could receive a lesser punishment than many misdemeanants, but was still subjected to the punitive procedures associated with trial for felony. For the evolution of felony and misdemeanour see Plucknett *Concise History* 442–53, 456–9; for the difference in procedural details, see Courtney J. Kenny *Outlines of Criminal Law* 3d ed. (Cambridge: University Press 1907) 97–9.

121 As Glanville Williams explains in the preface to his *Criminal Law*, the book was written to supply this need in English law; indeed, its subtitle is 'The General Part.'

122 Cairns to Statute Law Committee, 22 November 1877, LCO 1/42

123 Reilly's remarks are dated 6 December 1877. The committee submitted its memorandum on 2 January 1878: LCO 1/42.

124 (1877) 2 *The Nineteenth Century* 190–216

125 Ibid. 739–59

126 Stephen to Lytton, 2 January 1878, Stephen Papers, 14/1. The concept

was a logical advance on the civil law system, which had retained separate codes, and it was followed by most if not all common law jurisdictions, which have subsequently enacted such legislation. However, the idea may have been Cairns's, since a letter from his secretary to the Treasury stipulated that the Criminal Code was to have been 'prepared in the form of three Bills: but the three were afterwards under the directions of the Lord Chancellor united in one': 11 July 1878, LCO 1/42.

127 Stephen to Lytton, 3 May 1878, Stephen Papers, 14/1

128 (1873) 23 *The Contemporary Review* 5, 18. It is not likely that such criticism would have sounded good coming from a man with no practical experience of the system and who moreover, had been soundly beaten in a recent by-election when standing for a safe party seat: Stephen *Life* 344, 348.

129 (1877) 21 *Fortnightly Review* 362

130 Compare, for example, Stephen's remarks in 'A Penal Code,' especially at pages 364 and 373, with Holker's address, which introduced the last major item of the day. The House adjourned at 1:15 AM: Hansard, 15 May 1878, cols. 1936–57, 1959.

131 Hansard, 15 May 1878, col. 1950

132 There were 648 members in the Twenty-first Parliament (1874–80). Of these 123, or 19 per cent, were barristers, and 218, or 34 per cent, were magistrates or other legal personnel, for a total of 341, or 53 per cent. (These data were derived from *Dod's Parliamentary Companion* [London 1879].)

133 Hansard, 14 May 1878, col. 1957

134 Ibid. 17 June 1878, cols. 1671–3

135 James to Cairns, 24 June 1878, LCO 1/42

136 'The Criminal Code' *The Times* 27 June 1878. The introduction of the draft code generated considerable discussion, much of it favourable, in *The Times*, the *Law Times*, and other journals, and internationally. (See Radzinowicz *Stephen* 63–6 for citations.)

137 Hansard, 8 July 1878, cols. 950–2. Stephen was to receive fifteen hundred guineas for his service on the commission: Lord Chancellor to Treasury, 11 July 1878, LCO 1/42. It was also at this time that Stephen bargained with Cairns for a judgeship: Stephen to Lytton, 8 July 1878, Stephen Papers, 14/1.

138 Hansard, 15 August 1878, col. 2039

139 TUC Parliamentary Committee to Cairns, 7 July 1878, LCO 1/42

140 Hansard, 15 August 1878, col. 2040

141 *Parl. Papers* Report of the Royal Commission on the Law Relating to

Indictable Offences, 1878–9 [c. 2345] xx, 1–48; hereinafter Commissioners' Report 1879. Letter, Cairns to Stephen, 3 January 1879, Stephen Papers, 15/28. See also Stephen to Lytton, 7 February 1879, ibid.

142 Commissioners' Report 1879, 12–13. The draft code contained 8 titles, 45 parts and 552 sections. (It had more sections than its predecessor of 1878; see above, note 116, for comparison.)

143 Twenty-one members spoke in the debate – sixteen from the opposition and five Conservatives. Of the total, sixteen were barristers. (These data were generated from *Dod's Parliamentary Companion*.)

144 Hansard, 3 April 1879, cols. 310–24. The quotation is at col. 324.

145 Ibid. cols. 326, 330 et passim

146 Ibid. col. 325

147 Ibid.

148 Ibid. cols. 323, 346

149 'The Criminal Code' *The Times* 18 April 1879. It is noticeable in Stephen's correspondence with Lytton that references to the Criminal Code decline very sharply after his elevation to the bench. Moreover, another of the sources of information about the progress of legislation, the Lord Chancellor's Office File, is silent for this period. There is a gap of seven years – from 1879 to 1886 – in the correspondence.

150 Hansard, 5 May 1879, col. 1750

151 Ibid. col. 1751

152 Ibid. cols. 1576–8

153 Ibid. col. 1760

154 Ibid. col. 1772

155 Cockburn's criticism of detail runs to sixteen of eighteen printed folio sheets. His concern with summary offences is expressed on page 9: *Parl. Papers* copy of letter from Lord Chief Justice of England, dated 12 June 1879 concerning the Criminal Code Bill, 1878–9 [232] LIX, 233–57.

156 On the same day that Cockburn dispatched the letter, Sir Henry James asked that the letter be tabled in the Commons (Hansard, 16 June 1879, col. 1915). On 26 June an edited version appeared in *The Times*, after the letter had been published as a Parliamentary Paper, and yet another edited version came out in the *Law Journal* of 28 June. The news was soon given wide publicity in Canadian and American legal circles: see (August 1879) 2 *Montreal Legal News* 280; (August 1879) 15 *Canada Law Journal* 197; (August 1879) 20 *Albany Law Journal* 140.

157 Holker to Stephen, 8 July 1879, Stephen Papers, 15/95

158 Hansard, 23 February 1880, cols. 1239–40

159 Ibid. col. 1242

160 Ibid. cols. 1242–5
161 It is of interest to note that in this, the last attempt ever made to codify
English criminal law, the chief protagonists were, as they had been in the
past, the lord chancellor, his chief law officers, and the lawyers of the
opposition. Altogether there were forty speakers in the debates of 1878,
1879, and 1880, and many spoke several times; twenty-seven, or 70
per cent, were barristers, and eighteen of these were members of the
opposition. (These data were derived from *Dod's Parliamentary Companion*.)
162 For other interpretations, see A.H. Manchester 'Simplifying the Sources
of the Law' (1973) 2 *Anglo-American Law Review* 546–50; and Friedland
'Wright's Criminal Code' 324–5.

CHAPTER 3 THE ORIGIN AND DEVELOPMENT OF LEGAL SYSTEMS IN BRITISH NORTH AMERICA

1 Jonathan Belcher was appointed chief justice by the Crown in response to
a request from Governor Hopson after officers of the courts had been
accused of libel and partiality: *DCB* vol. 4, 50.
2 Charles Townshend *Historical Account of the Courts of Judicature in Nova
Scotia* (Toronto: Carswell 1900) 45
3 See *Blankard* v. *Goldy* (1694) 2 Salkeld 411, 91 ER 356 (KB); *Case 15 –
Anonymous* (1722) 2 P. Wms. 75, 24 ER 646 (KB); and *Campbell* v. *Hall* (1774)
1 Cowp. 204, 98 ER 1045 for a full discussion of how English possessions
were perceived to have received English law. For commentary on these
cases, see Thomas G. Barnes 'As Near as May Be Agreeable to the Laws
of This Kingdom: Legal Birthright and Legal Baggage at Chebucto,
1749' in Peter Waite, Sandra Oxner, and Thomas G. Barnes (eds) *Law in a
Colonial Society* (Toronto: Carswell 1984). In his analysis Barnes asserts
that Nova Scotia was 'a colony acquired by conquest confirmed by treaty'
(at 14). In terms of constitutional law, this is a debatable point. Certainly,
earlier authoritative commentators did not agree with Barnes: see Thomas
C. Haliburton *History of Nova Scotia* vol. 1 (1829; reprinted Belleville,
Ont.: Mika Press 1973) 8, 39; William Forsyth *Cases and Opinions on Constitutional Law* (London: Stevens and Haynes 1869) 26; George W. Burbidge
A Digest of the Criminal Law of Canada (Toronto: Carswell 1890) 12. See
also the Treaty of Utrecht, wherein there is no mention of the cession of
Acadia to Great Britain, but in which article 14 stipulates that '[i]t is
expresly [sic] provided, that in all the said Places and Colonies to be
yielded and *restored* by the most Christian King ... ' (my italics); in Fred L.
Israel (ed.) *Major Peace Treaties of Modern History* vol. 1 (New York:

Chelsea House 1967) 210. Of course, this is now of academic interest only. What is of continuing importance is that the people of Nova Scotia perceived themselves to be inhabitants of a colony acquired by peaceful settlement and developed their law accordingly. See, for example, the preamble to 1759, 33 Geo. II, c. 3 (NS), which states: '[T]his Province of Nova Scotia, or Acadie, and the property thereof did always of right belong to the Crown of England, both by priority of discovery and ancient possession.'

4 Lawrence M. Friedman *A History of American Law* (New York: Simon and Schuster 1973) 32. The following discussion is based on Friedman's excellent summary, 'American Law in the Colonial Period,' 29–90; see also 275–6.

5 For the English experience see CC 57–60.

6 Beamish Murdoch 'An Essay on the Origin and Sources of the Law of Nova Scotia, in *Law in a Colonial Society* 190, 193; and *HECL* vol. 1, 1–7

7 William S. MacNutt *The Atlantic Provinces* (Toronto: McClelland and Stewart 1965); Townshend *Courts* 46. For a more comprehensive account of the court system, see Haliburton *History* vol. 1, 162–4. Townshend and Haliburton differ in detail, however, and their accounts are sometimes difficult to reconcile. Haliburton's account is the more coherent of the two, but it is not documented. Townshend quotes copiously from cited sources.

8 Townshend *Courts* 46. The author states, 'It has not been made very clear to me exactly to what extent [Courts of General Sessions] exercised jurisdiction in civil and criminal matters.' If, however, their powers were similar to those of Quarter Sessions in England (Haliburton *History* vol. 1, 163; vol. 2, 336), then they had original criminal jurisdiction to try all indictable offences and very limited authority in a few minor civil causes. However, according to Madame Justice Oxner, '[t]he Sessions Court generally committed the more serious offences to the Supreme Court.' 'The Lower Courts of Nova Scotia' in *Law in a Colonial Society* 63

9 Townshend *Courts* 19–22, 46

10 Ibid. 64; Friedman *American Law* 47

11 Townshend *Courts* 24, 30

12 *DCB* vol. 4, 50

13 Fifteen individuals have been identified as being on the bench or at the bar in 1754. Apart from the chief justice, only two had legal training: Otis Little of the Massachusetts bar (*DCB* vol. 3, 404) and John Duport, an English attorney (Townshend *Courts* 32). Two others may have been trained in law: George Suckling, an Englishman (*DCB* vol. 4, 724) and

James Monk Sr of Massachusetts, the father of the future chief justice of Lower Canada. The eleven others were justices of the Common Pleas and comprised five army officers, a merchant, a schoolteacher, the governor's clerk, and three whose occupations are unknown. Five were born in England, two in the colonies, and one in Switzerland; the birthplaces of the other three are unknown. The balance soon tipped in favour of the colonial-born, for of twenty-seven persons identified as having served on the bench or at the bar by 1800, only ten are known to have been born in England.

14 1811, 51 Geo. III, c. 3 (NS)

15 Benjamin Russell 'Legal Education' in (1918) 3 *Proceedings of the Canadian Bar Association* 118–19. In Benjamin Russell's time the system was essentially the same as it had been in 1811 and before. Russell (1849–1935) was a lawyer, a jurist, and an author; he was educated at Mount Allison University (BA, MA, DCL), called to the Nova Scotia bar (1872), served as a member of Parliament from 1896, and was appointed puisne judge of Nova Scotia Supreme Court (1904). He died in office. His *Autobiography of Benjamin Russell* (Halifax: Royal Print and Litho 1932) is a valuable source of information on mid-nineteenth-century university education in general and legal education in particular.

16 Beamish Murdoch *Epitome of the Laws of Nova Scotia* vol. 1 (Halifax: Joseph Howe 1832) 6. Murdoch (1800?–1876) was known as 'Nova Scotia's Blackstone'; he was a lawyer, an author, a judge, and a politician. He was called to the bar in 1822. He served as an MLA from 1826 to 1830, and as recorder of Halifax from 1860 to 1870. He was also the editor of the *Acadian Recorder*. Although his *History of Nova Scotia* is said to be his major work, the first volume of his *Epitome* is a good read for a layman. Its language is non-technical and the style is lucid. Like his notional namesake (Blackstone *Commentaries* vol. 1, 30–4) Beamish was a staunch advocate of education in the liberal arts as a necessary preliminary to a legal career. His remarks on this subject are cogent and as true today as they were in 1832: *Epitome* vol. 1, 8–10.

17 Law Library, Halifax *Catalogue of Books in the Law Library at Halifax* (Halifax: J.S. Cunnabell 1835)

18 Haliburton *History* vol. 2, 344. In 1848 this interpretation of contemporary English law on the subject (*Case 15 – Anonymous*, note 3 above) was quoted with approval by Brenton Halliburton, chief justice of the province, in his judgment in *Uniacke* v. *Dickson* (James 1848) 2 NSR 287 at 289.

19 Murdoch 'An Essay' 191. Such learning would be made necessary by the

fact that Murdoch advocated the use of an American textbook as a legal primer for Nova Scotia law students: *Epitome* vol. 1, 10.

20 For the origin and development of the grand and petty jury systems see CC 31, 72–4. In Nova Scotia the grand jury was in place at least as early as 1749, and may even have been empanelled at an earlier date: Townshend *Courts* 5, 6, 10.

21 Forsyth *Constitutional Law* 18–20; Burbidge *Digest* 12 n1; *Uniacke* v. *Dickson* supra note 18, 291 et passim. The case involved two English statutes enacted in 1541 and 1571 respectively. They were held not to be in force in Nova Scotia by Halliburton CJ.

22 MacNutt *Atlantic Provinces* 59

23 1758, 32 Geo. II, c. 13 (NS); 1758, 32 Geo. II, c. 20 (NS)

24 *HECL* vol. 1, 50, 76

25 1758, 32 Geo. II, cc. 13, 17, 20 (NS). Many felonies could be committed by doing or omitting to do one or more of several specific acts: for example, one could be charged with the felony of treason for compassing the king's death, by levying war on him, or by adhering to his enemies. This was the reason there were many more capital offences than felonies.

26 1839, 2 Vict., c. 7 (NS); 1841, 4 Vict., cc. 4, 5, 6, 7 (NS); compare Peel's Acts.

27 RSNS 1851, cc. 155, 162. No substantial change was made to this system before Confederation; see appendix 2.

28 See above, chapter 2, note 29.

29 For instance, individuals convicted of the misdemeanour of remaining in a riotous assembly after the proclamation to disperse had been read were liable to four years' imprisonment (RSNS 1851, c. 160, s. 6), while those convicted of the felony of placing explosives in a public place were punished by a maximum of three years' imprisonment (c. 166, s. 6).

30 7 Co. Rep 18a; 91 ER 398. For amplification of the rule, see *Campbell* v. *Hall* (1774) 1 Cowp. 204; 98 ER 1045. Its later development is outlined in R. MacGregor Dawson *The Government of Canada*, 5th ed. (Toronto: University of Toronto Press 1973) 5.

31 Hilda Neatby *The Administration of Justice Under the Quebec Act* (Minneapolis: University of Minnesota Press 1937) 3

32 Governor Murray's instructions directed him to use Nova Scotia as a model: Adam Shortt and Arthur Doughty *Documents Relating to the Constitutional History of Canada 1759–1791* vol. 1 (Ottawa: King's Printer 1918) 187. For the constitution of the courts, see ibid. 205–9. For the confusing result, see Neatby *Administration* 3.

33 Chief Justice Gregory, an English barrister, was the only judge who had been educated for the law (*MDCB* 283); Shortt *Documents* vol. 1, 206n; Hilda Neatby *Quebec: The Revolutionary Age 1760–1791* (Toronto: Macmillan 1966) 34–7, 50; Neatby *Administration* 205; William R. Riddell *The Bar and Courts of Upper Canada or Ontario* vol. 1 (Toronto: Macmillan 1928) 7, 18. Note that two volumes are bound together in the latter work.

34 For the text of the royal proclamation, see RSC 1970, appendix, 123.

35 1774, 14 Geo. III, c. 83 (Imp.)

36 Shortt *Documents* vol. 2 680, 690

37 Ibid. 600; Neatby *Administration* 22, 351–4

38 Léon Lortie 'The Early Teaching of Law in French Canada,' (1975–6) 2 *Dalhousie Law Review* 522. Mabane was born in Scotland and educated at Edinburgh University (*MDCB* 427); Fraser was also Scottish-born but was educated in France (ibid. 246).

39 Shortt *Documents* vol. 2 641, 680

40 This statement is literally true. But it is an oversimplification of a complex situation which is discussed in detail in Neatby *Quebec* 125–41, 156–71.

41 Shortt *Documents* vol. 2 638, 690

42 Riddell *Bar and Courts* vol. 1 7, 18

43 Lortie 'Teaching of Law' 525

44 Riddell *Bar and Courts* vol. 1 6, 20, 30

45 For details of this incident see ibid., 20–3; see also 1785, 25 Geo. III, c. 4 (LC).

46 1785, 25 Geo. III, c. 4 (LC)

47 1849, 12 Vict., c. 44 (LC); details in Lortie 'Teaching of Law' 521; and see B.A. Testard de Montigney *Histoire du droit canadien* (Montreal 1869) 576.

48 It is unlikely that there were more than a thousand legal texts available in universities and other institutions at the turn of the century. In 1828 *La Bibliothèque du barreau* held only 325 volumes; over the next twenty-three years only 1,700 titles were added: Antonio Drolet *Les Bibliothèques canadiennes* (Ottawa: Le Circle du livre de France 1965) 55, 94, 111.

49 For details of these events, and the fascinating account of Maxmilien Bibaud's private law school, see Lortie 'Teaching of Law' 525–32.

50 1793, 23 Geo. III, c. 6. For detail see Testard de Montigney *Histoire du droit* 442–3.

51 1841, 4 & 5 Vict., c. 20 (Can.). For details of the many changes that took place in this period, see Testard de Montigney *Histoire du droit* 443–50.

52 1774, 14 Geo. III, c. 83, s. 12 (Imp.); Neatby *Quebec* 33

53 1801, 41 Geo. III, c. 9, s. 1 (LC)

54 Frank Mackinnon *The Government of Prince Edward Island* (Toronto: University of Toronto Press 1951) 11

55 Ibid. 15, 27

56 Alexander Warburton *A History of Prince Edward Island* (Saint John, NB: Barnes and Co. 1923) 415

57 *DCB* vol. 5, 776

58 Ibid.

59 Mackinnon *Government of PEI* 57. As in other British North American colonies, bench and bar were a heterogeneous group. Of six early PEI legal personages for whom biographical material is available, one was from Scotland, two from Ireland, one from England, and two from the old colonies.

60 1817, 57 Geo. III, c. 4 (PEI)

61 1842, 5 Vict., c. 21 (PEI)

62 1848, 11 Vict., c. 31, s. 12 (PEI)

63 1852, 15 Vict., c. 22, s. 2 (PEI)

64 Quoted in Mackinnon *Government of PEI* 14

65 1773, 13 Geo. III, c. 8 (PEI)

66 1792, 32 Geo. III, c. 1 (PEI)

67 1836, 6 Will. IV, c. 21 (PEI); compare 1826, 7 Geo. IV, c. 64 (Imp.) and 1827, 7 & 8 Geo. IV, c. 28 (Imp.).

68 1836, 6 Will. IV, c. 22 (PEI); compare Peel's Acts.

69 See appendix 1.

70 1860, 32 Vict., c. 19, s. 1 (PEI). See also appendix 2.

71 MacNutt *Atlantic Provinces* 95–7

72 Joseph W. Lawrence *Judges of New Brunswick and Their Times* (Saint John, NB: n.p. 1907) 16

73 Ibid. 17–18, 26. See also *Acts of the General Assembly of Her Majesty's Province of New Brunswick* (Fredericton: Queen's Printer 1838), appendix 1 ('Courts').

74 Lawrence *Judges of New Brunswick* 21, 39, 59; *MDCB* 764

75 Lawrence 21, 22. Of the fifteen names listed on these pages thirteen were born, were educated, and practised in the old colonies; one, Elias Hardy, was born and educated in England, although he subsequently practised in New York for ten years or more. While no biographical data has been found for the remaining individual, Samuel Denny Street, it would appear from casual references to him that he too was an old colonist. *DCB* vol. 5, 161, 353.

76 Reproduced in Lawrence *Judges of New Brunswick* 180

77 G.A. McAllister 'Some Phases of Legal Education in New Brunswick' (1955) 8 *University of New Brunswick Law Journal* 43, n74. In an order of 1835 the bench reduced the interval to one year for an attorney who held a degree.

78 *A Catalogue of Books Belonging to the Law Society of New Brunswick* (Fredericton, NB: John Simpson 1834)

79 McAllister 'Legal Education' 39, 43

80 All English law enacted before an arbitrarily selected 'reception date' is considered to be in force in a colony. Legislation enacted in Westminster after the reception date does not bind the colony unless it is specifically named in the enactment. See also note 3 above.

81 D.G. Bell 'A Note on the Reception of English Statutes in New Brunswick' (1979) 28 *University of New Brunswick Law Journal* 195. See 196–7 for Bell's discussion of arguments for reception dates other than 1660.

82 Between 1786 and 1829 only one capital felony was enacted. Individuals convicted of procuring a miscarriage 'shall suffer death': 1810, 50 Geo. III, c. 2 (NB). Considering the law in effect in England and other colonial jurisdictions at this time, punishments were relatively benign. For example, killing moose drew a fifteen-pound fine (ibid. c. 22), while the penalty for killing red and fallow deer was a five-pound fine.

83 1829, 9 & 10 Geo. IV, c. 2 (NB); 1831, 1 Will. IV, cc. 14, 15, 16, 17 (NB). The first two statutes of this series listed all the acts that had been repealed by the imperial legislation and recited that 'the Statutes or Acts of Parliament ... so repealed in England ... or such of them as are in force in this Province, be and the same are hereby declared to be repealed.'

84 See appendix 1.

85 See appendix 2.

86 For details, see Gerald M. Craig *Upper Canada: The Formative Years 1784–1841* (Toronto: McClelland and Stewart 1963) 1–19.

87 1791, 31 Geo. III, c. 31 (Imp.)

88 Riddell *Bar and Courts* vol. 2, 86

89 1794, 34 Geo. IV, c. 3, s. 1 (UC)

90 Ibid. s. 17

91 1794, 34 Geo. III, c. 3 (UC); 1792, 32 Geo. III, c. 6 (UC); Riddell *Bar and Courts* vol. 2 78–80, 93–4

92 1793, 33 Geo. III, c. 8 (UC)

93 For details and an analysis, see Riddell *Bar and Courts* vol. 2, 161–82.

94 David B. Read *The Lives of the Judges of Upper Canada and Ontario* (Toronto: Roswell and Hutchinson 1888) 17, 43, 53; Riddell *Bar and Courts* vol. 1, 35, 64

95 Patrick Brode *Sir John Beverley Robinson: Bone and Sinew of the Compact* (Toronto: Osgoode Society 1984) 104

96 Of twenty-seven men who have been identified as members of the bar in Robinson's time and for whom biographical information has been found, only four are known to have been born and educated for the law in England. Of the remaining twenty-three, six received their legal education in Upper Canada, five in old Quebec, and four in the old colonies. No biographical data have been found for the remaining eight.

97 Brode *Robinson* 162

98 1797, 37 Geo. III, c. 13 (UC); Riddell *Bar and Courts* vol. 1 47. It will be noted that there is no mention of the 'solicitor' in early Upper Canadian records. This is not an omission. The solicitor was an officer of the Court of Chancery, and since there was no such court in Upper Canada until 1837, there was likewise no solicitor until then.

99 1797, 37 Geo. III, c. 13, ss. 5, 6 (UC)

100 The terms were the same in England. The only difference was that the intending English attorney was not a member of an Inn, and his education and admission to practice were controlled by the courts. See *HEL* vol. 6, 431–75 for the historical development of the profession, and vol. 7, 22 and 54 for the situation at the end of the eighteenth century.

101 1797, 37 Geo. III, c. 13, s. 2 (UC)

102 Individual donations or bequests rarely exceeded half a dozen volumes. If research indicated that a given set of volumes would involve a substantial outlay, the purchase was not made. Moreover, like Chief Justice Stewart's law books, shipments to the Law Society were lost at sea or elsewhere in transit: William R. Riddell *The Legal Profession in Upper Canada* (Toronto: Law Society of Upper Canada 1916) 83–104. All the information in the text following concerning the Law Society is taken from this publication.

103 See Charles Durrand *Reminiscences of Charles Durrand* (Toronto: Hunter Rose 1897) 60, 76, 121; James C. Hamilton *Osgoode Hall Reminiscences of the Bench and Bar* (Toronto: Carswell 1904) 26–31, 147–60; Edward Gillis 'Legal Education in Ontario' (1905) 4 *Canadian Law Review* 101–5; J.E. Farewell 'The Student at Law in the Early Sixties' (1915) 35 *Canadian Law Times* 53–6; D.G. Kilgour 'A Note on Legal Education in Ontario 125 Years Ago' (1959–60) 13 *University of Toronto Law Journal* 270–2.

104 1822, 2 Geo. IV, c. 5, s. 3 (UC)

105 Riddell *Legal Profession* 18

106 Ibid. 20, 21; for statistics on the attorneys' decline, see the table at page 32.

107 For a detailed examination of this topic, but viewed from a different perspective, see G. Blaine Baker 'Legal Education in Upper Canada 1795–1889; The Law Society as Educator' in David H. Flaherty (ed.) *Essays in the History of Canadian Law* vol. 2 (Toronto: The Osgoode Society 1983) 49–142, particularly 129, n. 73.

108 1792, 32 Geo. III, cc. 1, 2 (UC)

109 1779, 19 Geo. III, c. 74, s. 3 (Imp.). By this act 'branding was practically abolished, though the words of the act are not absolute.' *HCL* vol. 1, 463.

110 It must be remembered that the substantive English criminal law of 1792 was hardly more enlightened than that of 1763. This is amply demonstrated in the records of the times. For example, in his fall circuit of the Eastern District in 1820, Powell CJ sentenced three persons to hang – one for horse theft, one for rape, and one for murder. Only the last, an Indian boy of ten, was reprieved. Several more were banished for life for what would now be considered minor offences. William R. Riddell *Upper Canadian Sketches* (Toronto: Carswell 1922) 33–7. See also the examples cited in Brode *Robinson* 106.

111 1800, 40 Geo. III, c. 1, s. 1 (UC)

112 For a discussion of this movement, see Brode *Robinson* 107, 184.

113 1832, 2 Will. IV, cc. 1, 4 (UC); 1833, 3 Will. IV, cc. 2, 4 (UC)

114 1833, 3 Will. IV, c. 3 (UC)

115 1840, 3 & 4 Vict., c. 35, s. 46 (Imp.)

116 Elizabeth Gibbs (née Nish) (ed.) *Debates of the Legislative Assembly of United Canada* (Montreal: Centre d'Études du Québec 1978) 27 August 1841, 710–11, 713. Henry Black was a supporter of the administration and had been a member of Sydenham's special council: *DCB* vol. 10, 68.

117 1841, 4 & 5 Vict., c. 24 (Can.)

118 Consolidated Statutes of Canada (CSC) 1859, Commissioners' Report, vi. The statutes were 1841, 4 & 5 Vict., cc. 25, 26, and 27 (UC).

119 For example, procuring an abortion was a capital felony under 1829, 9 Geo. IV, c. 31, s. 13 (Imp.), whereas by the analogous Canadian act, 1841, 4 & 5 Vict., c. 27, s. 14 (Can.), a convicted felon was liable only to imprisonment.

120 See appendices 1 & 2.

121 1851, 14 & 15 Vict., cc. 95, 96 (Can.). These were largely modelled on the English statutes of 1848, 11 & 12 Vict., cc. 42 and 43 (Imp.). However, many specifically Canadian innovations made in the intervening years were included in the criminal procedure acts in CSC 1859, cc. 99–103 inclusive.

122 By RSBC 1899, c. 135

123 1863, 26 & 27 Vict., statute 8 (BC)

124 See appendix 4.

125 For the law of Assiniboia and the Northwest Territories, see Desmond Brown 'Unpredictable and Uncertain: Criminal Law in the Canadian North West Before 1886' (1979) 17 *Alberta Law Review* 497–507.

126 See appendix 2.

127 *R. v. Bertrand* (1867) LR 1 PC 520, at 530. See also the precedents cited by the minister of justice, Sir John Thompson, in his report to the governor general on criminal appeals to the Judicial Committee of the Privy Council. Canada, Parliament, Sessional Papers, 1889, no. 77.

128 Judgments from 134 criminal appeals prior to 1867 are printed in the following reports: NS Rep. (15); LC Rep. (27); PEI Rep. (1); NB Rep. (32); UCQB Rep. (44); and UCCP Rep. (15). These do not include all the reports of the time, but they indicate the trend.

129 One result of decentralization was that the opportunity for advancement was restricted. A place on the provincial bench or in the leadership of the bar was the most a lawyer could hope for if he stayed within the system – a future as a big fish in a little pond. (See details at the end of this note.) If he aspired to greater fame or fortune in the legal arena, he had to leave the colony for a place within the imperial system or move to the United States. Alternatively, for the man who hoped for greater glory but who wished to retain the security of his income from the bar and his ties with colonial society, there was the possibility of combining the law with politics (as did, for example, John A. Macdonald). This is no doubt the reason there were forty-seven lawyers, who made up 25 per cent of the membership, in the first House of Commons after Confederation. See Henry J. Morgan *Canadian Legal Directory* (Toronto 1876) 274–9 for details of Canadians who attained eminence as judges on colonial benches outside North America; and Durrand *Reminiscences* 396 on the migration of Canadian lawyers to the United States.

In 1867 there were approximately 1,480 lawyers in British North America, dispersed as follows: Nova Scotia 140; Lower Canada 340; Prince Edward Island 30; New Brunswick 310; Upper Canada 650; and British Columbia 10. In contrast, there were only forty-five seats on the senior benches of the colonies. (All figures are derived from the data in Morgan *Legal Directory*.)

130 *Parliamentary Debates on Confederation* (Quebec: Hunter, Rose 1865) 41

131 Canada, Senate *Report Concerning the Enactment of the British North America Act of 1867* (Ottawa: King's Printer 1939) annex 4, 52, 70, 91

132 Christopher Dunkin, the Conservative MLA for Brome, mentioned the

subject in passing in the course of his speech criticizing the proposed union, and two questions were asked concerning the jurisdiction of the federal government in criminal matters after Confederation. Apart from these utterances and John A. Macdonald's speech, the *Confederation Debates* are silent on the subject: see 508, 576–7.

133 1867, 30 & 31 Vict., c. 3, s. 91 (Imp.)

134 See, for example, 1881, 44 Vict., c. 5 (Ont.), which abolished the separate superior courts of the province and erected in their place the High Court of Judicature for Ontario, and otherwise transformed the whole system. Nova Scotia enacted similar legislation in 1884, 47 Vict., c. 25 (NS); Quebec in RSQ 1883, articles 2289–2776; New Brunswick in 1897, 60 Vict., c. 24 (NB).

135 1875, 38 Vict., c. 11, s. 16 (Can.)

136 Apart from the fact that it was more convenient and less expensive for an appellant's counsel to go to Ottawa rather than directly to London, the Supreme Court was, in many respects, a judicial 'spare wheel' until 1949, when appeals to the Privy Council were abolished. For background on this question, see Michael J. Harmon 'The Founding of the Supreme Court of Canada and the Abolition of the Appeal to the Privy Council' (1976) 8 *Ottawa Law Review* 7-31. For more detail, see James G. Snell and Frederick Vaughan *The Supreme Court of Canada: History of the Institution* (Toronto: The Osgoode Society 1985) 145–71.

137 See Frank R. Scott *Essays on the Constitution* (Toronto: University of Toronto Press 1977) 46–8 for a short discussion on this subject, and Peter B. Waite *Canada 1874–1896* (Toronto: McClelland and Stewart 1971) 116–19, for a discussion of specific cases.

138 'Grand Juries' (1891) 27 *Canada Law Journal* 6

139 For a detailed account of how the grand jury and the magistrates controlled expenditures on public works, see *HEL* vol. 10, 147–51. Nova Scotia (RSNS 1851, c. 46) and New Brunswick (RSNB 1854, cc. 54 and 56) followed this model closely. In the special circumstances obtaining in Quebec after the conquest the system could not be made to function as it did in an English environment (see Neatby *Administration of Justice* 342–4). After the separation of the province there were legislative modifications. A system was set up which gave greater authority to magistrates but which made mandatory the appointment of a special jury from the grand jury panel to decide questions relating to public works when so required by property owners of the jurisdiction. See 1796, 36 Geo. III, c. 9, ss. 45, 46 (LC). Upper Canada's legislation followed closely that of Lower Canada: 1810, 50 Geo. III, c. 9, s. 3 (UC). In *Study of the Civil*

Jury and the Grand Jury in Ontario (Toronto: Ontario Law Reform Commission 1971) 78–103, S.N. Lederman sketches the early history of the criminal side of the grand jury and gives a detailed account of its development in late nineteenth-century Ontario, but its civil side is dismissed in one sentence. For the historical development of the civil and criminal functions of the grand jury see CC 72–3, 81.

140 1840, 4 Vict., c. 4 (LC). For details, see A.D. DeCelles 'The Municipal System of Quebec' in A. Shortt and A.G. Doughty (eds.) *Canada and Its Provinces* vol. 15 (Toronto: Brook and Co. 1914) 291–5.

141 Peter B. Waite *The Man from Halifax* (Toronto: University of Toronto Press 1985) 114; J. Murray Beck *The Government of Nova Scotia* (Toronto: University of Toronto Press 1957) 302; John Castell Hopkins *Life and Work of the Rt. Hon. Sir John Thompson* (Toronto: United Publishing 1895) 63

142 Waite *Man from Halifax* 437

143 Miller to Thompson, 9 April 1879, PAC, John Sparrow David Thompson papers, microfilm, reel c9235; Waite *Man from Halifax* 87. For biographical detail on Miller, see Henry J. Morgan *The Canadian Men and Women of the Time* (Toronto: William Briggs 1912) 804. For the multifarious duties of the grand jury and the concomitant opportunities for profit under the old system, see RSNS (3rd ser.) 1864, c. 45.

144 The Canadian system paralleled the contemporary English practice. See 'Grand Juries' (1891) 27 *Canada Law Journal* 4–9 for details.

145 Discussion in the *Upper Canada Law Journal* was remarkably impartial for that time and place: in 'Abuse of the Grand Jury System' (1859, vol. 5, at 51) the author catalogues the defects of the system and advocates legislation to correct them; 'Grand Juries' (1856, vol. 2, at 237) supports the status quo; and 'Grand Juries' (1860, vol. 6, at 274) reprints an article from an English periodical, *The Jurist*, which is critical of attempts to abolish the institution and with which the editor of the *Journal* is in complete agreement.

146 1848 11 & 12 Vict., c. 42 (Imp.); 1851, 14 & 15 Vict., c. 96 (Can.); 1857, 20 Vict., c. 59 (Can.). For the fascinating story of the genesis of the Crown Attorney Act, see Marvin R. Bloos 'The Crown Prosecutor in Alberta: An Unfinished Hybrid' (LLM thesis, University of Alberta 1987) 141–50.

147 See, for example, the letter from Hubert McDonald, a county court judge from Brockville, to Senator James R. Gowan (7 March 1889, PAC, James R. Gowan Papers, reel m1938), in which McDonald cites several instances where grand juries refused to bring in a true bill after both crown attorney and magistrate had in effect committed individuals for trial.

148 The first jurist to be openly critical of the grand jury is reported to have

been Mr Justice Gwynne of the Ontario Court of Common Pleas. At the Kingston assizes in 1869 he told the grand jury that their 'second preliminary investigation seems questionable,' and that, in fact, they would be better employed following their own pursuits. Quoted in John Kains *How Say You* (St. Thomas, Ont. 1893) 11. (Kains was a lawyer from St Thomas.)

149 James Robert Gowan (1815–1909) was born in Ireland, and emigrated to Upper Canada with his parents. He articled under James E. Small, and served as a volunteer in the Rebellion of 1837. He was called to the bar in 1839, and appointed to the bench by the Lafontaine-Baldwin government in 1843. At twenty-seven, Gowan was the youngest judge ever commissioned in British North America. He retired from the bench in 1883 and was called to the Senate in 1885. For an interesting and informative biography of Gowan, see Mark W. Fisher 'Sir James Robert Gowan' (MA thesis, University of New Brunswick 1971)

150 Arthur Colquhoun *The Hon. James R. Gowan: A Memoir* (Toronto 1894) 22, 65–75

151 Bloos 'Crown Prosecutor' 149. Although Gowan had changed his political allegiance from Tory to Reform in his early years (Fisher 'Gowan' 13), he was a dedicated and apolitical servant of the government in power during his judicial career. While he was John A. Macdonald's personal legal draftsman for well over thirty years, he was at the same time an intimate of Oliver Mowat and performed the same services for him. (See the correspondence between Gowan and Mowat, particularly Mowat to Gowan, 8 July 1876, in the James Small and James Gowan Papers, Archives of Ontario.) And if he was later to press Attorney General Thompson to codify the criminal law, it was no more than he was to do to Edward Blake when Blake was attorney general in the Mackenzie government.

152 Senate *Debates* 25 February 1889, 56–7. Under the provisions of the Speedy Trials Acts of 1875 [38 Vict., cc. 45 and 47 (Can)], persons charged with indictable offences could, in many cases, elect to be tried summarily. Evidently, many so elected.

153 Senate *Debates* 25 February 1889, 57

154 Quoted in Kains *How Say You* 64

155 In 1879 and 1892 the Ontario Legislature enacted statutes regulating the composition and duties of grand juries, but no proclamation was issued to bring the statutes into force.

156 For details, see Kains *How Say You* 63–4. The constitutional question was

never resolved in a court. Jurisdiction remained with the provinces, most of which enacted legislation on grand juries well into the twentieth century. In Ontario, for example, the last such statute was the Juries Act, so 1974, c. 63, ss. 48, 49.

157 Macdonald to Gowan, 24 January 1885, Gowan Papers, reel m1898
158 Thompson to Gowan, 21 April 1886, ibid., reel m1938; Thompson to Gowan, 25 May 1886, ibid. reel m1899
159 Senate *Debates* 25 February 1889, 52–65
160 It may have been well researched and well delivered, but it received scant coverage in the national press, and certainly nothing like the coverage the topic was accorded in England, where it generated many editorials and innumerable letters to the editor (see cc 80–2). In contrast, apart from a short paragraph in the Toronto *Globe*, Gowan's speech was ignored by Liberal party organs, and the only Conservative newspaper to give the speech more than a couple of lines was the *Halifax Herald* of 26 February 1889, which published a well-reasoned editorial supporting Gowan's views and advocating the abolition of the grand jury in Nova Scotia, if not elsewhere in Canada. But the appeal obviously fell on deaf ears, for it produced no letters to the editor in the following weeks.
161 cc 66–8
162 Thompson to Gowan, 11 March 1889, Gowan Papers, reel m1938
163 Gowan to Thompson, 4 and 19 April 1889, PAC, Sir John Sparrow David Thompson Papers, microfilm, reel c9252; Thompson to Gowan, 20 April 1889, Gowan Papers, reel m1938
164 Gowan to Macdonald, 26 September 1890, PAC, Sir John A. Macdonald Papers, microfilm, reel c1600
165 Canada, Parliament, Sessional Papers, 1891, no. 66 'Correspondence between the Department of Justice and the Judges Respecting the Grand Jury' 7
166 While discussing coverage of the grand jury question in the press, Thompson commented to Gowan: 'On a matter like this I cannot help thinking that while the press may be of great service to us in helping to guide the public mind, *if we are able to come to the conclusion to abolish the present system*, it is of little value as indicating what ought to be done, in advance of our decision' (my italics). 26 November 1890, Gowan Papers, reel m1938
167 Senate *Debates* 23 June 1891, 105. In view of Thompson's reluctance to interfere with the grand jury system, he must have been pleased to note that the press ignored Gowan's speech. The only comment on the

debate was reported in the Toronto *Mail* of 24 June 1891. It did not deal with the substance of the senator's remarks, but reported that it was the first speech to be recorded for Hansard on an Edison phonograph.

168 Canada, Parliament, Sessional Papers, 1891, no. 66 'Judges' Replies' 6, 62–9. It is instructive to note that no replies from the provincial attorneys general were published. What, one wonders, would their opinions have been?

169 See Murdoch *Epitome* vol. 1, 8–10; McAllister 'Legal Education' 37, 39, 49; and Gillis 'Legal Education in Ontario' 102–5. This is a representative sampling; many other publications could be cited that reflect the sentiments expressed above.

170 John Willis *A History of Dalhousie Law School* (Toronto: University of Toronto Press 1979) 6–7, 20–1

171 For a contemporary view of this process, see James M. Young 'The Faculty of Law' in *The University of Toronto and Its Colleges 1827–1906* (Toronto: University of Toronto Library 1906) 149–67. For a modern perspective, see Brian Bucknall, Thomas Baldwin, and J. David Lakin 'Pedants, Practitioners, and Prophets: Legal Education at Osgoode Hall to 1957' (1968) 6 *Osgoode Hall Law Journal* 149–59.

172 N.W. Hoyles 'Legal Education in Canada' (1899) 19 *Canadian Law Times* 261–73. The table of variation is at page 267.

173 'Dominion Bar Society' (1877) 13 *Canada Law Journal* 9

174 *Report of the Canadian Bar Association 1915* (no publication information) 1

175 For details of the founding of this organization, see (1921) 8 *Canadian Bar Association Proceedings* 268–9. Reports have been issued annually, except for 1940, by the commissioners with the title [year] *Proceedings of the [number] Annual Meeting of the Conference of Commissioners on Uniformity of Legislation in Canada*. Since 1974 the reports have been entitled *Uniform Law Conference of Canada: Proceedings of the Annual Meeting*.

176 For details of the origin and development of the attorney, solicitor, and barrister see CC 62–4.

177 *HEL* vol. 15, 224

178 1881, 44 Vict., c. 5, s. 74 (Ont.)

179 Excepting British Columbia, all contemporary jurisdictions in Canada continued to use the term 'attorney' well into the twentieth century. British Columbia dropped the term in 1895: RSBC 1895, c. 24.

180 In 1890, for example, incest was a misdemeanour in Nova Scotia, punishable by two years' imprisonment; a conviction in New Brunswick could result in fourteen years' imprisonment, and in Prince Edward Island

in twenty-one years' imprisonment. In British Columbia it was a misdemeanour punishable by three years' imprisonment to conceal any relevant information from a registrar with intent to deceive when registering a title to land. Such an action was not an offence elsewhere in Canada. Burbidge *Digest* articles 215, 456

181 1869, 32 & 33 Vict., c. 36 (Can.) schedule B

182 Henri-Elzéar Taschereau *The Criminal Law Consolidation and Amendment Acts* 1st ed. (Montreal: Lovell 1874) vol. 1, iv

183 Greaves *Criminal Law Acts* xxxvi

184 See appendix 3.

185 Piracy was also a capital crime. But Canadian admiralty courts, which tried such offences, sat under the authority of the imperial statute 1869, 32 & 33 Vict., c. 29, and charges were laid according to its provisions. For discussion, see Samuel R. Clarke and Henry P. Sheppard *A Treatise on the Criminal Law of Canada* 2d ed. (Toronto: Hart and Co. 1882) 89.

186 House of Commons *Debates* 6 June 1887, 798–801. See especially the remarks of David Mills at 801.

187 *HCL* vol. 3, 367

188 (1873) LR 4 PC 599. Not included are the appeals brought under the Canada Temperance Act, 1878, 41 Vict., c. 16 (Can.), which was not a criminal statute as such, although it did provide for punishments.

189 The question that concerned the Quebec attorney general had to do with a conflict between a Lower Canadian and a dominion statute. *R. v. Coote*, supra, at 608. Their Lordships did not give judgment on this question, however.

190 *R. v. Riel* (1885) 10 App. Cas. 675 at 677

191 Frank Mackinnon 'The Establishment of the Supreme Court of Canada' (1946) 27 *Canadian Historical Review* 270–2

192 House of Commons *Debates* 16 March 1875, 745

193 Robert Cassels *A Digest of Cases Determined by the Supreme Court of Canada* (Toronto: Carswell 1893) 192–8

194 The following reported criminal appeal cases were heard in provincial courts between 1867 and 1892: NS Rep. 54; Ramsay's AC (Que.) 47; PEI Rep. 2; NB Rep. 42; UCQB Rep. 38; UCCP Rep. 15; Terr. L. Rep. 20; BC Rep. 7; and O. Rep. 140. This is by no means an exhaustive list of reported cases, for many of the reports of the time, such as the Ontario Practice Reports and the Quebec Law Reports were not consulted once the trend was apparent. Nor were all criminal appeals reported, for, as C.H. Stephens, the editor of Ramsay's Appeal Cases, makes clear with respect

to his own volume, '[t]he number of unreported cases is unexpectedly large, comprising nearly, if not quite, one half of the total number of judgements in Appeal' (at vi).

195 This quotation is taken from a twenty-page brief prepared by Senator Gowan for Sir John Thompson sometime in May 1892. It is undated and unsigned, but the draft is in the Gowan Papers (reel m1939): Canada, Department of Justice, file 63/94, item 117.

CHAPTER 4 CONSOLIDATION AND CODIFICATION
BEFORE CONFEDERATION

1 See appendix 5.
2 For the origin and development of the form of the English statute see CC 64–70.
3 *HEL* vol. 2, 440; Lord Brougham's Act, 1865, 13 & 14 Vict., c. 21, s. 2 (Imp.)
4 1759, 33 Geo. II, c. 3 (NS)
5 1809, 49 Geo. III, c. 4 (UC)
6 *HCL* vol. 2, 218n
7 Nova Scotia, House of Assembly *Statutes at Large 1758–1804* (Halifax 1805) ix
8 Several editors have compiled collections of the statutes under this title, the first being Barker's collection of 1587. The format that the Nova Scotian editors followed was introduced by Owen Ruffhead, an English barrister, in his edition published between 1762 and 1765.
9 New Brunswick *Acts of the General Assembly* (Fredericton: Queen's Printer 1838) preface
10 Upper Canada, House of Assembly *Journal* 2 April 1817, 416
11 Ibid. 6 March 1818, 499
12 Ibid. 21 March 1818, 543
13 Ibid. 5 November 1825, 9
14 Ibid. 9 February 1830, 46; 19 February 61
15 Ibid. 5 December 1831, 30
16 Ibid. 15 December 1831, 121
17 1841, 4 & 5 Vict., c. 15 (Can.)
18 Gibbs (née Nish) *Debates of the Legislative Assembly* vol. 1, 27 August 1841, 710–11, 713, 727
19 Canada (Province) *Statutes of Upper Canada* (Toronto 1843). The report of the commissioners (vol. 1, 1–3) is dated 8 March 1843.
20 Report of the commissioners, 1

21 *Canada Gazette* 21 March 1842, 248
22 Canada (Province) *Revised Acts and Ordinances of Lower Canada* (Montreal 1845) iii; Canada, Legislative Assembly *Journal* 1843, appendix o.o., 1
23 Canada (Province) *Revised Acts and Ordinances of Lower Canada* xiv
24 Canada, Legislative Assembly *Journal* 1843, appendix o.o., 3
25 1849, 12 Vict., c. 29 (NB).
26 The New Brunswick act borrowed Brougham's phrase to cover the substantive provisions: section 2 reads, in part, 'And be it enacted, that the Schedule to this Act annexed, shall be deemed ... to be parcel to this Act ... as if such [schedule] had been expressly ... recited with the usual words and in the usual forms of enactment.' Compare *Parl. Papers* Fourth Report on Criminal Law, 1848 [940] XXVII, 70.
27 1849, 12 Vict., c. 29; c. 5, s. 1, article 6 (NB)
28 *Parl. Papers* Report of the Royal Commission on Indictable Offences, 1878–9 [2345], XX, 14
29 Commissioners' Report, RSNS 1851, vii
30 William Young was an MLA and a Speaker of the assembly; Jonathan McCully was an MLC: *MDCB* 435, 820.
31 RSNS 1851, viii. The extracts quoted in this section are taken from this volume.
32 The act is not included in the Statutes of the session, and is identified only by the date of its enactment – 7 April 1851. For Lord Brougham's Act, see above, chapter 2, note 70.
33 As an example of the potential developments when the definition of an important term was left to a judge, see Desmond Brown 'The Craftsmanship of Bias: Sedition and the Winnipeg Strike Trial 1919' (1984) 14 *Manitoba Law Journal* 1–33.
34 RSNS 1851, c. 170, s. 2
35 RSNB 1854, c. 162, s. 13. The content of the remainder of this paragraph is derived from the New Brunswick Commissioners' Report of 22 March 1853; ibid. vii–xv.
36 RSNB 1854, c. 147, s. 1
37 1843, 7 Vict., c. 29 (Can.). So far as can be ascertained, this is the first appearance of this innovation in any British jurisdiction. Subparagraphs were not seen in English statutes until Lord Thring introduced them a decade later, in 1854; Ilbert *Legislative Forms* 69.
38 Gibbs (née Nish) *Debates of the Legislative Assembly* vol. 9, 1139–41
39 *DCB* vol. 11, 41
40 Gibbs (née Nish) *Debates of the Legislative Assembly* vol. 9, 1141
41 Ibid. vol. 10, 1276, 1632

42 1855, 18 Vict., c. 88, s. 2 (Can.)

43 Canada, Legislative Assembly *Journal* 28 February 1855, 603

44 Canada, Legislative Assembly *General Index to the Journals of the Legislative Assembly 1841–1851* 508; *1851–1866* 827

45 Canada, Legislative Assembly *Journal* 1859, appendix no. 9, First Report of the Commissioners appointed to revise and consolidate the Statutes of Upper Canada. Note that appendix 9, which consists of the first report and a supplementary report with a total of thirty-two pages, is unpaginated. For Lower Canadian statistics, see the second report of the 1843 Commission printed in *Revised Acts and Ordinances of Lower-Canada* vi.

46 Canada, Legislative Assembly *Journal* 11 July 1851, 156

47 Ibid. 28 September 1854, 132; 1859, appendix 9, First Report

48 Editorial (1858) 4 *Upper Canada Law Journal* 147; see also 124–5.

49 Canada, Legislative Assembly *Journal* 1859, appendix 9, First Report

50 According to (then) Senator Gowan, the commissioners' 'first process in drafting the revision was to strike out all the unnecessary words in an enactment' in accordance with Arthur Symons *Mechanics of Lawmaking* (London 1835). But Macdonald did not approve, 'and so we had not the free hand, as draftsmen we desired.' They also produced a much thicker volume than would otherwise have been the case. Gowan to Thompson, 9 November 1892, Thompson Papers, reel c9259.

51 Macaulay to Macdonald, 23 April 1858, Macdonald Papers, reel c1707. Macaulay (1793–1859), a former chief justice of the Court of Common Pleas, had also been a member of the commission that had drafted the 1843 edition of the Revised Statutes of Upper Canada. He was knighted for his work on the 1859 edition, and died soon thereafter.

52 Macaulay to Macdonald, 29 May 1858; 31 May 1858 (two letters), Macdonald Papers, reel c1707

53 Macdonald to Gowan, 31 January 1857, in J.K. Johnson (ed.) *The Letters of Sir John A. Macdonald 1836–1857* (Ottawa: Public Archives of Canada 1968) 421; 5 February 1858, in J.K. Johnson and Carole Stelmack (eds.) *The Letters of Sir John A. Macdonald 1858–1861* (Ottawa: Public Archives of Canada 1969) 18

54 Macaulay to Macdonald, 31 May 1858, Macdonald Papers, reel c1707

55 Canada, Legislative Assembly *Journal* 1859, 151, 169, 343, 379, 590

56 Gowan to Thompson, 21 April 1892, in a letter of advice on the tactics that should be used to put through the Criminal Code: Thompson Papers, reel c9257

57 Unfortunately, this important and interesting development is beyond the scope of this study, but those who wish to learn about its historical

development could not do better than to read John Brierley's informative 'Quebec's Civil Law Codification' (1968) 14 *McGill Law Journal* 521–89.

58 Oliver Mowat to Macdonald, 1 December 1856, Macdonald Papers, reel c1673

59 Canada, Legislative Assembly *Journal* 1859, appendix 9, First Report

60 1841, 4 & 5 Vict., c. 26, s. 6 (Can.)

61 csc 1859, c. 93, s. 5

62 Seven went to chapter 99 (procedure in criminal cases) and three to chapter 103 (summary convictions): csc 1859, schedule B.

63 Commissions to revise the statutes of Prince Edward Island were issued in 1861 and 1890, and reports from the commissioners were published, but no legislative action to implement a revision was taken until the Revised Statutes of Prince Edward Island were enacted in 1951: Olga B. Bishop *Publications of the Governments of Nova Scotia, Prince Edward Island and New Brunswick* (Ottawa: National Library 1957) 107. In contrast, the Revised Statutes of British Columbia came out in 1888, only four decades after the erection of the jurisdiction. To round out the account, the Council of Assiniboia codified the ordinances of the jurisdiction as early as 1832. For details of this last development, see Brown 'Criminal Law before 1886' 506–7.

CHAPTER 5 PREPARATION FOR CODIFICATION IN CANADA

1 Macdonald set the precedent for this action when he assumed the portfolio of minister of militia in addition to that of attorney general in 1862, as the Fenian problem began to loom.

2 Macdonald to Richard Snelling, 29 February 1868, Macdonald Papers, reel c26. Snelling was a Toronto lawyer who had written to Macdonald concerning such a commission.

3 Gowan to Macdonald, 28 January 1862, Macdonald Papers, reel c1600. The suggestion of Gowan was made with respect to the assimilation of the criminal law of the two Canadas, but from the context of the letter and the plan Macdonald followed, there is little doubt that it was this suggestion which Macdonald acted on in 1867.

4 Macdonald to Gowan, 12 October 1871, Macdonald Papers, reel c30. See also the prime minister's remarks in the debate on the criminal law bills in 1869: House of Commons *Debates* 27 April 1869, 89.

5 Bernard to Gowan, 3 March 1868, Gowan Papers, reel m1937

6 Wicksteed to Gowan, 23 April 1868, Gowan Papers, reel m1938; Gowan to Thompson, 21 April 1892, Thompson Papers, reel c9257

7 Taschereau *Consolidation Acts* vol. 1, iv
8 Bernard reported to Gowan that he had gone over the bills with Senator Jonathan McCully of Nova Scotia and John H. Gray, a New Brunswick MP, to ensure that no items from those provinces were missed. Bernard to Gowan, 3 March and 30 May 1868, Gowan Papers, reel m1937.
9 John Sandfield Macdonald to Sir John A. Macdonald, 29 May 1868, Macdonald Papers, reel c1659; Bernard to Gowan, 3 March 1868, Gowan Papers, reel m1937
10 House of Commons *Debates* 6 May 1868, 642
11 Ibid. 643
12 The only mention of the passage of these bills I have been able to find in the popular press was in the *Ottawa Citizen* of 15 May 1868; the bare facts – the titles of the bills – were reported, nothing else. The *Toronto Globe* of the same date devoted four lines to the Summary Jurisdiction Bill. At this early date few newspapers outside Quebec and Ontario carried parliamentary news. Moreover, the large majority of those that did were organs of the political parties, and their coverage was badly skewed: the Conservative journals could be depended upon to ignore or denigrate good news for the opposition and to inflate items favourable to the government, and, of course, Liberal papers responded in kind. By the 1890s there was much more impartial reporting, but even then more than half the newspapers in Canada were party organs. See Paul Rutherford *A Victorian Authority* (Toronto: University of Toronto Press 1982) 214.
13 In the Commons the ratio of members from Ontario and Quebec to those from Nova Scotia and New Brunswick was nine to one; in the Senate it was two to one.
14 Senate *Debates* 4 June 1869, 264
15 Ibid. 261. The full report is printed in Canada, Senate *Journal* 7 May 1868, 260–1 (hereinafter Senate *Journal*).
16 Senate *Debates* 15 May 1868, 320
17 Ibid. 321
18 Ibid. 288, 321; 16 May 325, 327. The *Toronto Globe* of 18 May 1868 was the only newspaper to report this fact, without comment. But it did follow the Liberal party line the next day when its parliamentary correspondent criticized the government for rushing an inordinate number of bills through late in the session, when it was apparent that members hardly had time to 'read and consider' them: 19 May 1868.
19 Monck to Macdonald, 17 May 1868, Macdonald Papers, reel c1513; House of Commons *Debates* 22 May 1868, 763
20 Wicksteed to Gowan, 23 May 1868, Gowan Papers, reel m1938

21 See the *Ottawa Citizen* of 23 May 1868 and the Toronto *Globe* of the same date for typical treatments of prorogation ceremonies of the time.

22 For example, the *Toronto Mail* devoted almost all of pages 1, 2, and 3 to the Bunting conspiracy case on 4 April 1884, while the *Halifax Herald* took all of page 3 to detail the opening events of the Buchanan poison trial on 12 June 1892. In contrast, the only mention of the criminal law debates of 1868 and 1869 was a thoughtful and critical analysis of the Speedy Trials Bill published in an editorial in the *Toronto Globe* of 22 May 1869.

23 See, for example, Macdonald to John M. McMullen, the historian from Brockville, 1 June 1868, Macdonald Papers, reel c26; Macdonald to William J. Ritchie, chief justice of Nova Scotia, 25 May 1868, ibid.

24 House of Commons *Debates* 27 April 1869, 89

25 Ibid. 4 May 1869, 171

26 Again, the bare fact of the second reading of the criminal law bills en bloc was reported in the *Ottawa Citizen* of 30 April 1869, and in an even shorter form in the *Toronto Globe* of 24 April 1869.

27 Senate *Debates* 4 June 1869, 262–77. In a six-inch column paraphrasing the debate on the Offences against the Person Bill, the *Toronto Globe* of 5 July 1869 made an oblique allusion to the senator's acid comments. No other major newspaper reported this debate.

28 The main debates on these bills in the Senate took place between 1 and 7 June: Senate *Debates* 1869, 246–87.

29 Canada, *Acts of the Parliament of the Dominion of Canada Relating to Criminal Law* (Ottawa: Queen's Printer 1874)

30 For details see Taschereau *Consolidation Acts* vol. 1, iv et passim.

31 1869, 32 & 33 Vict., c. 22, s. 15 (Can.)

32 Compare 1861, 24 & 25 Vict., c. 100, s. 56 (Imp.), and 1869, 32 & 33 Vict., c. 20, s. 69 (Can.).

33 See RSC 1886, II, appendix no. 2, 2447, which details the disposition of the forty-five sections to procedural chapters in that revision.

34 Andrew Horne *The Mirror of Justices* edited and translated by William Whittaker [ca. 1290] (London: Bernard Quaritch 1895) 25

35 *HCL* vol. 3, 146

36 *In re Bellencontre* [1891] 2 QB 122, at 137

37 Stephen *Digest* 194, n1

38 Samuel R. Clarke *A Treatise on the Criminal Law as Applicable to the Dominion of Canada* 1st ed. (Toronto: Carswell 1872) 289

39 Ibid. 79

40 Friedland 'Wright's Code' 307

41 Gowan to John A. Macdonald, 12 October 1870, 15 May 1871, Macdonald

Papers, reel c1600; Gowan to Thring, draft, 25 July 1892, Gowan Papers, reel m1938; Henry Ardagh *Life of Hon. James R. Gowan* (Toronto: University Press 1911) 178

42 Friedland 'Wright's Code' 308; Gowan to Mr Justice Taschereau, Supreme Court of Canada, draft, 17 April 1880, Gowan Papers, reel m1938

43 It was not 1872, as Friedland ('Wright's Code' 340, n282) was led to believe by Gowan's letter to Wright of 19 January 1891 (draft) in which he reminds him of their meeting 'in 1872.' Gowan Papers, reel m1900.

44 Friedland 'Wright's Code' 312; Gowan to Wright, draft, 19 January 1891, reel m1900

45 See Barton to Gowan, fall 1872, and Gowan to Barton, draft, 9 April 1873, Gowan Papers, reel m1897.

46 Canada, *Criminal Law Acts 1874*

47 Henri-Elzéar Taschereau (1836–1911) was born in Ste Marie de la Beauce, LC. He studied at Quebec Seminary and was called to the bar in 1857. In 1871 he was appointed puisne judge of the Superior Court of Quebec. In 1874 Taschereau was thirty-eight and had been on the bench of the Superior Court for four years. He was promoted to the Supreme Court of Canada on 8 October 1878 by the Mackenzie government as one of its final appointments. He was elevated to chief justice by the Laurier government in 1902.

48 Taschereau *Criminal Law Acts* vol. 1, iv

49 Ibid. vi

50 The letter is reproduced in the preface to volume 2 of Taschereau's *Criminal Law Consolidation and Amendment Acts* (Toronto: Hunter Rose 1875) iii

51 1869, 32 & 33 Vict., cc. 29, 30, 31, and 32 (Can.)

52 Mowat to Gowan, 5 February 1876, Small and Gowan Papers

53 See the correspondence between the two men over a two-year period especially Gowan to Mowat, 28 March 1876, and Mowat to Gowan, 8 July 1876, ibid. See also the detailed but incomplete account of the labours of the commission in Fisher 'Pioneer Judge' 59–64. For less detail, but a more complete picture, see the account in RSO 1877, II, 2467.

54 Gowan to Mr Justice Taschereau, draft, 17 April 1880, Gowan Papers, reel m1938

55 Friedland 'Wright's Code' 313

56 House of Commons *Debates* 27 February 1877, 327

57 Ibid. 21 April 1887, 1668. The *Toronto Globe* of 23 April 1877 reported this item and paraphrased the portion of the debate in which Blake explained that he would follow the plan used to produce the Revised Statutes of Ontario. No other newspaper recorded either the item or the debate.

58 Although research in Blake's papers has failed to turn up Gowan's letter, the facts in it are attested to by Blake's reply. There is little doubt that Gowan offered Blake Wright's code, because Blake describes it as 'the draft in your possession' (Blake to Gowan, 28 June 1877, Gowan Papers, reel m1937), which is essentially the way Gowan described it when he offered to lend it to Taschereau in 1880; this is discussed below. See also Gowan to Taschereau, draft, 17 April 1880, Gowan Papers, reel m1938.

59 Blake to Gowan, 28 June 1877, Gowan Papers, reel m1937

60 Friedland 'Wright's Code' 307

61 Ardagh *Gowan* 71, 182

62 Carnarvon to Gowan, 27 June 1878; Cairns to Gowan, 14 July 1878, Gowan Papers, reel m1897

63 Cairns to Gowan, 18 July 1878, Gowan Papers, reel m1897

64 Zebulon A. Lash, deputy minister of justice, to James Cockburn, MP, 28 April 1881; Canada, Parliament, Sessional Papers, 1883, no. 17, 9. Cockburn was appointed commissioner of the dominion statute consolidation project in 1881, and wrote to the minister of justice asking for the drafts Langton had prepared.

65 Henry J. Morgan *The Canadian Men and Women of the Time* (Toronto: William Briggs 1898) 760; Donald Creighton *John A. Macdonald: The Old Chieftain* (Toronto: Macmillan 1965) 154

66 Gowan to Macdonald, 15 November 1878, Macdonald Papers, reel c1600.

67 Ibid. Nor is there any correspondence between this most prolific letter-writer and James MacDonald.

68 (1879) 2 *Legal News* 13, 19–24, 27–31; see also (1878) 1, at 69 and 431, and (1880) 3, at 113 and 169.

69 House of Commons *Debates* 16 March 1879 223

70 Gowan to Macdonald, 8 April 1879, Macdonald Papers, reel c1600

71 Savary to Macdonald, 24 February 1879, Macdonald Papers, reel c1715

72 Senate *Debates* 7 May 1879, 427–73

73 Ibid. 474–5

74 A paraphrase of part of the debate was published in the *Toronto Globe* of 9 May 1879. Of five newspapers consulted, the *Globe* was the only one to mention this item.

75 Economic questions, the preliminary moves in the effort to build the Canadian Pacific Railway and prospective immigration to the northwest all bulked large in John A. Macdonald's mind at this time. See Creighton *Old Chieftain* 243–305.

76 House of Commons *Debates* 1 March 1880, 306; Gowan to Macdonald, 31 December 1879 and 19 May 1880, Macdonald Papers, reel c1600

77 Snell and Vaughan *Supreme Court of Canada* 26

78 Taschereau to Gowan, 15 March 1880, Gowan Papers, reel m1899
79 The words in parentheses were crossed out by Gowan, and the draft ends with an incomplete sentence: Gowan to Taschereau, draft, 12 April 1880, Gowan Papers, reel m1938.
80 Gowan to Taschereau, draft, 17 April 1880, Gowan Papers, reel m1938
81 Taschereau to Gowan, 21 April 1880, Gowan Papers, reel m1938
82 Canada *Acts of the Parliament of Canada Relating to the Criminal Law* (Ottawa: Queen's Printer 1881)
83 Creighton *Old Chieftain* 284–316
84 See Macdonald Papers, reel c1659 'Correspondence between Sir John A. Macdonald and the Hon. James MacDonald 1875–1881.' P.B. Waite asserts that James MacDonald 'was no political lion,' and quotes Sir Hector Langevin as saying that MacDonald 'was an utter failure in politics.' *Man from Halifax* 102. Sir John Thompson, who served on the bench with MacDonald for four years, did not hold him in high regard as a judge either: Thompson to Prime Minister Macdonald, 20 August 1888, Macdonald Papers, reel c1683.
85 House of Commons *Debates* 10 March 1881, 1328
86 Ibid. Although there was extensive coverage of the estimates in the press, the only specific mention of this item was in the *Halifax Herald* of 11 March 1881.
87 House of Commons *Debates* 10 March 1881, 1328
88 Macdonald to Cockburn, 30 March 1881, Macdonald Papers, reel c33
89 *DCB* vol. 11 196
90 Macdonald to Cockburn, 30 March 1881, Macdonald Papers, reel c33
91 Canada, Parliament, Sessional Papers, 1883, no. 17, 8
92 Zebulon Lash to Cockburn, 28 April 1881, 5 November 1881, ibid. 11
93 James MacDonald to Prime Minister Macdonald, 7 April 1881, Macdonald Papers, reel c1659
94 Campbell, who was an effective postmaster general before his move to Justice, was prevailed upon by Tupper and Langevin to take the job, but Campbell was not confident that he had the qualifications for it (Campbell to Macdonald, 17 May 1881, Macdonald Papers, reel c1590). On the face of it, the main drawback to the appointment was that Campbell was in the Senate. But in this case the drawback was more apparent than real. Macdonald and Campbell, as they had in the past, formed a very effective team. Campbell did the work in Justice and controlled debate in the Senate, while Sir John was freed of detail but was Justice spokesman in the Commons.

95 Cockburn to Campbell, 7 June 1881 and Lash to Cockburn 8 June 1881, Canada, Parliament, Sessional Papers, 1883, no. 17, 9

96 Lash to Cockburn, 17 November 1881, Lash to J.L. MacDougall, auditor general, 18 November; and Lash to Cockburn, 28 November, ibid. 11, 12

97 Ibid. 6

98 The number 1,294 was calculated by Gustavus Wicksteed, who published some of the commission reports that had not been printed as sessional papers. The total included statutes from the following jurisdictions: dominion 612; Nova Scotia 86; Prince Edward Island 173; New Brunswick 147; the Canadas 215; British Columbia 61: 'The Revised Statutes of Canada' (1887) 10 *Legal News* 187–92 and (1888) 11, 57–9.

99 Canada, Parliament, Sessional Papers, 1883, no. 17, 1–5. For an exhaustive analysis of the commissioners' work, see Campbell's speech in the Senate: *Debates* 16 March 1885, 304–22.

100 Alexander Ferguson to Campbell, 1 May and 1 August 1882; Canada, Parliament, Sessional Papers, no. 17, 7, 8

101 Campbell to Macdonald, 7 September 1882, Macdonald Papers, reel c1590

102 Biographical material on Burbidge has been culled from a variety of sources, but principally from Russell *Autobiography* 80, 81ff.; 'Graduate of Mount Allison' (1891) 21 *The Argosy* 28; and C[harles] M[orse] 'The Late Mr Justice Burbidge' (1908) 28 *Canadian Law Times* 222.

103 Campbell to Macdonald, 1 April 1882, Macdonald Papers, reel c1590. The name is indecipherable. It appears to be 'Connally.' The problem with this interpretation is that there is no 'Connally' or close variation of this name in any law list of the period.

104 In the Department of Justice letterbook, which was in use when Burbidge was appointed, there are twelve letters from Burbidge to Cockburn concerning the consolidation, and most enclose letters from all and sundry advocating change: PAC RG13, A3, Department of Justice Letterbooks, microfilm, reel c14331. See, for example, pages 467, 488, 499, and 507.

105 Campbell to Macdonald, 7 September 1882, Macdonald Papers, reel c1590; Burbidge to Cockburn, 12 October 1882, PAC RG13, A3, Department of Justice Letterbooks, reel c14332

106 House of Commons *Debates* 21 February 1883, 57. Several newspapers reported on events in Parliament for this date, but only the *Toronto Globe* and the *Toronto Mail* of 22 February 1883 mentioned the exchange between Macdonald and Blake, and then only in passing. There was no editorial comment then or later.

107 Burbidge to Privy Council, 28 April 1883, PAC RG13, A3, Department of Justice Letterbooks, reel c14335; Campbell to Macdonald, 17 June 1883, Macdonald Papers, reel c1589

108 Burbidge to Carswell, the legal publisher, 30 April 1883, PAC RG13, A3, Department of Justice Letterbooks, reel c14335

109 Burbidge to Courtney, ibid., 18 May 1883, reel c14334. It is to be noted that Burbidge says 'I,' not 'the Department' or 'the Government.'

110 Burbidge to Joseph Colmer, High Commission Secretary, 9 August 1883, ibid., reel c14336; Burbidge to Carswell, 15 September 1883, ibid.

111 Campbell to Macdonald, 17 June 1883, Macdonald Papers, reel c1589; Senate *Debates* 16 March 1885, 311

112 Senate *Debates* 16 March 1885, 312

113 Ibid. 2 April 1884, 404

114 A copy of Burbidge's draft has not yet been discovered. The information on its content is taken from 'A New Penal Code,' published in the *Toronto Globe* of 30 August 1884. This article is the longest and most detailed treatment of the criminal law in the popular press during the period of this study. It is an excellent piece of exposition and analysis, and is marred only by the fact that its author takes the government to task for expending the entire subvention since the beginning of the revision process on the code when, in fact, it was only a small part of the consolidation. In an editorial in the same issue it is made plain that a code that defines offences is necessary. The editorialist, having reviewed the proposed definition of sedition and its possible application by the courts, is not sure that the proposed legislation will fill the bill in all respects. But he is willing to withhold judgment until he sees the final form of the legislation. In view of the excellence of the *Globe*'s treatment, the two comments in professional journals, albeit favourable, are superficial. See 'The Consolidation of the Statutes' (1884) 4 *Canadian Law Times* 432 and 'Report of the Commissioners' (1884) 7 *Legal News* 358–9.

115 Senate *Debates* 2 April 1884, 404

116 Ibid. 405, 404

117 Ibid. 16 March 1885, 312

118 Burbidge to Campbell, 11 December 1884, PAC RG13, A2, Department of Justice, letters received, microfilm. For the report see 'The Revised Statutes of Canada' (1887) 10 *Legal News* 188. This may not be the full text. The actual report was part of sessional paper no. 21 for 1885, which was not published.

119 In essence: the Senate did not have the authority to initiate money bills. The consolidation was a money bill in that public revenue was appropri-

ated to enforce its provisions. But because it was a consolidation and made no changes in existing law, the Senate would not have been initiating these measures; rather, it would have been transposing them from one form to another.

120 The first edition of his *Parliamentary Procedure and Practice* (Montreal: Dawson Brothers) was published in 1884.

121 John Bourinot 'Memorandum as to the right of the Senate to consider in the first place the Consolidated Statutes of Canada,' 19 January 1885, Macdonald Papers, reel c1701

122 Senate *Debates* 13 February 1885, 48

123 There were joint committees on the library and on printing, of course, but this was the first joint committee struck to examine substantive law.

124 Senate *Debates* 16 March 1885, 306. The debate runs from 304 to 322.

125 Campbell's speech received a good press in Conservative organs: see, for example, the *Toronto Mail* of 17 March 1885 and *La Presse* of 18 March; but there was no mention of it in Liberal journals. They were engaged in a running battle with the Senate because of their alleged exclusion from that chamber by the Speaker. See 'The Senate Press Censorship' in the *Toronto Globe* of 19 March and the *Ottawa Free Press* of 17 and 18 March.

126 See, for example, Macdonald to Campbell, 19 May 1885, PAC, Sir Alexander Campbell Papers and 'The Riel Trial' *Toronto Globe* 11 July 1885.

127 Creighton *Old Chieftain* 409–17; Waite *Man from Halifax* 126–33

128 House of Commons *Debates* 21 April 1885, 1226. Macdonald's announcement was reported without comment in several Conservative newspapers. See, for example, *La Presse* of 22 April 1885. Apart from the *Toronto Globe*, the Liberal papers were full of the franchise bill and the Riel rebellion.

129 House of Commons *Journal* 1885, appendix 2, 2–7

130 Campbell to Macdonald, 20 May 1885, Macdonald Papers, reel c1591

131 House of Commons *Journal* 30 June 1885, 504

132 Waite *Man from Halifax* 128–33

133 Alexander Ferguson had been retained to integrate the statutes of the 1885 session in the Revised Statutes and to make the amendments proposed by the joint committee. When he wanted advice and direction during the early days of Thompson's tenure, he wrote directly to the prime minister concerning his work. See, for example, his report to Macdonald of 22 October 1885, Macdonald Papers, reel c1773.

134 House of Commons *Debates* 3 March 1886, 38

135 Ibid. 39. The debate was given good coverage in the Conservative press,

particularly in *La Presse* 4 March 1886, but was ignored by Liberal papers, except for the *Toronto Globe* of the same date.

136 House of Commons *Debates*, 6 April 1886, 513, 514, 516

137 Again, Thompson's speech was reported favourably in the Conservative press and largely ignored by Liberal journals. However, although the *Ottawa Free Press* was silent on the Revised Statutes, it did give prominence to a criminal law amendment enacted by the imperial Parliament (7 April 1886.)

138 House of Commons *Debates* 7 April 1886, 555. The title of a short editorial, 'The Bumptious Minister Bends,' gives some indication of how Thompson's performance was reported by the *Toronto Globe* (8 April 1886). In turn, the *Globe*'s editorialist was subjected to some acid comments by the *Toronto Mail* (9 April). However, as with most items to do with statute law revision, the journalists ignored the substance and concentrated on the personalities involved.

139 Ardagh *Gowan* 188–91

140 Gowan to William Hartpole Lecky, a British historian, 10 March 1885, Gowan Papers, reel m1937; Senate *Debates* 16 March 1885, 304

141 From 21 April onward, a steady exchange of letters between Gowan and Thompson continued until Thompson's death in 1894. In 1886 the primary topic was the summary conviction bill that Gowan had drafted the previous year. See Thompson to Gowan, 21 April 1886, Gowan Papers, reel m1938. Gowan does mention the Revised Statutes, but only in passing, so it seems that the statutes did not arouse any controversy after second reading in the Commons; Gowan to Thompson, 28 May 1886, Thompson Papers, reel c9238.

142 But it was greeted by editorial silence in the press. After the exchange between the *Globe* and the *Mail* subsequent to second reading, several papers noted the bare fact of third reading in the Commons. Apart from a short paragraph in the *Ottawa Free Press* of 21 May 1886 detailing Senator Scott's criticism that the commissioners had interpreted some parts of the statute law incorrectly, there was silence on events in the Upper Chamber.

143 Nearly 1,300 Dominion and colonial acts running to several thousand pages had been compressed into 185 chapters covering 2,246 pages. An additional 260 pages recorded in detail the history and disposition of the original enactments.

144 In terms of bulk, the situation in Canada was still much different from that in England, where the eighteen volumes of the imperial collection took up the best part of a bookshelf. In Canada the legal professional

could, with the addition of the one or two similar volumes of provincial enactments, provide himself with a complete set of the statute law of his jurisdiction that would occupy no more than nine or ten inches of shelf space at a cost of less than $20. For example, the two volumes of the RSO 1877 cost $6; the CSC 1859, which was larger than either of the volumes of the RSC 1886, could be had for $5, so it is unlikely that one of the latter would have cost more than $5. Thus, the total outlay for an Ontario lawyer would have been about $16. Morgan *Canadian Legal Directory* annex, Carswell's catalogue, 7, 19.

145 Thompson to D.D. Field, 14 April 1887, Thompson Papers, reel 10572. Unfortunately, a correspondence did not develop between Thompson and Field; at least, there is no trace of one in the Thompson Papers.

146 House of Commons *Debates* 3 March 1886, 39

147 Ibid. This statement was incorrect, but no one challenged Thompson on the issue.

148 The criminal statutes are RSC 1886, c. 60 and cc. 139–85.

149 RSC 1886, c. 147, s. 9

CHAPTER 6 THE CRIMINAL CODE

1 Morgan *Canadian Men and Women 1912* 739. Thompson to Privy Council, 27 July 1887, PAC RG13, A3, Department of Justice Letterbooks, reel c14348

2 Morgan *Canadian Men and Women 1912* 739

3 Canada, *Acts of the Parliament of the Dominion of Canada Relating to Criminal Law* (Ottawa: Queen's Printer 1887)

4 Taschereau to Thompson, 2 November 1887, Thompson Papers, reel c9242. Taschereau knew whereof he spoke in this respect. Delivery of the volumes for the government was probably made early in 1888, but the publisher was still waiting for payment two years later: Thompson to Taschereau, 9 January 1890, Thompson Papers, reel c10576.

5 Thompson to Taschereau, 9 January 1890, Thompson Papers, reel c10573

6 Henri-Elzéar Taschereau *The Criminal Statute Law of Canada* 2d ed. (Toronto: Carswell 1888). For reviews see (1888) 8 *Canadian Law Times* 148 and (1888) 24 *Canada Law Journal* 391.

7 Taschereau *Criminal Statute Law* 2d ed., iv–vi

8 This was a persuasive argument. According to Taschereau, his first edition, though well received by the profession, had incurred a substantial financial loss: Taschereau to Thompson, 2 November 1887, Thompson Papers, reel c9241.

9 Taschereau to Thompson, 23 October 1889, Thompson Papers, reel c9246

10 One of the most recent manifestations of this trait had been demonstrated when he had cleared up the legal chaos in the North-West Territories by the sweeping legal reforms he had introduced in 1886 and 1887. See Brown 'Unsure and Uncertain' 512. For an assessment of this aspect of Thompson's career, see Waite *Man from Halifax* 437–8.

11 There was no love lost between Taschereau and Burbidge either, since the latter had advised the Privy Council to refuse Taschereau's application for leave in April 1884 on the grounds that the judge's application had requested that the approval be forwarded to him in Hamilton, Bermuda, and had been postmarked in New York: Burbidge to Privy Council, 2 March 1884, PAC RG13, A3, Department of Justice Letterbooks, c14337.

12 Taschereau to Thompson, 23 October 1889, Thompson Papers, reel c9246

13 It may well be that Governor General Frederick Stanley got wind of such a scheme and warned Thompson, because on 30 October he asked Thompson to come and see him 'in reference to *an important Criminal matter.*' Memorandum, Robert Sedgewick, deputy minister of justice, to Thompson, 30 October 1889, Thompson Papers, reel c10576.

14 Hansard, 6 February 1880, col. 145

15 See the debate on the Criminal Evidence Bill in 1891 for a succinct summary of Cameron's efforts to have such legislation enacted. House of Commons *Debates* 27 July 1891, col. 2955.

16 Graham Parker asserts that Taschereau wrote to Thompson concerning the Criminal Code Bill of 1891 ('Origins of the Criminal Code' 273). This is incorrect. Taschereau's letter refers to the Supreme Court Bill (1891, 54 & 55 Vict., c. 26), which, as Thompson pointed out in his reply, had then passed 'all its stages except third reading.' Bill 32, the draft Criminal Code, was read the first time on 12 May; it was never read a second time. Taschereau to Thompson, 31 July 1891, Thompson Papers, reel c9254; Thompson to Taschereau, 11 August 1891, ibid. reel c10698.

17 For example, see Burbidge to Thompson, 21 February 1888, with which Burbidge sent a draft bill to abolish forfeiture on conviction of felony, and discussed proposals to make the rules of English law uniform in Canada: Thompson Papers, reel c9242.

18 On the title page of his *Digest*, Burbidge wrote: 'Founded by permission on Sir James Fitzjames Stephen's Digest of the Criminal Law.' An extensive search in the Stephen Papers failed to turn up a mention of this project, and no reference to it has been found in the few papers of Burbidge that have been discovered.

19 Article 86, 'Riotous Demolition of Houses' (Burbidge *Digest* 72), for

example, contains only 54 words, in contrast to the 233-word sentence in RSC 1886, c. 147, s. 9.

20 Dominion legislation had by no means subsumed all the criminal law of the provinces. See chapter 3, note 180.

21 Thompson told Gowan that Masters 'had done a good deal of work on the preparation of a digest of Procedure in Criminal Cases similar in plan to Burbidge's book.' But since the latter was modelled on Stephen, it is a reasonable assumption that Masters, too, would have followed the same practice, using as his model Stephen's *Digest of the Law of Criminal Procedure* published in 1883 (London: Macmillan). Thompson to Gowan, 3 May 1892, Gowan Papers, reel m1938.

22 Burbidge to Thompson, 16 November 1889, Thompson Papers, reel c9246

23 For detail see CC 43.

24 Charles Morse, review of *A Digest of the Criminal Law of Canada* (1890) 13 *Legal News* 81–3; review (1890) 10 *Canadian Law Times* 90–4; review (1890) 26 *Canada Law Journal* 599

25 Canada, Parliament, Sessional Papers, 1891, no. 66, 7

26 Like Sir Alexander Campbell before him, Thompson was determined to select his deputy on the basis of ability, since he 'could not afford to take a man about whose fitness [he] could entertain a doubt': Thompson to Sir John A. Macdonald, 21 September 1887, Macdonald Papers, reel c1683. For details of the five-month search that eventuated in the appointment of Sedgewick, see Waite *Man from Halifax* 188. Sedgewick (1848– 1906) was a former colleague of Thompson's at the Nova Scotia bar and a co-founder of and lecturer at Dalhousie Law School. At the time of his appointment he was the recorder of Halifax. He was promoted to the bench of the Supreme Court of Canada by Thompson in 1893.

27 Thompson to Gowan, 3 May 1892, Gowan Papers, reel m1938

28 Bourinot *Parliamentary Procedure* 172

29 Sedgewick to F.A. McCord, law clerk of the House of Commons, 22 October 1890, PAC RG13, A3, Department of Justice Letterbooks, reel c14358; House of Commons *Debates* 30 June 1891, col. 1559

30 Canada, House of Commons, Bill no. 32, An Act Respecting the Criminal Law, 1891; hereinafter DC 1891

31 In DC 1891 the provenance of each section is printed in the margin adjoining the section. The main English source is the draft code of 1880; twenty-eight sections are taken from the draft code of 1879 and from various imperial statutes. RSC 1886 is the prime Canadian source; several sections are condensed from subsequent dominion legislation and old

colonial statutes; five sections are from Burbidge's *Digest*, and four are new legislation. Two sources are cited for several sections of DC 1891: the first source indicated, imperial or Canadian, has been taken as the prime source of each of these sections in the compilation of the statistics in the text.

32 DC 1891, s. 303. This definition is essentially the same as that given in the Criminal Code today; see RSC 1970, c. 34, s. 283.

33 DC 1891, ss. 213, 215, 255, 264. For the common law development of sedition, see Brown 'Craftsmanship of Bias' 7–26.

34 For an example of how a judge was able to exercise quasi-legislative authority, see the account of the trial for sedition of the Winnipeg Strike leaders in 1919, ibid. 1–6.

35 As to bail, compare RSC 1886, c. 174, s. 81, and DC 1891, s. 597. With regard to standing trial in the dock: before the enactment of the Criminal Code, a misdemeanant was a 'defendant' as in a case of tort; after 1892, his status became that of 'prisoner at the bar' and he was put in the dock in the charge of the jury. See Kenny *Criminal Law* 99; Hardinge Giffard in *Halsbury's Laws of England* 1st ed. (London: Butterworth 1907–17) vol. 9, 362; W.J. Tremeear *The Criminal Code* 1st ed. (Toronto: Canada Law Book Company 1902) 590n.

36 For the origin and development of felonies and misdemeanours, see CC 71–4; for summary conviction offences, see ibid. 75–6.

37 For a review of the common law pertaining to grand juries and indictments, see Blackstone *Commentaries* vol. 4, 299–306. For the imperial commissioners on the subject of the proposed changes, see *Parl. Papers* 1879 [2345] XX 32.

38 For a thorough discussion of this subject and an enumeration of the few obscure offences that were held to be punishable at common law, see Allen B. Harvey (ed.) *Tremeear's Annotated Criminal Code* 5th ed. (Calgary: Burroughs 1944) 42–9; for an abbreviated discussion, see Alan W. Mewett 'The Canadian Criminal Law, 1867–1967' (1967) 45 *Canadian Bar Review* 727–8.

39 Germany, Statutes, *Strafgesetzbuch für das deutsche Reich* (Königsberg 1891); *Strafprosessordnung für das deutsche Reich* (Berlin 1892). France, Statutes, *Code pénal* (Paris 1881); *Code d'instruction criminelle* (Paris 1898)

40 For a partial list of other alterations in the penal law, see Henri-Elzéar Taschereau *The Criminal Code of Canada* (Toronto: Carswell 1893) iv–x.

41 Canada *Acts of the Parliament of the Dominion of Canada Relating to Criminal Law* (Ottawa: Queen's Printer 1891)

42 Gowan to Thompson, 24 November 1890, Thompson Papers, reel c9250

43 For example, Gowan urged Thompson not to attempt to enact the
   1891 bill, but rather to use it to 'invite fair criticism' which would be
   reflected in subsequent legislation (Gowan to Thompson, 18 May 1891,
   Thompson Papers, reel c9253). The minister had adopted this policy at
   least a month previously: Sedgewick to Judge Thomas McGuire of Prince
   Albert, PAC RG13, A3, Department of Justice Letterbooks, reel c14360.
   However, he took the trouble to answer Gowan, and the impression his
   letter leaves is that he had considered the senator's suggestion carefully
   in arriving at his decision: 22 May 1891, Gowan Papers, reel m1938.
44 Thompson to Adamson, 24 November 1890, Gowan Papers, reel m1938
45 Bourinot *Parliamentary Procedure* 517
46 House of Commons *Debates* 12 May 1891, col. 156
47 In the newspapers consulted for this study, I have been unable to find
   any trace of the discussion of 'fundamental changes' in the criminal
   law noted by Thompson.
48 House of Commons *Debates* 12 May 1891, col. 156
49 13 May 1891. Most newspapers mentioned the introduction of Bill 32 in
   passing, but only the *Toronto Mail* and *Globe* of 13 May 1891 gave an overview of its content.
50 Hansard, 14 May 1878, cols. 1936–59; 3 April 1879, cols. 310–47
51 See the briefing sheets prepared for Thompson by Sedgewick in which he
   refers specifically to Holker's speeches of 1878 and 1879. Canada, Department of Justice, file 63/94, item 117. This special file consists of several
   hundred heterogeneous items pertaining to the Criminal Code bills
   of 1891 and 1892, and contains a full index of the names of correspondents. It was assembled from items stripped from regular departmental
   files. The topics ranged from selling tobacco to minors (item 15) to a classification scheme for degrees of homicide (item 24), and included much
   of Senator Gowan's correspondence for these years, and his 'extended
   suggestions' for amending the bills (items 49 and 49$^1/_2$). I am indebted to
   the Honourable Jean Chrétien, the former minister of justice, for allowing
   me to review this and other historical files held by the department.
52 Joseph Pope *Memoirs of the Right Honourable Sir John Alexander Macdonald*
   (Toronto: Musson Book Company n.d.) 628. See also the account in
   Creighton *Old Chieftain* 561.
53 Hector-Louis Langevin was a senior Quebec minister in the Conservative
   Cabinet. It was alleged that he was implicated with Thomas McGreevy,
   a Quebec MP and a building contractor, in illegal contracts and patronage
   hand-outs. The scandal dragged on for years. Eventually, McGreevy
   was expelled from the House, charged, convicted, and given a prison

sentence. For details, see Waite *Man from Halifax* 287–8, 304–13. Honoré Mercier, premier of Quebec, was implicated in the Baie Des Chaleurs scandal, another drawn-out process. He was removed from office by the lieutenant-governor; for details see ibid. 308, 381.

54 Senator Gowan finally received a copy on 18 May, a week after first reading in the Commons. This appears to have been a special case, since it was forwarded to him at his home in Barrie by the Senate postmaster: Gowan to Thompson, 18 May 1891, Thompson Papers, reel m9253.

55 House of Commons *Journal* 31 July 1891, 368

56 Haskins to Arthur Boyle, MP, 21 April 1892, Canada, Department of Justice, file 65/92

57 Roderick C. Macleod 'The Shaping of Canadian Criminal Law, 1892 to 1902' Canadian Historical Association, *Historical Papers 1978* 70

58 Canada, Department of Justice, file 63/94, items 4, 49, and 49$^1/_2$

59 Ibid. items 59, 66, 14, 24, and 97. One notable group which is not represented is the professional press. Apart from a short comment in (1891) 14 *Legal News* 137 to the effect that a criminal code bill had been mentioned in the throne speech, there was no direct comment, no analysis, and no criticism from this source, either to the Justice Department directly or in the editorial pages of legal journals during 1891. It was not until 16 May 1892, when the code had been before Parliament for over two months, that the *Legal News* gave it a brief mention [(1892) 15, 145]. Nothing further appeared in any legal periodical until after the enactment of the code.

60 House of Commons *Debates* 8 March 1892, col. 106

61 Although parliamentary and press attention were focused on the Quebec general election, which was held on the same day as the introduction of Bill 7, most newspapers made passing mention of it. The *Toronto Mail* of 9 March 1892, whose correspondent must have been well briefed by Thompson, ran the longest account, which included information that was not in the *Debates* and which, in fact, was not true – namely, that '[t]he grand jury system, which has been the subject of a great deal of public criticism, is left unchanged.'

62 Dawson to Sedgewick, 5 April 1892; McCord to Thompson, 6 April; circular memorandum, Dawson to all concerned, 6 April Thompson Papers, reel c9257

63 House of Commons *Debates* 12 April 1892, col. 1312 (my italics)

64 *Parl. Papers* 1879 [2345] xx 7

65 House of Commons *Debates* 12 April 1892, col. 1313

66 Ibid. col. 1314

67 Ibid. col. 1316

68 David Mills (1831–1903) attended local schools and the University of Michigan. He was called to the Ontario bar in 1883, and named queen's counsel in 1890. He was a professor of constitutional and international law at the University of Toronto from 1888. He served as a Liberal MP and Justice critic from 1878 and as minister of justice in the Laurier government from 1897; he was appointed to the Supreme Court of Canada in 1902.

69 Waite *Man from Halifax* 185, 437

70 See Sedgewick's briefing sheets: Canada, Department of Justice, file 63/94, item 117.

71 He could have easily done so, had he wished to. Senator Gowan had prepared for him a closely written twenty-page brief on the subject. The minister may well have had it with him when he delivered his speech, because it is paper-clipped to Sedgewick's briefing sheets, which Thompson did follow closely during the first half of his presentation (ibid.).

72 A measure of Thompson's success in lulling the opposition to sleep on his bill can be seen in a remark of Senator Gowan. A month after second reading, he told Thompson, 'I fancy there can be few who are really making the question *a study*. Otherwise a book I took away with me from the library [containing papers and reports which criticized the Imperial codification bills] and have [,] would have been *in request*.' He obviously intended to keep it out, since, in his opinion, it 'would have been a *rich find* for the enemy, in attacking your bill (*futor arma ministrat*).' However, since Thompson had been careful to anticipate all the objections the English critics had made, Gowan's initiative was well meant but unnecessary. Gowan to Thompson (the letter is undated, but it was received in the Justice Department on 19 May 1892): file 63/94, item 49.

73 As the distance from Ottawa increased, interest in Bill 7 decreased. The *Victoria Daily Colonist* of 13 April 1892 gave second reading twelve lines, while the *Halifax Herald* of the same date told its readers that 'the house adjourned at 6 o'clock till Tuesday next.' The *Manitoba Free Press* was silent. *La Presse* (same date) and the Ottawa and Toronto papers ran extended paraphrases of the debate, but of course gave prominence to the speeches of their political mentors. But regardless of its political bias or whatever else it reported, each account stressed Thompson's announced intention to retain the grand jury, and most reported the satisfaction with which this announcement was received by Laurier and Mills.

74 Senate *Debates* 12 April 1892, 156

75 Ibid.

76 Ibid. 157

77 There is no account of the Senate debate in any newspaper consulted for 13 April, or for a week afterwards. This raises the question of what kinds of accounts would have been written if parliamentary correspondents had audited both Thompson's and Gowan's speeches.

78 Gowan to Thompson, 21 April 1892, Thompson Papers, reel c9257

79 Sedgewick to Bourinot, 27 April 1892, Canada, Department of Justice, file 63/94, item 97

80 Senate *Debates* 12 April 1892, 156; House of Commons *Debates* 12 April, col. 1319

81 William Mulock (1844–1944) attended local schools and the University of Toronto. He was called to the Ontario bar in 1868 and named queen's counsel in 1890. He served as a Liberal MP from 1882, and as postmaster general from 1896. He was appointed chief justice of the Exchequer Division, High Court of Ontario, in 1905, and chief justice of Ontario in 1923. Lawrence Geoffrey Power (1841–1921) attended St Mary's College, Halifax, and Harvard University. He was called to the Nova Scotia bar in 1866, and named king's counsel in 1905. He served as clerk of the House of Assembly in Nova Scotia from 1867 to 1877. He was called to the Senate in 1877, and served as Speaker of the Senate from 1901 to 1905. Richard William Scott (1825–1913) was called to the Upper Canada bar in 1848, and named queen's counsel in 1867. He served as an MLA in the Province of Canada from 1857, and in Ontario from 1867. He was appointed Speaker of the Ontario House of Assembly in 1871, and called to the Senate in 1874. He served as secretary of state in the Mackenzie government from 1874; in opposition from 1878 to 1896; and as secretary of state in the Laurier government from 1896 to 1908.

82 William Miller 'Incidents in the Political Career of the Late Sir John Thompson' (n.p., n.p. 1895) 20. A copy of this pamphlet is included in PAC William Miller Papers.

83 Senate *Debates* 4 July 1892, 386

84 See Sedgewick to Gowan, 25 May 1892, Gowan Papers, reel m1938; Miller 'Incidents' 20. For details of Miller's part in introducing Thompson to politics above the local level, see Waite *Man from Halifax* 70–4. On Miller's drinking problem, see Sir John A. Macdonald to Thompson, 8 December 1888, Macdonald Papers, reel c9246. On his quest for honours, see, for example, Miller to Gowan, 9 January 1892, Gowan Papers, reel m1938; Miller to Thompson, 4 July 1892, Thompson Papers, reel c9258, and the many letters that precede and follow these.

85 Thompson to Gowan, 3 May 1892, Gowan Papers, reel m1938
86 Thompson to Gowan, 3 May 1892, ibid. This was not an isolated opinion;
   see Sedgewick to Gowan, 18 May 1892, ibid.
87 Senate *Debates* 6 July 1892, 476
88 House of Commons *Journal* 16 May 1892, 318
89 House of Commons *Debates* 17 May 1892, col. 2701
90 Thompson to Gowan, 18 May 1892, Gowan Papers, reel m1889
91 Louis Henry Davies (1845–1924) was educated at Prince of Wales Acad-
   emy, Prince Edward Island. He was admitted to the Inner Temple
   and called to the English bar in 1866; he was called to the PEI bar in 1867
   and named queen's counsel in 1880. He served as a Liberal MP from 1882.
   Davies was appointed to the Supreme Court of Canada in 1901, and
   named chief justice of Canada in 1918.
      Thompson was not impressed with the quality of the opposition
   speakers. 'Mills,' he said, 'is well read, Laurier far from it and Davies a
   mere gabbler of phrases picked up in a very inferior practice': Thompson
   to Gowan, 1 June 1892, Gowan Papers, reel m1900. Considering his
   command of the detail of the legislation and the tactics he used so successfully to keep the opposition in ignorance, Thompson was too acid in
   his comment. It is significant, too, that he did not mention William
   Mulock, whose arguments were always well reasoned and well articulated
   and who stopped Thompson cold during the debate on the sedition
   sections: *Debates* 19 May 1892, cols. 2831–33.
92 Thompson to Gowan, 18 May 1892, Gowan Papers, reel m1889
93 House of Commons *Debates* 19 May 1892, cols. 2830, 2834
94 Ibid. col. 2831
95 Ibid. col. 2833
96 For details of the development of the crime of sedition, see Brown
   'Craftsmanship of Bias' 7–26.
97 House of Commons *Debates* 13 June 1892, cols. 3649, 4228
98 John Ward *The Hansard Chronicles* (n.p. Deneau and Greenberg 1980)
   148–9
99 26 May 1892
100 18 May 1892
101 20 May 1892
102 This figure was given by Senator Scott, who discussed the matter exhaus-
    tively in debate. Textual comparisons made for this study support his
    information: Senate *Debates* 5 July 1892, 399.
103 Telegram, Thompson to Gowan, 27 June 1892, Gowan Papers, reel m1900.
    Third reading in the Commons passed almost unnoticed in the press.

104 Miller to Gowan, 2 July 1892, Gowan Papers, reel m1938
105 Although the Revised Statutes had been sent to a joint committee in 1885, it will be recalled that the bill of that year was withdrawn before it reached the Senate. During my research on the question of the joint committee I talked to the law clerk of the House of Commons. He was intrigued when he learned of the event, and informed me that it was a most unusual procedure. He knew of no other later instance where a joint committee had been struck to consider substantive legislation.
106 Scott's speech is reported in Senate *Debates* 4 July 1892, 385–7.
107 Sedgewick to S.E. Dawson, queen's printer, 20 April 1892, Canada, Department of Justice, file 63/94, item 97; Bourinot *Parliamentary Procedure* 172
108 Senate *Debates* 4 July 1892, 385–7
109 Ibid. 387–98
110 Scott's searching and wide-ranging remarks got scant attention in the press: four lines in the *Manitoba Free Press* of 5 July 1892, fifteen in *La Presse* of the same date, and four in the *Toronto Mail* of the same date. Otherwise there was silence. The criminal law got even less attention during the final days of debate when the Senate divided its attention between the code and the Redistribution Bill.
111 Senate *Debates* 6 July 1892, 465
112 Ibid. 466–9
113 Ibid. 4 July 1892, 386. There is no doubt that Scott was a busy man during the period of the joint committee meetings. As leader of the opposition he had a number of administrative tasks. In addition, at least seven major and contentious bills, ranging from land grants to railroads in Manitoba and the North-West, to ocean mail service, to the Bell Telephone Bill, and the Internal Economy of the Senate Bill were passed by the Senate. Scott made major interventions in the debates on most of these bills.
114 Senate *Debates* 9 July 1892, 523
115 10 July 1892, and 12 July 1892, respectively
116 They are enumerated in House of Commons *Journal* 9 July 1892, 488–91.
117 Sedgewick to Dawson, 3 November 1892, PAC RG13, A3, Department of Justice Letterbooks, reel c14365
118 All the correspondence on this incident, including Taschereau's letter and the detailed departmental rebuttal, comprise item 107 in Canada, Department of Justice, file 63/94.
119 2 February 1893
120 9 February 1893
121 11 February 1893

122 Editorial (1893) 16 *Legal News* 55
123 'The Criminal Code' (1893) 23 *Canada Law Journal* 94–5
124 Draft, Gowan to Governor General Frederick Stanley, 25 March 1893, Gowan papers, reel m1938; unaddressed draft, undated, Gowan papers, reel m1939
125 House of Commons *Debates* 13 February 1893, 607

CHAPTER 7 EPILOGUE

1 Editorial (1894) 30 *Canada Law Journal* 447
2 Letter 'The Criminal Code' (1893) 13 *Canadian Law Times* 204–5. In felony trials the jurors were sworn individually, and their oath obliged them to try 'the *prisoner* at the bar'; jurors who were to try a misdemeanour were sworn as a group, and promised to 'truly try the issue between our sovereign Lord the King and the *defendant*': Kenny *Outlines* 99.
3 Norman W. Hoyles 'The Criminal Law of Canada' (1902) 38 *Canada Law Journal* 225–60
4 Report (1898) 43 *The Solicitor's Journal* 120
5 1861, 24 & 25 Vict., c. 96, s. 31 (Imp.)
6 Hoyles 'Criminal Law' 245
7 For example, Hoyles criticized at length section 227 (d), by which a person who unintentionally killed another while engaged in unlawful activity was guilty of culpable homicide, or murder. In his view the codifiers had adopted Lord Coke's 'cruel and monstrous' early seventeenth-century doctrine, and were out of touch with contemporary Canadian society: 'Criminal Law' 252–4.
8 See chapter 6, note 15 supra.
9 Macleod 'The Shaping of Canadian Criminal Law, 1892 to 1902' 68, 69
10 Ibid. The Justice Department still retains several thick files (no. 63/1894 'Suggested Amendments to the Criminal Code') of the correspondence that began to inundate parliamentarians and the department after the code came into force.
11 'An opium joint is a house, room or place to which persons resort for the purpose of smoking or inhaling opium': An Act to Amend the Criminal Code, 1909, 8 & 9 Edw. VII, c. 9 (Can.).
12 1910, 9 & 10 Edw. VII, c. 11, s. 1; c. 13, s. 2 (Can.)
13 Alan W. Mewett 'The Criminal Law' (1967) 45 *Canadian Bar Review* 740. Stephen would no doubt be pleased to see that the governing regulations of the Canadian Armed Forces, *Queen's Regulations and Orders*, constitute a code. Moreover, volume 2, the subcode of criminal law, follows exactly

the format introduced by Macaulay in the Indian Criminal Code, and perfected by Stephen in his *Digest*, in that each substantive section is followed by one or more examples that illustrate its application.

14 'Restructuring' is used advisedly. It is the term used by Allen J. MacLeod, the draftsman of the 1954 edition of the Criminal Code. In a letter to me dated 11 May 1988, he said: '[T]he Department of Justice view was that the exercise was to be not so much a "revision" as a "restructuring" of the Code, i.e., more form by far than substance.'

15 An Act to Amend the Criminal Code, 1919, 9 & 10 Geo. v, c. 46, s. 1 (Can.). In more peaceful times the Justice Department was able to repel such pernicious attempts to breach the integrity of the code. For example, offences concerning narcotics, which also placed the burden of proof on the defendant, were gathered together in a separate statute, the Narcotics Act, rather than in the Criminal Code: Roderick C. Macleod (ed.) *Lawful Authority* (Toronto: Copp Clark Pitman 1988) 153.

16 *Canada Gazette* no. 14, vol. LII, 1278–80

17 The clause of the order in council relating to printing and distributing seditious material was much influenced by similar legislation in the United States, which was also caught up in the 'Red Scare.' Compare the order in council, clause 9, and the u.s. Espionage Act, Statutes at Large, Title XII, s. 1, 217 (1917). To get some idea of how the war and the Russian Revolution caused mass paranoia, see 'Art and Politics, Dissent and Repression: The Masses Magazine versus the Government, 1917–1918' (1988) 32 *American Journal of Legal History* 42–78, in which John Sayer successfully evokes the temper of those troubled times.

18 *Canada Gazette* no. 14, vol. LII, clause 4, 1279 (my italics)

19 For a short but informative account of the period see Robert C. Brown and Ramsay Cook *Canada 1896-1921* (Toronto: Macmillan 1976), 309–14; for a detailed account of the strike and its antecedents, see Donald C. Masters *The Winnipeg General Strike* (Toronto: University of Toronto Press 1973).

20 House of Commons *Debates* 1 May 1919, 1956

21 Ibid. 10 June 1919, 3291; 14 February 1933, 2101; 19 June 1936, 3898

22 Ibid. 10 June 1919, 3289. See also the discussion on sedition in chapter 6.

23 House of Commons *Debates* 27 June 1919, 4134

24 Ibid. 1 July 1919, 4355, 4356

25 Ibid. 5 July 1919, 4661

26 See, for example, Masters *General Strike* 134, and David J. Bercuson *Confrontation at Winnipeg* (Montreal: McGill-Queen's University Press 1974) 178.

27 *The King* v. *R.B. Russell* case No. 2/2171-8, 23 December 1919, Mr Justice
   Metcalf's charge to the jury (Winnipeg: Prothonotary's Office, Manitoba
   Law Courts) 1–48. For a detailed account of Thomas Metcalf's research for
   his charge, see Brown 'Craftsmanship of Bias' 2–6.
28 The two sections were merged and renumbered as section 98 of chapter
   36 in the 1927 edition of the Revised Statutes of Canada.
29 House of Commons *Debates* 13 February 1933, 2106; 18 June 1935, 3898
30 As read into the parliamentary record, section 12 of the 'Regina Mani-
   festo', the program of the CCF, advocated the repeal of section 98: House
   of Commons *Debates* 5 February 1934, 270.
31 *R.* v. *Buck* [1932] 3 DLR 97 (Ont. CA)
32 House of Commons *Debates* 14 February 1933, 2096, 2102
33 Ibid. 18 June 1936, 3897–3938
34 This surprising finding was made by a trial judge at the time, and his
   judgment was quoted with approval by the Archambault Commission:
   Report of the Royal Commission to Investigate the Penal System of Canada
   (Ottawa: Queen's Printer 1939) 74.
35 Ibid. 79, 80
36 Ibid. 97
37 House of Commons *Debates* 30 June 1934, 4587
38 In 1934 Macphail was not in a position to know all the facts uncovered by
   the Archambault Commission during the period from 1936 to 1938. For
   a more thorough and less subjective account of Buck's case, see *Report on
   the Penal System* 74–100.
39 House of Commons *Debates* 27 February 1936, 613
40 *Report on the Penal System* 358
41 House of Commons *Debates* 11 May 1936, 2675
42 Ibid. 28 January 1937, 345–6
43 Ibid. 20 May 1940, 26
44 *1944 Proceedings of the Twenty-sixth Annual Meeting of the Conference of
   Commissioners on Uniformity of Legislation in Canada* 342. I am indebted to
   Professor Emeritus Wilbur F. Bowker, past director of the Alberta Institute
   of Law Research and Reform and past president of the Conference of
   Commissioners on Uniformity of Legislation in Canada, for drawing this
   event to my attention.
45 Ibid. 343
46 The following list of provincial law reform organizations and the dates of
   their founding is taken from Thomas W. Mapp 'Law Reform in Canada:
   The Impact of the Provincial Law Reform Agencies on Uniformity' (1982–
   3) 7 *Dalhousie Law Journal* 277: Law Reform Commission of British Colum-

bia (1970); Alberta Institute of Law Research and Reform (1968); Law Reform Commission of Saskatchewan (1974); Manitoba Law Reform Commission (1971); Ontario Law Reform Commission (1964); Director General, Legislative Affairs, Department of Justice of Quebec (1977); Law Reform Division, Department of Justice of New Brunswick (1971); Law Reform Commission of Prince Edward Island (1971); and Nova Scotia Law Reform Advisory Commission (1972).

47 *Proceedings of the Twenty-sixth Meeting of the Conference of Commissioners on Uniformity* 342
48 House of Commons *Debates* 3 July 1947, 5027
49 Ibid. 19 June 1948, 5489. The commissioners' terms of reference were comprehensive. They were given eight specific tasks, which included a direction to 'adopt uniform language throughout ... rearrange provisions and parts [and] endeavour to make the Code exhaustive of the criminal law: *Report of Royal Commission on the Revision of [the] Criminal Code* (Ottawa: Queen's Printer 1954) 3.
50 House of Commons *Debates* 21 February 1949, 727ff; 3 May 1950, 2139ff
51 Ibid. 1 April 1949, 2256–7
52 Ibid. 2 May 1950, 2086
53 In passing, it is worthy of note that the Canadian Code of 1954 was considerably shorter than what had theretofore been the model in this respect, namely, the 1953 edition of the combined West German penal and procedural codes, which ran to at least 844 sections.
54 *Report on the Criminal Code* 4
55 House of Commons *Debates* 19 June 1936, 3905, 3929; 1954, 2 & 3 Eliz. II, c. 51, s. 60 (4)
56 *Report on the Criminal Code* 10
57 House of Commons *Debates* 15 December 1953, 945
58 Ibid. 23 January 1953, 1272–6. Like Peel, Garson had good reason to emphasize this point. Like their English predecessors, Canadian politicians and legalists of the time were very resistant to change. An interesting example of this resistance is related by the legal draftsman Allen J. MacLeod, who found it difficult 'to persuade the commissioners that "sexual intercourse" could be substituted for "carnal knowledge" without doing violence in any way to the history or substance of the law relating to sexual offences.' Letter, A.J. MacLeod to D.H. Brown, 8 December 1981.
59 House of Commons *Debates* 15 December 1953, 945
60 Ibid. 939–47
61 Ibid. 12 January 1954, 1020–37. For informed commentary on this process,

see the four articles commissioned by the editor of the *Canadian Bar Review* for the first issue of the 1955 volume. 'The first is on the history, organization and mechanics of the revision; the second on some of the more significant changes made in the substantive law of offences and punishments; and the third on the sometimes overlooked, but no less important subject of criminal procedure.' These were written by Department of Justice officials, A.J. MacLeod and J.C. Martin, who researched and drafted the revision. The fourth came from the pen of Joseph Sedgwick, a distinguished practitioner of criminal law, who usually acted for the defence: G.V. Nicholls 'Canada's New Criminal Code' (1955) 33 *Canadian Bar Review* 1.

62 House of Commons *Debates* 23 February 1970, 3966
63 See the letters from W. Kent Power, then the editor in chief of the *Western Weekly Reports*, and L.R. MacTavish, then the president of the Conference of Commissioners on Uniformity of Legislation in Canada in (1954) 32 *Canadian Bar Review* 929–31, 1060–1. See also the article 'Law Reform' by R.E. Megarry, then the assistant editor of the *Law Quarterly Review*, who gave a systematic review of law reform institutions in England, and made detailed suggestions for the organization of similar bodies in Canada: (1956) 34 *Canadian Bar Review* 691–712.
64 Letter from Stuart Garson, (1955) 33 *Canadian Bar Review* 129–32
65 'Report of the Committee on Legal Research' (1956) 34 *Canadian Bar Review* 1036–7
66 1957, *Proceedings* 176
67 Pierre Normandin *Canadian Parliamentary Guide 1988* (Ottawa 1988) 37
68 House of Commons *Debates* 24 January 1966, 140
69 Ibid. 11 May 1967, 60
70 Ibid. 7 July 1967, 2388
71 Ibid. 20 September 1968, 263
72 Roger Ouimet, G. Arthur Martin, J.R. Lemieux, Dorothy McArton, and W.T. McGrath *Toward Unity: Criminal Justice and Corrections* report of the Canadian Committee on Corrections (Ottawa: Queen's Printer 1969)
73 See Allen M. Linden and Patrick Fitzgerald 'Recodifying Criminal Law' (1987) 66 *Canadian Bar Review* 529–45: Patrick Healy 'The Process of Reform in Canadian Criminal Law' (1984) 42 *University of Toronto Faculty of Law Review* 1–24 and the references provided therein.
74 House of Commons *Debates* 23 February 1970, 3960–75
75 Law Reform Commission Act, SC 1970, c. 64, ss. 3, 4, 11, 18
76 A list of the commission's reports and working papers can be found in Law Commission Report 32 *Our Criminal Procedure* (Ottawa 1988) 2.

77 These three volumes comprise Reports 30, 31, and 32.
78 Linden and Fitzgerald 'Recodifying' 535
79 Law Commission Report 31 *Recodifying Criminal Law* 169: 'crime' is defined as 'an offence that is liable to be punished by imprisonment, otherwise than on default of payment of a fine.'

Index

Senate 225 n125; Bill 7 debate 135–6,
143–5, 234 n77; debate on consolidation of statutes 94–5, 97, 103–4,
219 n28; regional representation
in 218 n13; right to initiate
legislation 112, 224 n119, 225 nn119,
121
sexual offences 240 n58
Sheridan, Richard Brinsley 86
Simcoe, John Graves 51
Snelling, Richard 217 n2
solicitor 45, 55, 67, 205 n98
Special Committee of the House of
Commons on the Revision of the
Criminal Code (1953) 160
Speedy Trials Acts 1875 (Ont.) 210
n152
Stanley, Frederick Arthur, Baron
Stanley of Preston 228 n13
statute-books: British 189 n44, 190
n44, 215 n37, 226 n144; Brougham's
draft 19; colonial volumes 71–91;
Statutes of the Realm 14
Statute Law Committee 28, 194 n103
Statute Law Revision Act 1827
(UK) 14, 189 n43
Statute of Treasons and Felonies 1758
(NS) 43, 48
Statutes at Large of Nova Scotia 71
Statutes of the Province of Upper
Canada (1831) 74
Statutes of the Realm (England) 14,
16
statutory law 132–3
Stephen, Sir James Fitzjames 68, 84,
98, 121, 191 n76, 192 nn77, 82,
194 n101, 195 n116, 196 nn128, 137,
197 n149; biographical sketch
23–4, 192 nn80, 86; draft code of

1878 29–33; draft code of 1879 34–
6; *Digest of the Criminal Law* 24–6
Stephen, Leslie 192 n79
Stewart, Peter 47–8
Street, Samuel Denny 203 n75
substantive law 7, 19, 49, 56, 67, 125,
163
Suckling, George 199 n13
summary conviction offence 125, 152,
163
Supreme Court Bill 1891 (Can.) 228
n16
Supreme Court of British Columbia 58
Supreme Court of Canada 60–1, 68–9,
208 n136, 229 n26
Supreme Court of New Brunswick
49–50
Supreme Court of Nova Scotia 38, 40
Supreme Court of Prince Edward
Island 47

Taschereau, Sir Henri-Elzéar 93,
105–6, 121, 130, 228 n16; and
Burbidge 228 n11; biographical
sketch 220 n47; open letter on
Criminal Code (1892) 146–8; writings of 100, 119–20, 227 nn4, 8
Taylor, Sir Henry 99, 105
theft. *See* larceny
Thompson, Sir John Sparrow
David 11, 61–4, 114, 119–21, 151,
159, 211 n166–7, 222 n84, 226 n138,
228 nn13, 16, 229 n26, 232 n43,
233 nn71–72, 235 n91; legal reform
in North-West Territories 228 n10;
moves to codify criminal law
122–3, 126–48; pilots Bill 7 through
Commons 131–42; pilots revised
statutes through Commons 115–18